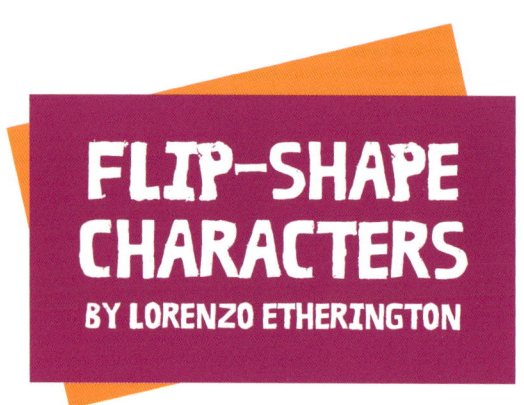

FLIP-SHAPE CHARACTERS
BY LORENZO ETHERINGTON

FOR MORE **COMPLEX DESIGNS,** THE FLIPPED SHAPES CAN ALSO BE REPEATED FOR **FEET,** ETC.

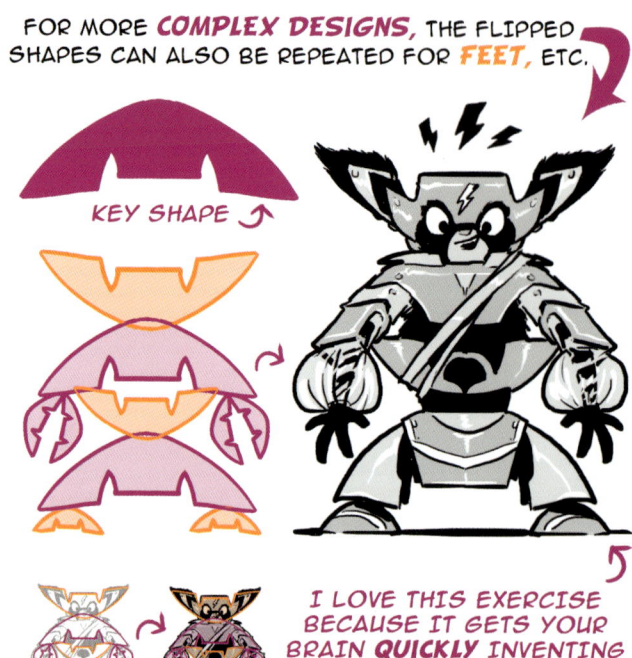

KEY SHAPE ↗

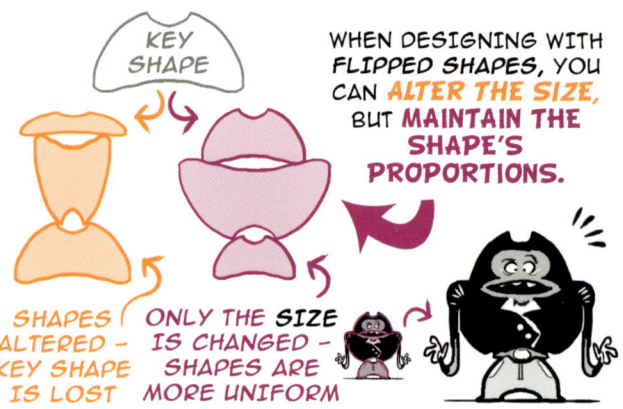

KEY SHAPE

WHEN DESIGNING WITH **FLIPPED SHAPES,** YOU CAN **ALTER THE SIZE,** BUT **MAINTAIN THE SHAPE'S PROPORTIONS.**

SHAPES ALTERED – KEY SHAPE IS LOST

ONLY THE **SIZE** IS CHANGED – SHAPES ARE MORE UNIFORM

I LOVE THIS EXERCISE BECAUSE IT GETS YOUR BRAIN **QUICKLY** INVENTING CHARACTERS IT MAY **NEVER THINK UP** OTHERWISE!

TRY FLIPPING A DIFFERENT WAY BY **ROTATING 180 DEGREES** – THIS IS PARTICULARLY EFFECTIVE WHEN USING **ASYMMETRICAL** SHAPES.

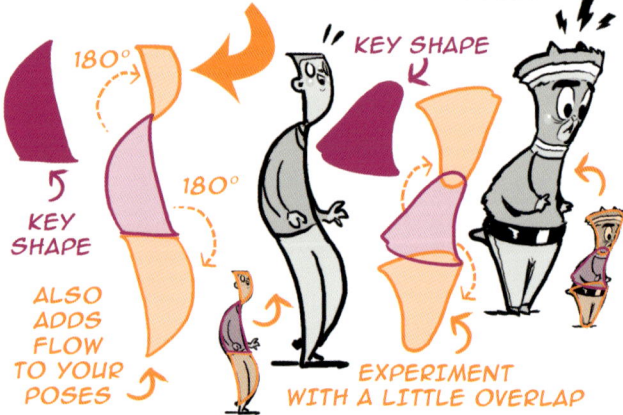

180°

KEY SHAPE

180°

KEY SHAPE

ALSO ADDS FLOW TO YOUR POSES

EXPERIMENT WITH A LITTLE OVERLAP

TRY TAKING **ONE SET** OF FLIPPED SHAPES, AND MAKING AS MANY **DIFFERENT CHARACTERS** AS YOU CAN!

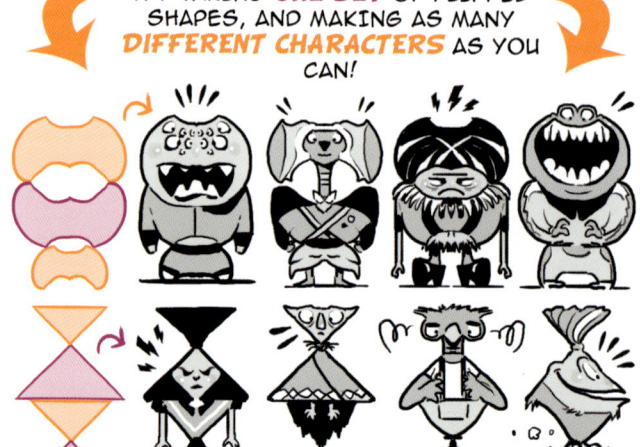

KENNETH ANDERSON
Illustrator / Character Designer
charactercube.com

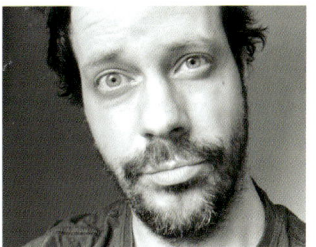

Kenny is a freelance character designer and illustrator based in Glasgow. He has made art for children's television, books, and the odd board game.

JACKIE DROUJKO
Freelance Character Designer
jackiedroujko.com

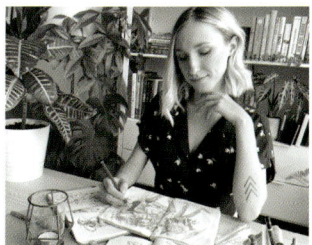

Sheridan Animation graduate Jackie Droujko is a character designer based in Vancouver, who has worked with Netflix, Dreamworks, and others.

NATHANNA ÉRICA
Illustrator at Disney
Publishing Worldwide
nathannaerica.com

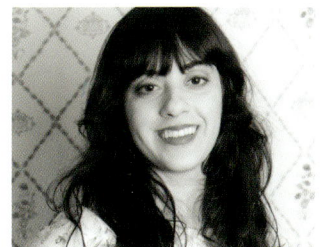

Nathanna is an illustrator, paper artist, and visual development artist from Brazil. She is currently working with Disney Publishing Worldwide.

MICHAELA NIENABER
Art Lead at Well Told
Entertainment
mnienaberart.com

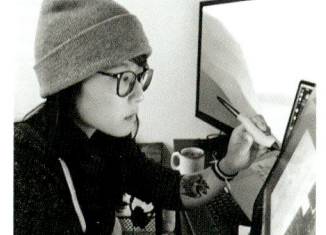

Michaela has been working in the game industry for 8 years. Past clients include Blizzard, Warchief Gaming, Night School Studio, and others.

DAVE GUERTIN
Art Director & Concept Artist
daveguertin.com

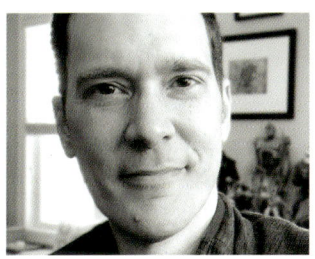

Dave is most notably the co-founder of CreatureBox and Principal Artist for the acclaimed *Ratchet & Clank* franchise.

ELÉONORE PELLUAU
Illustrator at Juratoys
eleonorepelluau.wixsite.
com/eleonorepelluau

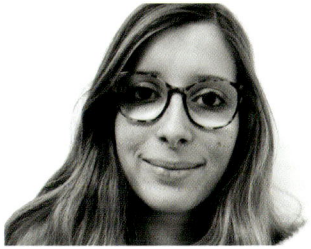

Eléonore is a French illustrator who works on illustrations for wooden and cardboard toys, and illustrates children's books.

ANGEL REN
Student at Sheridan
College Animation
instagram.com/gigiboom__

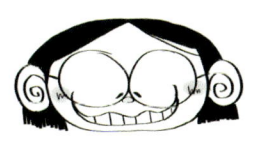

Angel is a Sheridan Animation student who was born in China and enjoys dancing, reading comics, and seeing people's silly and happy faces.

MARJOALINE ROLLER
Illustrator and Concept Artist
instagram.com/marjolaineroller

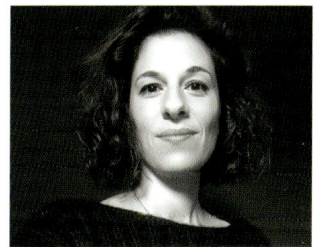

Marjolaine is a French artist working on storyboard, illustration, and concept art. She works with digital and traditional techniques.

KAINING WANG
Concept Designer at
Meta Reality Labs
kningart.com

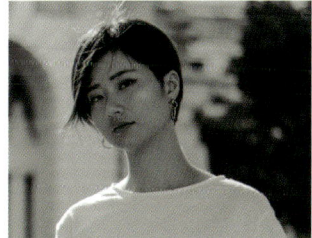

Kaining Wang is a visual development artist based in LA, currently working as a concept designer for Facebook Reality Labs.

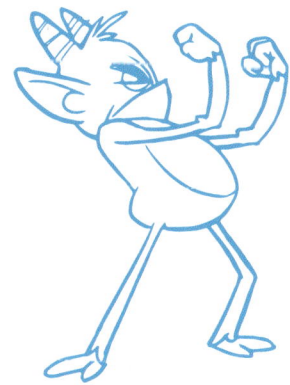

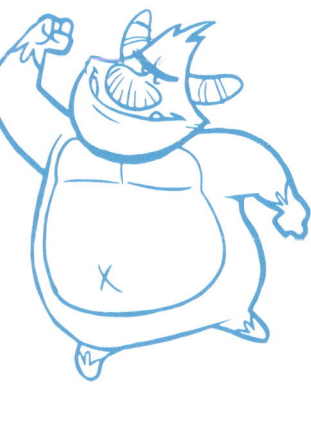

WELCOME TO *CHARACTER DESIGN QUARTERLY 23*

One of the great pleasures of editing *CDQ* is having the opportunity to pick the brains of so many wonderful artists that feature in the magazine. This issue's cover artist, Kenneth Anderson, has previously lit up the pages of *CDQ* with his wondrously colorful drawings – we had the chance to chat with Kenny about the childhood influences behind his unique designs, and gain some valuable insight into his process.

Another artist returning to *CDQ* is Dave Guertin, who created our very first cover image. We caught up with Dave to discuss his career and gained some fascinating insights into the principals behind his character designs. We also talked to Jackie Droujko about creating characters for some of the biggest studios in the business.

And, of course, we have our usual insightful collection of tutorials. Nathanna Érica explores how color choices are important to character design, Eléonore Pelluau shows us how to design a character for very young children, and Marjolaine Roller creates a stunning re-imagination of a classic character.

There's so much more to discover inside, so turn the page, let yourself be inspired, and then get creating! Who knows, maybe one day we'll be speaking to you, too?

SAM DRAPER
EDITOR

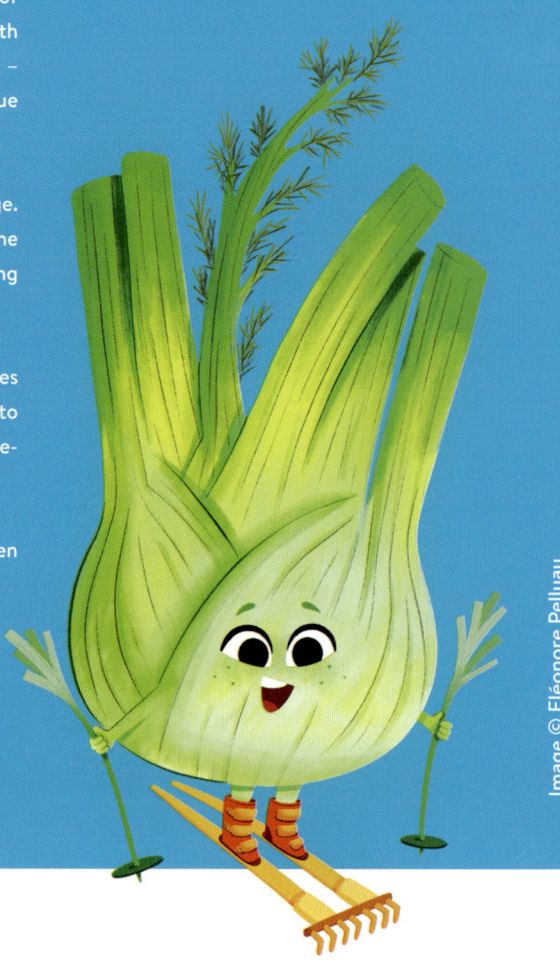

Image © Eléonore Pelluau

---

76   86   90

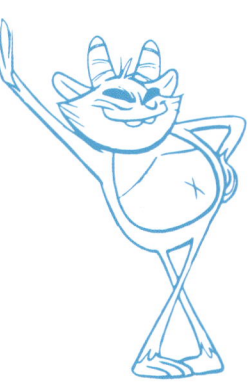

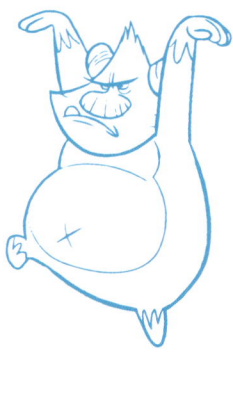

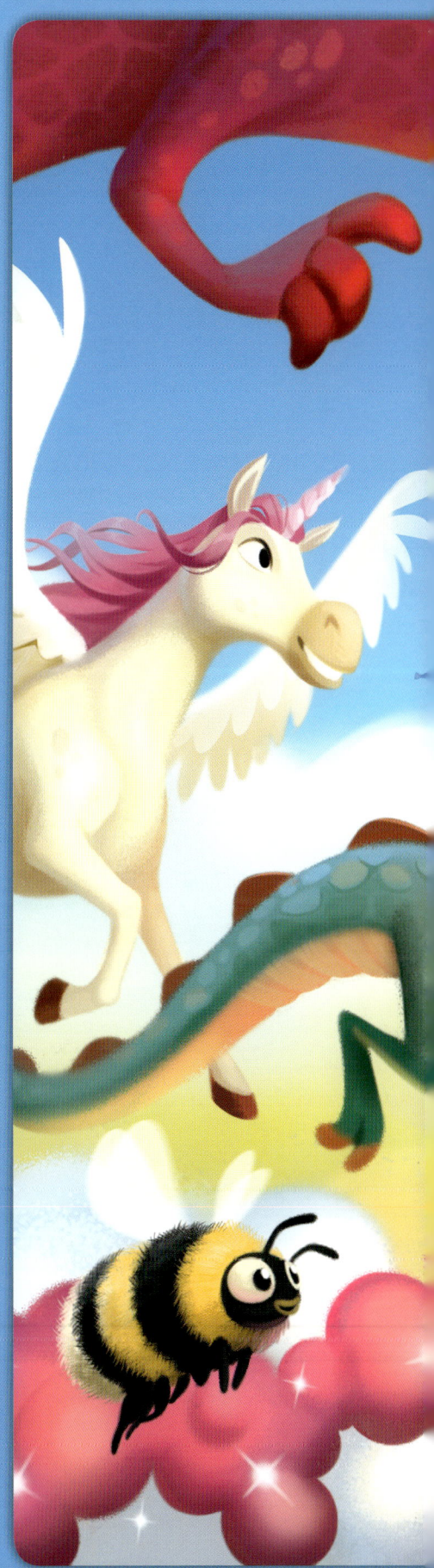

BEHIND THE COVER ART
KENNETH ANDERSON

This issue's spectacularly colorful cover was created by Kenny Anderson, a freelance character designer and illustrator based in Glasgow. Kenny is no stranger to the pages of *CDQ*, and we were thrilled to welcome him back for a chat about his varied career to date, and for a look at how he created the bright and fun-filled cover art.

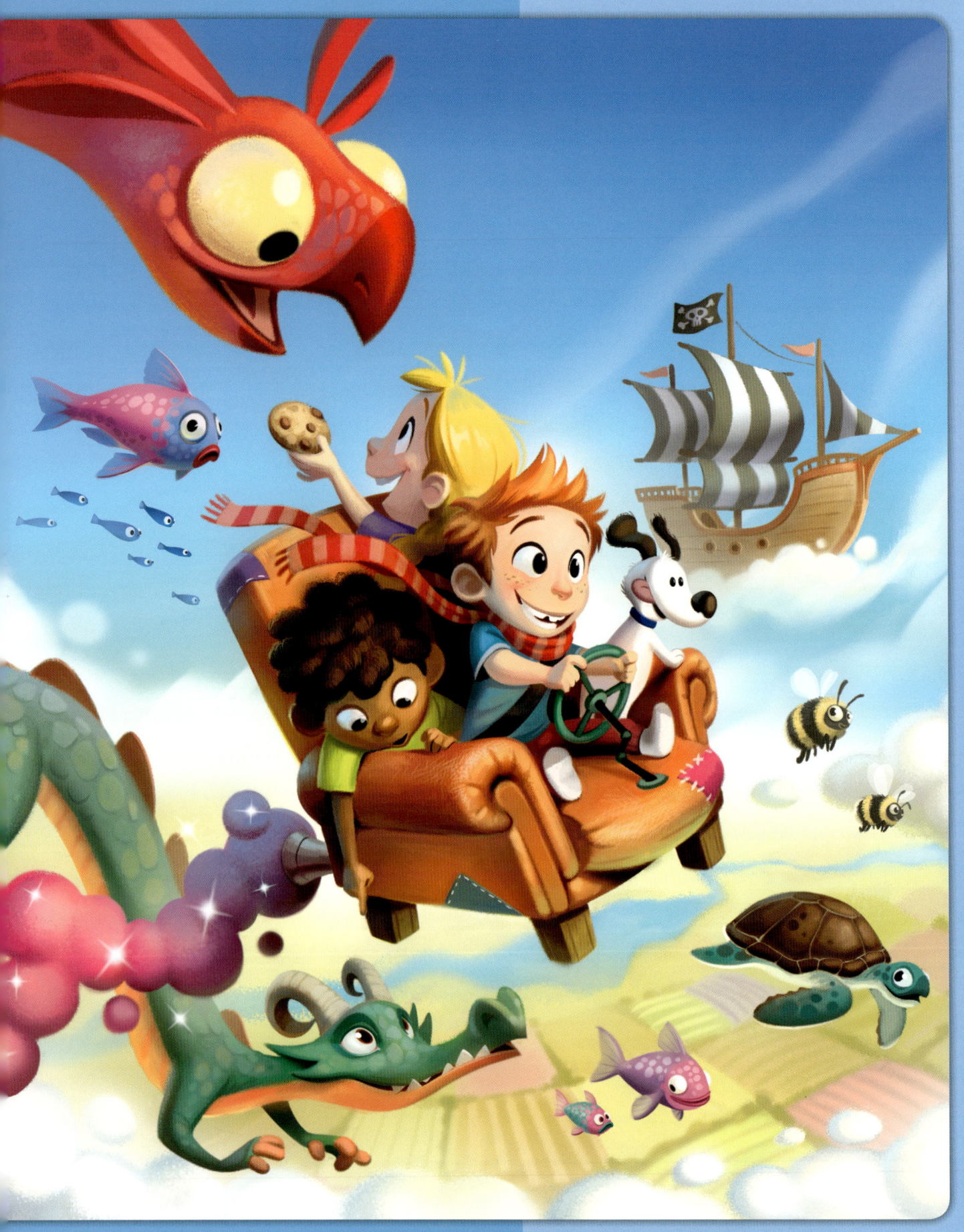

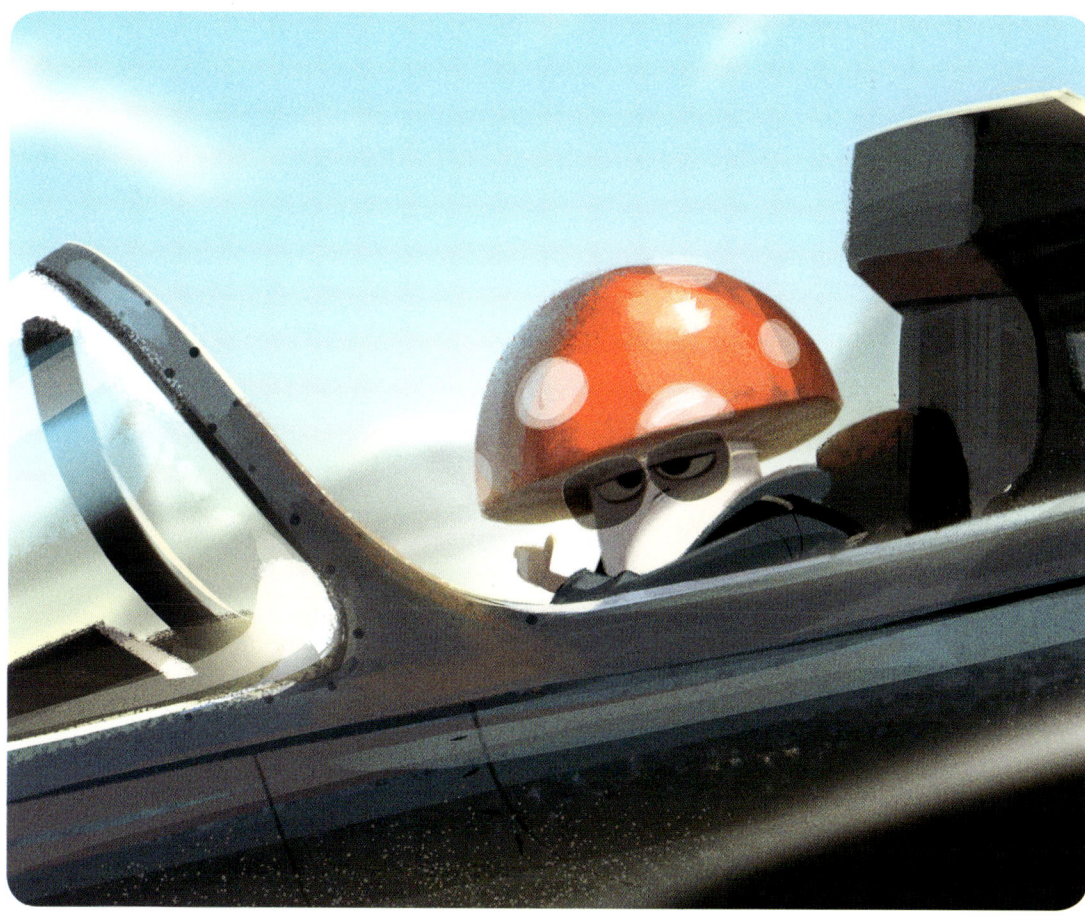

This page: *Mushroom Fighter* – This was made for a character design challenge – I went with a *Top Gun* theme for my mushroom fighter

Opposite page: *Crabby Island* – This image was part of a series of exploratory drawings, trying to flesh out an idea I had for a world filled with child pirates

Hi Kenny, welcome back to *CDQ*. Could you start by letting our readers know a little about yourself?

Hello, thank you for having me. As a fan of your magazine, it was a real honor to create this month's cover (even if it was a little bit intimidating).

I am a freelance illustrator and character designer based in Glasgow. I grew up here, and like most kids, I spent a lot of time drawing, doodling silly characters, and making my own poorly drawn comics. I was just the kid that kept drawing when all the others had stopped. After high school, I studied traditional animation up the road at Duncan of Jordanstone Art College in Dundee, graduating in 2005. I've been lucky enough to work pretty much consistently since then, starting out in the games industry, before moving into traditional 2D animation. I went freelance in 2009, and these days I mainly contribute to children's TV animation design. Recently, I've started branching out into kids books and book-cover illustration, while still dabbling in the odd bit of game design.

The focus of my work is always on characters and storytelling – I love creating little moments where characters are interacting or going on adventures. And pirates. I love drawing pirates.

Your character designs are full of emotion and say so much in a single image. Do you have any tips for conveying so much in just one drawing?

Thanks, that's great to hear. I guess that is a goal of mine when it comes to my work, to try and convey a story moment or a character's state of mind in one image. I think it comes from having worked as an animator in the past, except now I'm just trying to distill all that energy down into a single key drawing.

I think the secret might be to convey something very simple but put every part of the character into it. For example, take an emotional state such as anger – the characters pose and gesture, combined with the facial expression and the subtleties of what the hands and especially the eyes are doing will all help to build up that feeling you're trying to convey. If everything is working in harmony, then the emotion should come through for the audience, and it can feel like a lot is happening while the statement or story is really something very simple. Fundamentally, it's all about showing an emotion in that one statement with absolute clarity.

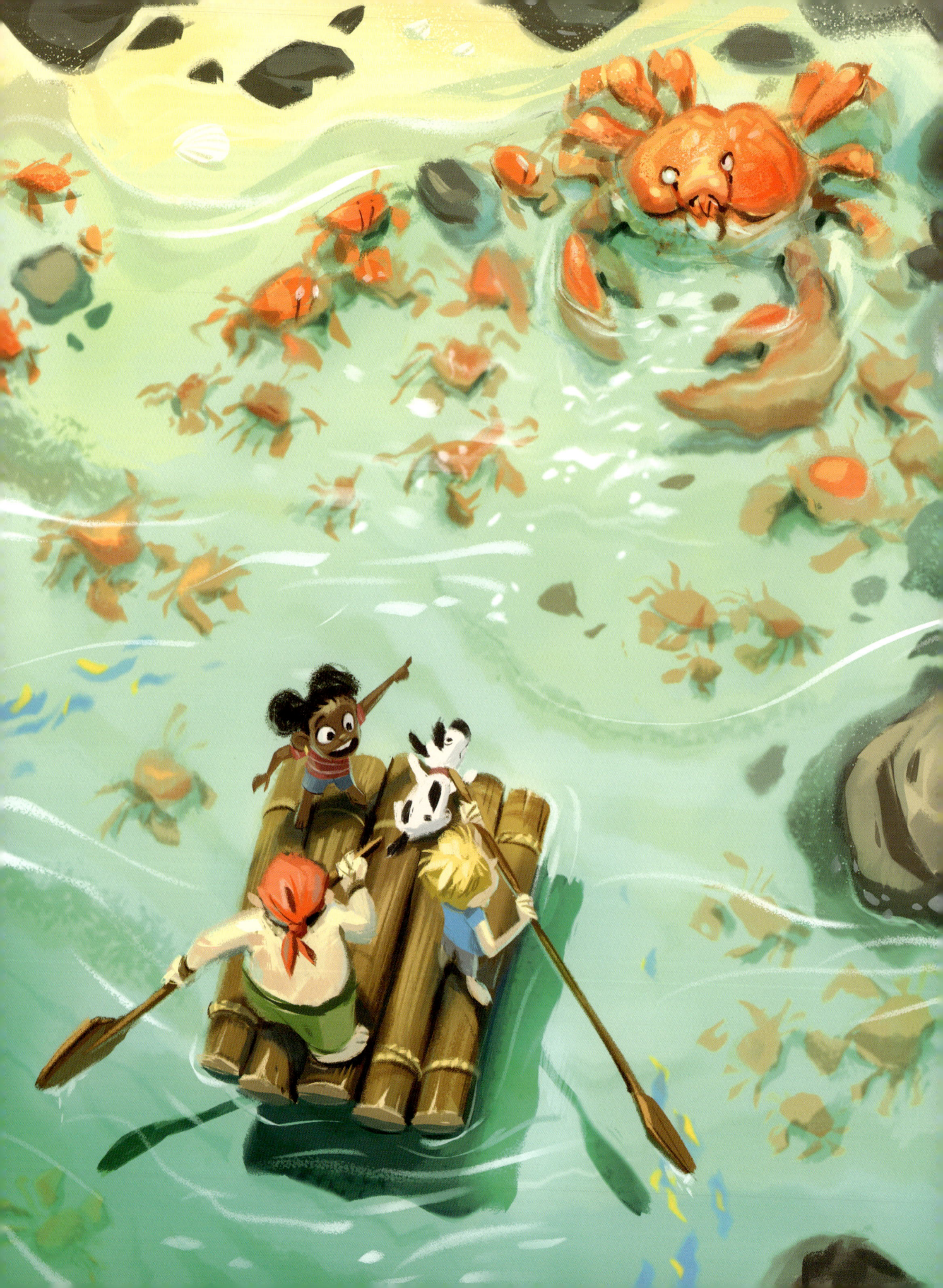

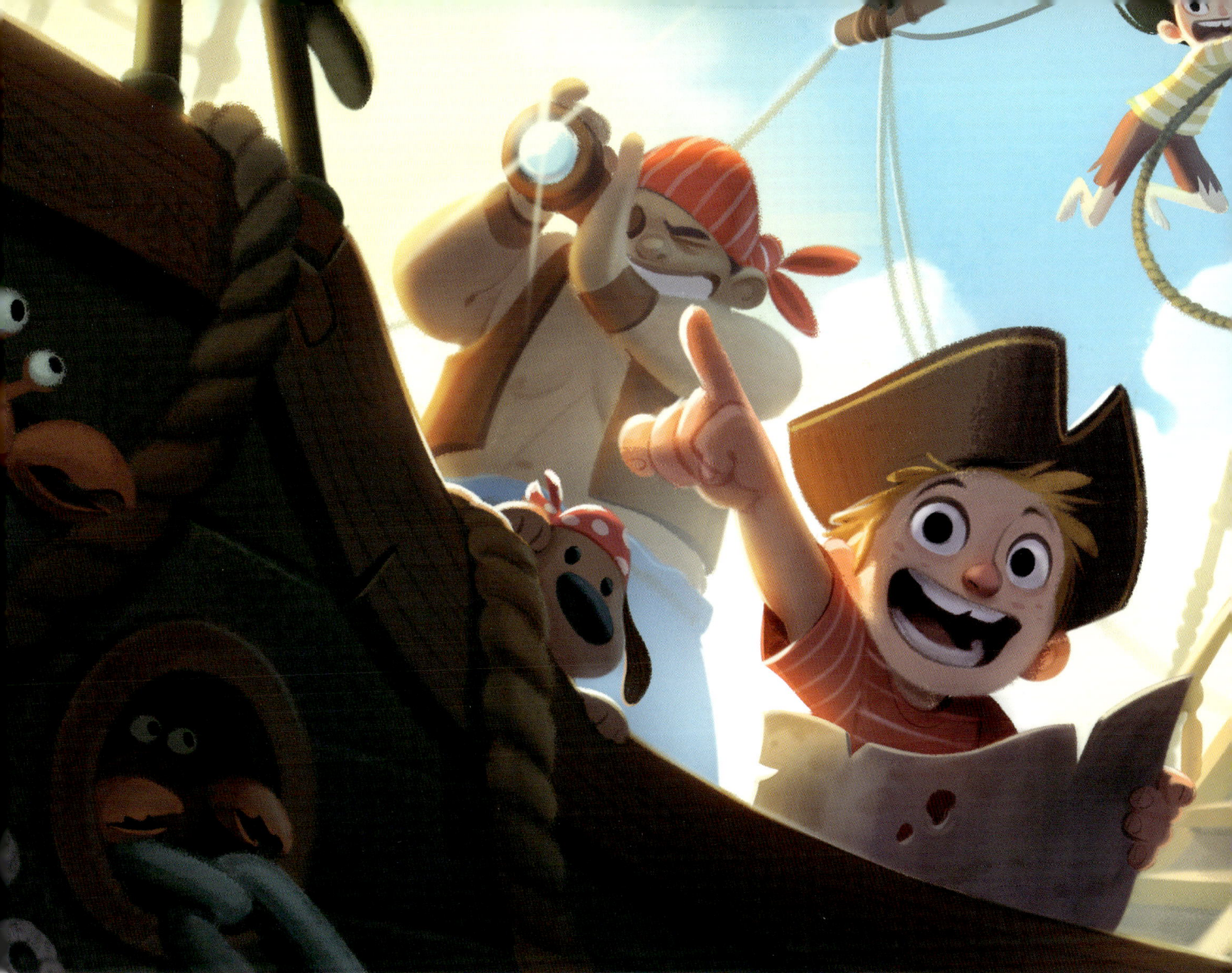

You've worked across all sorts of different mediums, from board games, to children's books, TV, video games, and more. Do you have a favorite industry to work in? Are there many differences with how you approach character design for different disciplines?

I've had quite a varied career so far – I get bored easily, you see! Thankfully, the thread that connects most of these different things is character design, and so while the mediums are widely different, really the end goal each time is pretty much the same.

I tend to enjoy working on particular projects more than particular mediums, however I do love the freedom involved in the world of illustration. As an illustrator, I feel like I have much more control and can put my own creative vision into the end product – it's a bit like being an art director, character designer, and environment artist all at once. However, that can be difficult, as it means making more creative decisions yourself. There is also a bit more freedom when it comes to

interpreting a brief or designing characters when illustrating, whereas in animation design, there are so many other factors or voices pushing and pulling designs in different directions. While the level of input may be best for the project, sometimes I might dislike the direction, from a personal point of view.

Illustration also comes with less technical constraints than animation or games – the only limitation to a design on a page is space, and maybe color, depending on if it's a black-and-white or color print. In animation and games, you are constantly struggling with the limitations and technical restraints of the medium. For example, some character designs just won't be riggable or cost effective for a particular production. Illustration escapes most of these problems, which is very freeing.

Generally, I approach character design in much the same way regardless of medium – I consider the constraints of each project at the outset and make sure it informs each step of my design process. The major difference might be if I am designing for a 3D medium or a 2D one –

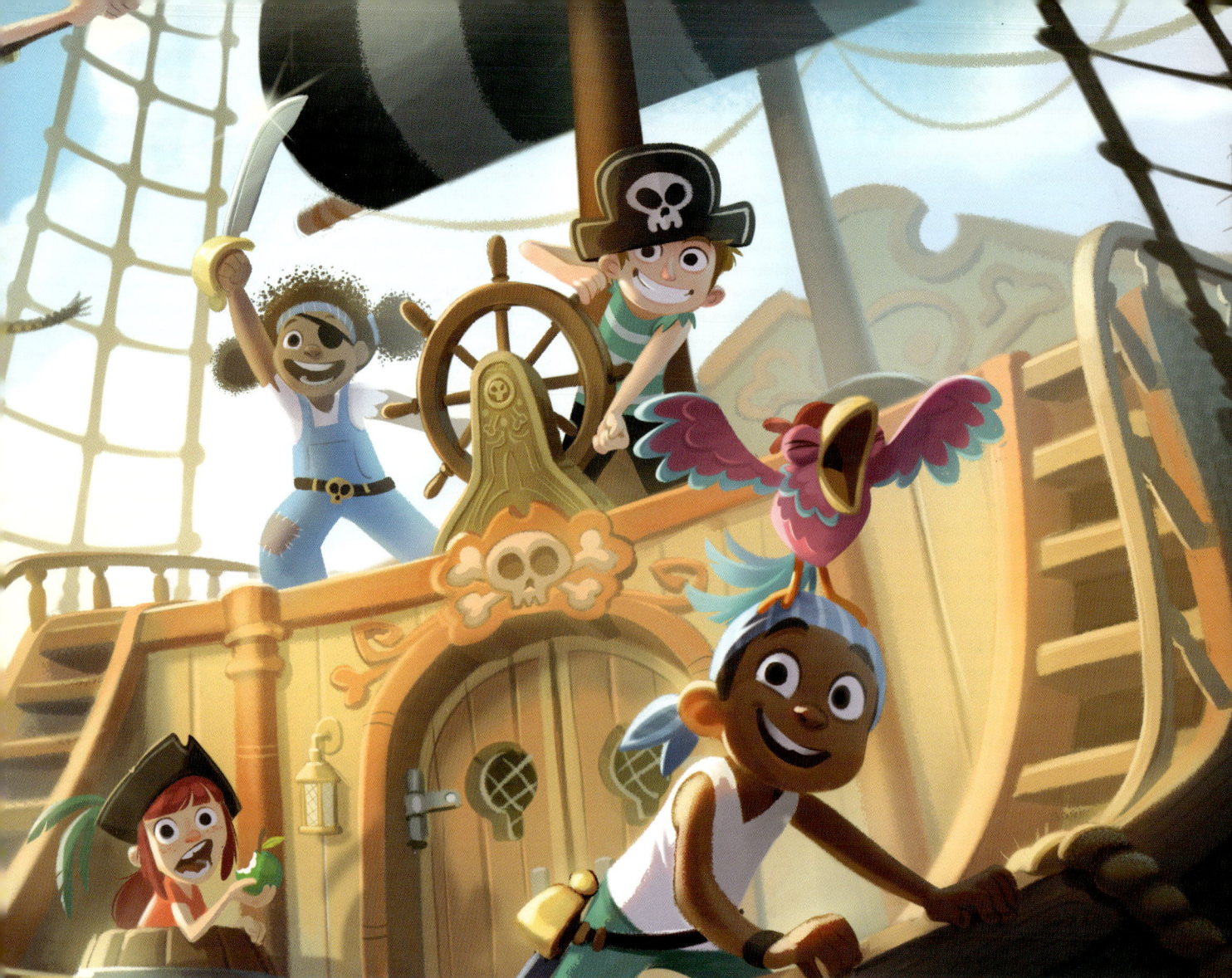

the rules of the game can change drastically depending on which it is. Overall, I'm always designing with the end goal, whatever that may be, in mind.

Could you talk a little bit more about the differences between designing for 2D and 3D and how the process for each differs?

In general, the process for designing characters is the same: start with a design brief, do some sketches, problem solve the design, take on feedback, and iterate to the final character. The key differences are in the technical restraints and mindset while designing. For example, if I'm designing for 3D I know I can play with textures and complexity a lot more (depending on style of course) than in a 2D medium. Complexity and 2D don't often go hand in hand, especially in traditional 2D animation – someone must draw every frame. More modern puppet or riggable 2D animated characters are starting to break that limitation a bit.

The other mindset shift is thinking in terms of how the characters are going to move and perform, and bringing that into the design. For example, a traditionally 2D animated character can be exaggerated, squashed, and stretched easily. The only limit here is what the artist can draw. In 3D and puppet-style 2D, that becomes more of a challenge, as it requires more complex character rigs. As a designer it's important to consider if a design can perform rather than if they look good from one angle and pose. I also tend to visualize my characters a bit differently depending on the medium I am designing for – I see them in my head differently, imagining them in their final form. For 3D characters, I draw them as if they were 3D already, while for 2D characters I may end up thinking a lot less volumetrically, or at least abstracting volumes to simpler shapes. Again, this also depends on style.

These pages: *Land Ahoy!* – This image sums up my work – pirates and kids going on adventures. A lot of my work is just channeling the spirit of the film *The Goonies*

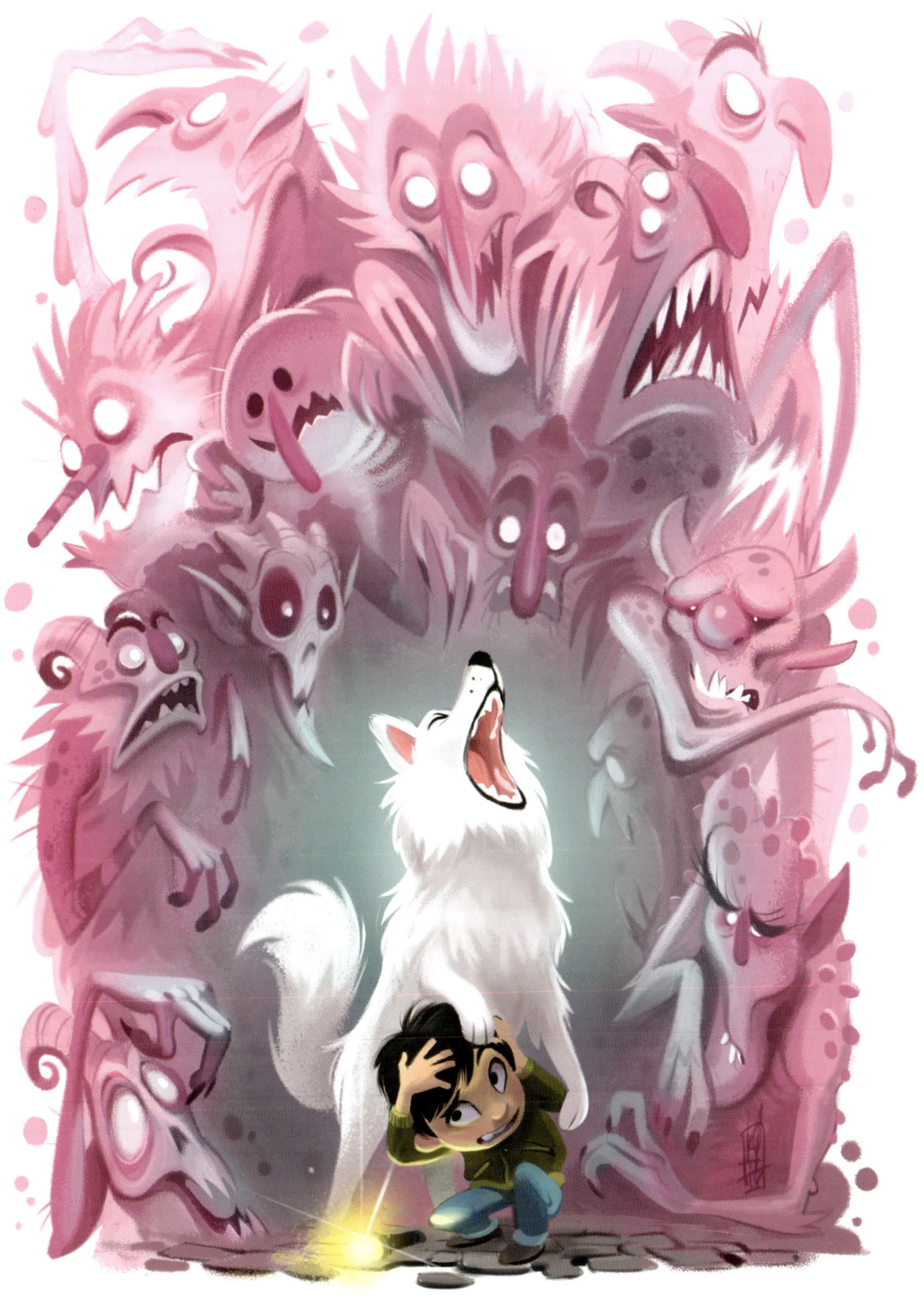

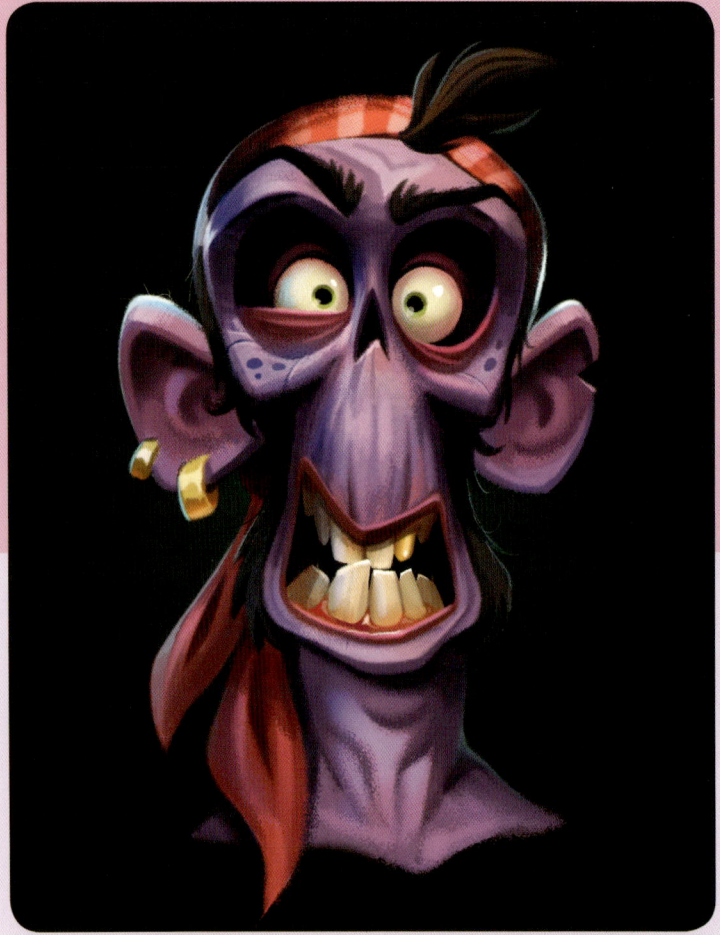

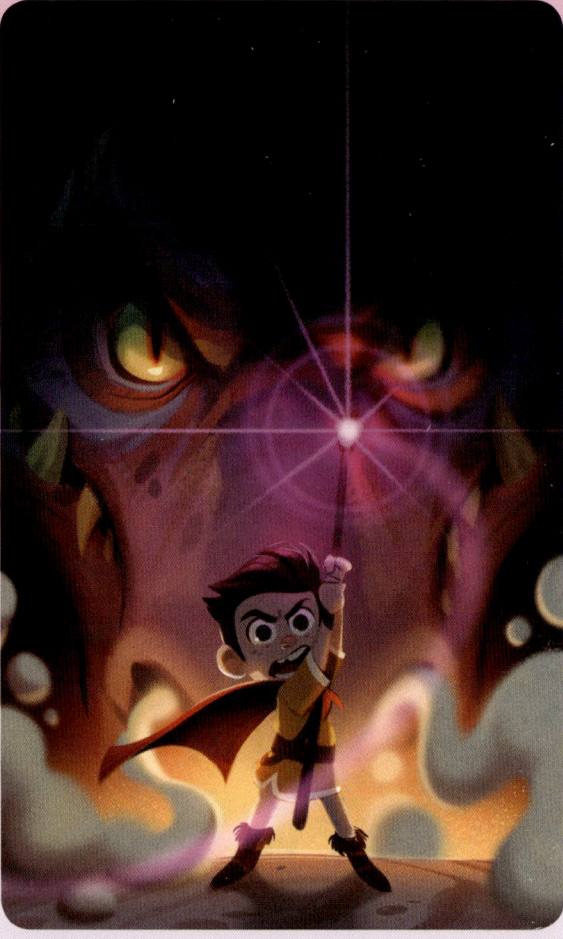

Where did you originally find inspiration for your art style, and how has it evolved throughout your career so far?

Everything I absorbed as a child has influenced my style and the things I like to draw. I grew up watching *Postman Pat*, *Bertha*, and *Trapdoor* on TV, and later on I got into *Teenage Mutant Ninja Turtles*, and games such as the *Monkey Island* series, and *Day of the Tentacle*. The surreal humor of these games is something that still appeals to me today, and I love the character design style. I was also a big fan of *Calvin and Hobbes* growing up, which I think has influenced the way I try to draw characters moving and performing – Bill Watterson is a genius when it comes to that. And, of course, my biggest influence of all would be *Wallace and Gromit* – discovering the short films, and the world of animation as an eleven-year-old, set me on the path I am on today. I was obsessed with the characters growing up, and would experiment with my own stop motion films, full of characters who looked uncannily like Wallace and Gromit. My career as an actual animator was very short lived, but I think I still carry that influence with me, in terms of Nick Park's quirky humor, storytelling, and love of character.

My style has definitely evolved over the years. I first realized character design was a possible career path when I discovered the work of Stephen Silver. His art really helped me start to abstract forms and think about what designing characters actually meant. For a while, people would look at my sketches and say it looked similar to his style. As time has gone on, my look has evolved as I've discovered artists such as Carter Goodrich, Nico Marlet, Lynn Chen – way too many to mention. Friends and peers have also inspired me with their work. So many artists have had an influence on me and nudged my work in new directions over the years, consciously and subconsciously – I have no idea how I will be drawing ten years from now.

Opposite page: *A Boy's Best Friend* – This image is a combination of two of my favorite things: dogs and drawing monsters

This page (left): *Zombie Pirate* – When I don't know what to draw, I often find myself drawing zombie pirates

This page (right): *The Dragon Whisperer* – Dragons are a lot of fun to draw – this is one of a series of illustrations with a different kid and dragon each time

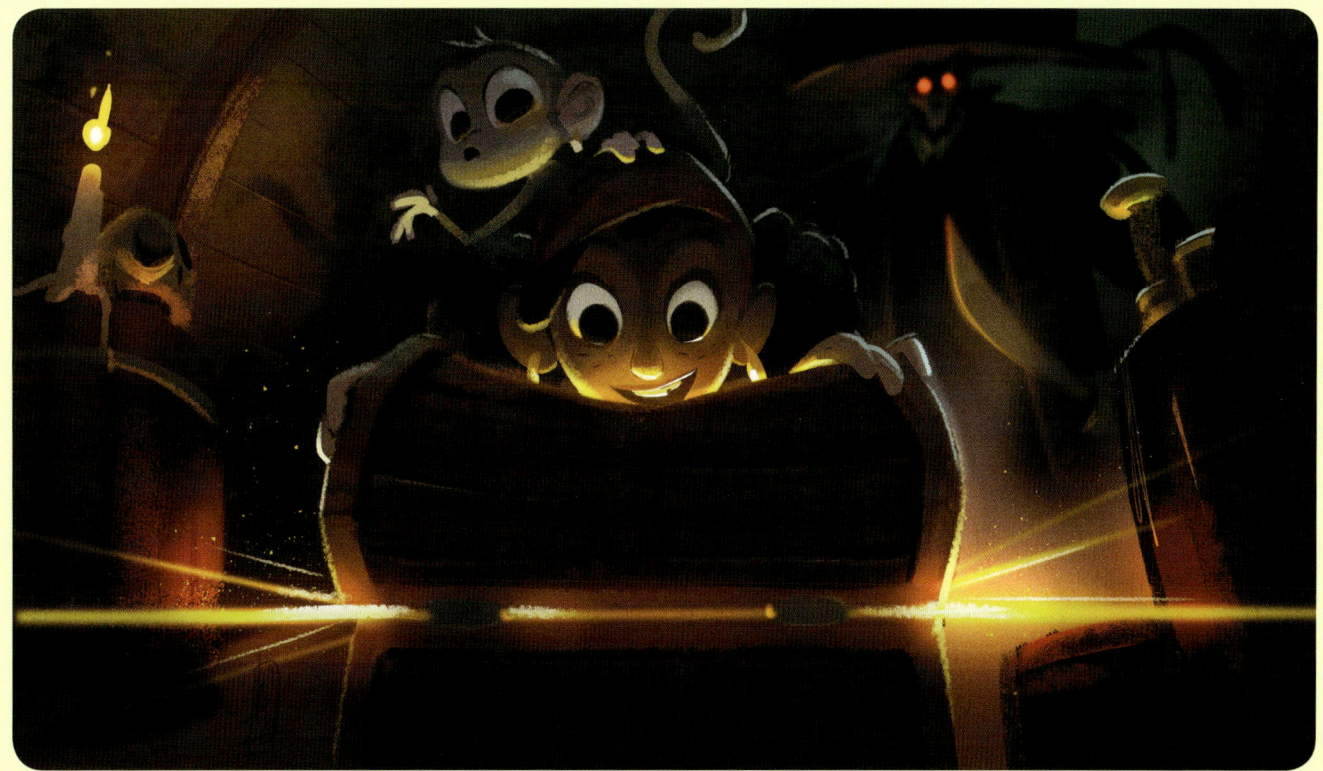

Social media can make the number of other artists seem a bit overwhelming these days. With so much competition, do you have any advice about how to stand out from the crowd?

Draw what you love. It's great to be inspired by the work of other artists and synthesize it into your work, but you have to put something of yourself into what you do, and make it your own. Consider your style as your unique selling point. That said, a unique style isn't something I would necessarily recommend chasing – I prefer to let my look evolve as I grow as an artist. I think for most people starting out in the world of character design it can be useful to be a bit of a style chameleon, at least until you start to gain your own unique voice through experience, practice, and osmosis. Over time you will no doubt find your voice and you will stand out without much effort – your passion and unique perspective will be appealing to many, and there is always room out there for new creative visions. Of course, there will always be the exceptional few among us who naturally develop a strong, unique style early on – that unfortunately wasn't me! I've certainly struggled through many years of drawing in what I feel was a very derivative style, and not having my own voice. I'm not even sure I really have a unique voice in my art even now.

Personally speaking, I don't really chase standing out from the crowd on social media – in fact, I try not to think about it. I do the best work I can, or whatever I am inspired to do in the moment, and put it out there. I have the passion to create art, something beyond the world of commercial work, with meaning and purpose, and while it would be nice for that to be appreciated out in the wild, that isn't necessarily what motivates me to do it. And while the number of artists and the amount of talent out there today can be overwhelming, right now there are more opportunities than ever before for character designers to find work.

Finally, are there details of any upcoming projects you can share with us?

I'm working on some fun projects at the moment and a few things that should be released in due course, but the nature of the job means I can't say too much until it's all out there. I've been developing some personal projects too, my main one being a graphic novel set in a fantasy version of Scotland. I've been working on it on and off for five years now – I would really like to get some momentum behind it soon and get it done. Aside from that, I am toying with the idea of creating an "Art Of" book, and maybe a short film. Unfortunately, there's just not enough time in the day!

This page: *The Magic Chest* – This image just happened spontaneously one day – it was the perfect moment where everything just seemed to come together. That doesn't happen often for me, so I appreciate it when it does

Opposite page: *The Treehouse* – A lot of my work revolves around capturing some nostalgia from my childhood – this was the treehouse I never had

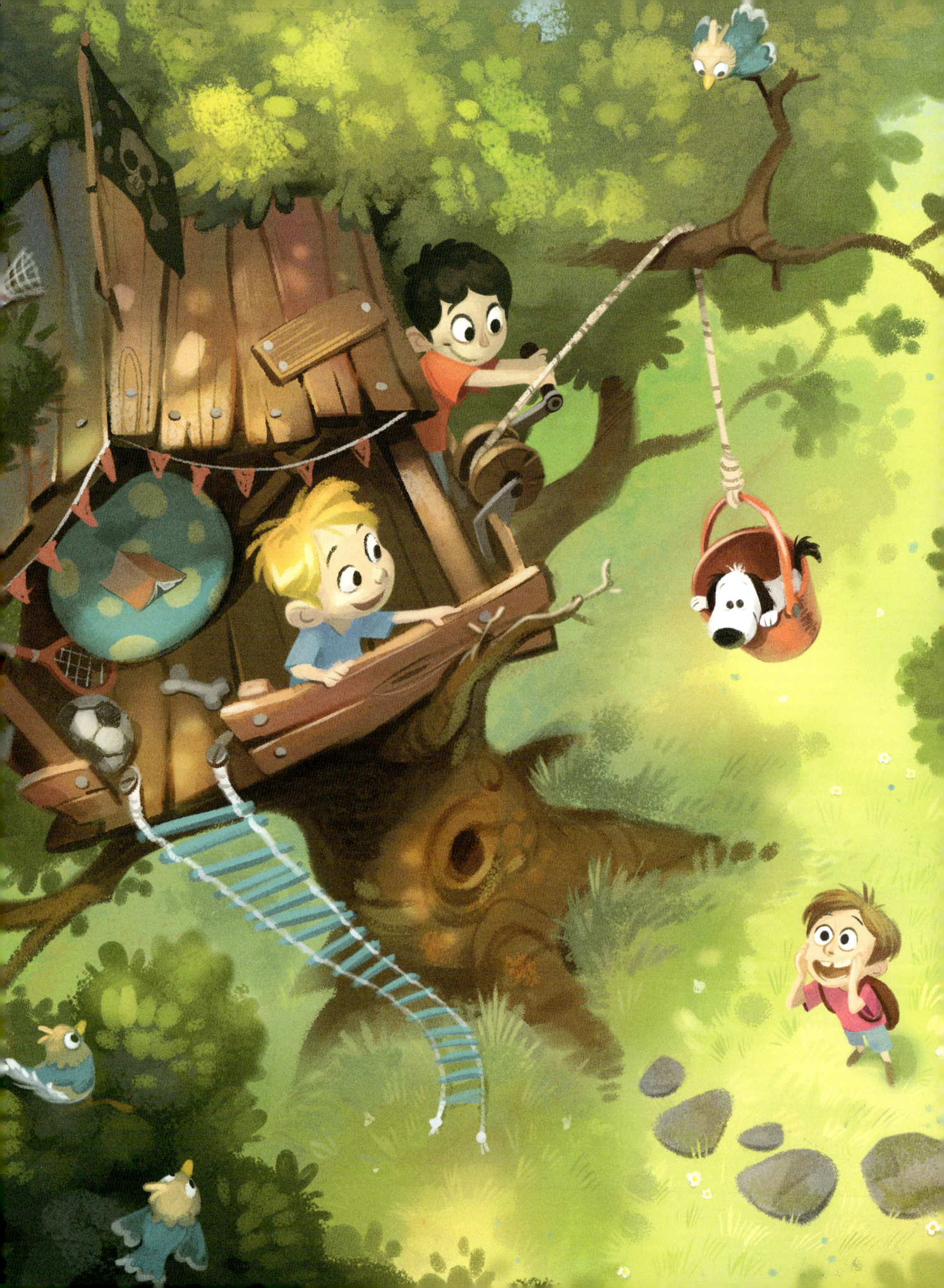

CRAFTING THE COVER

This tutorial covers my general process when it comes to character-based illustration, from sketching out ideas, to refining them into a thoughtful composition that sells a simple story moment. I like to keep my process as simple as possible, working from something very general to very specific. I will also touch on some things to bear in mind when illustrating for print media.

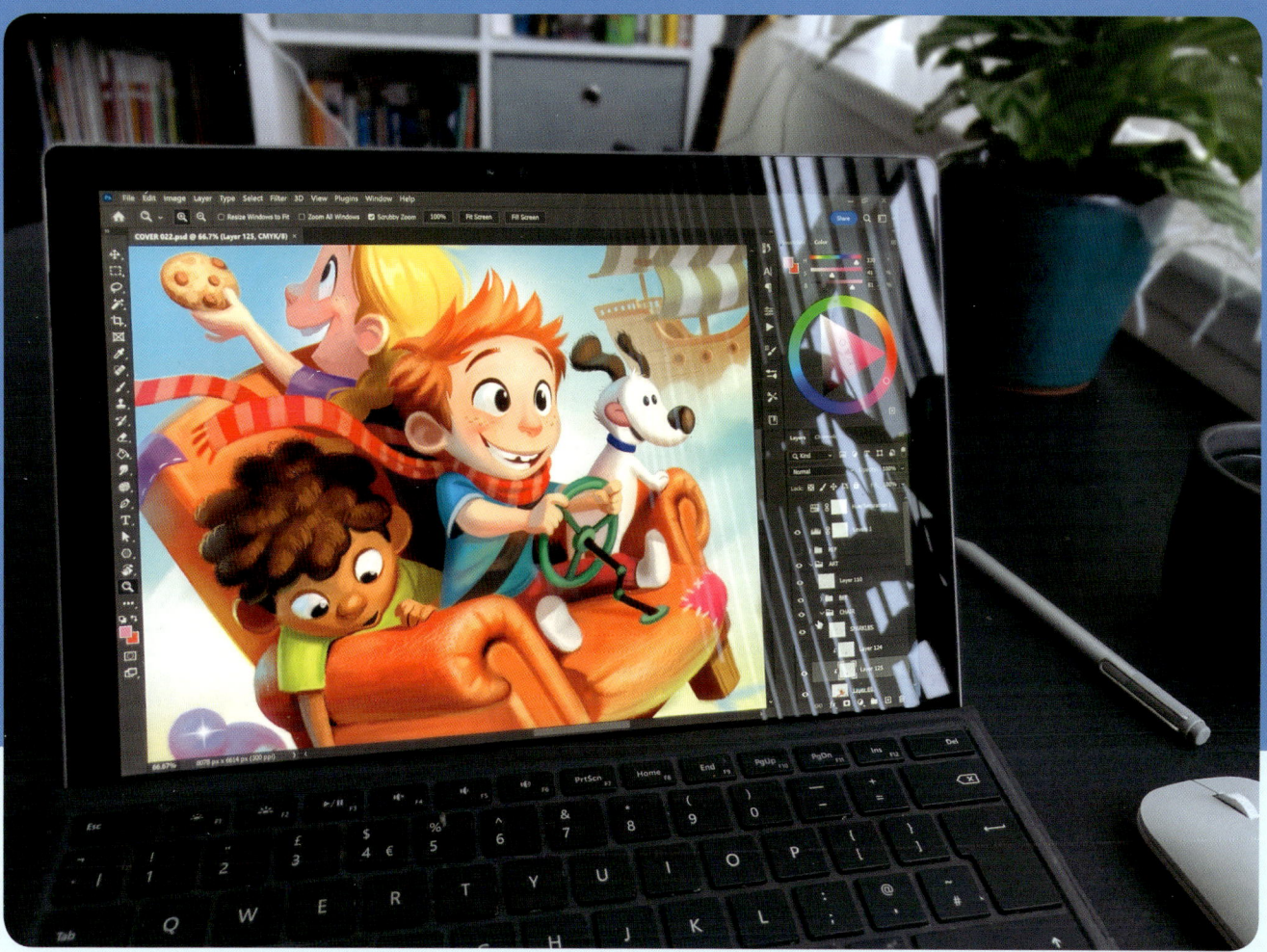

EXPLORING IDEAS

I start by playing around with ideas that are typical of my work and that I think will work nicely as a cover, while also being a bit different to previous *CDQ* cover art. Coming up with an idea is sometimes the hardest part for me. Much of my work involves a group of kids exploring or having fun in a simple story moment – I want this piece to be similar, so I explore a variety of ideas along these lines. I eventually settle on a silly but fun concept: three kids imagining themselves on a flying chair, surrounded by animals, monsters, and an airborne pirate ship. The idea is a bit of an homage to things I enjoyed as a child, such as *Calvin and Hobbes* and *The Wishing Chair*.

PREPARING THE CANVAS

Illustrating for print brings with it some unique requirements, so I prepare my image at the start carefully. I make sure the rough sketch fits the correct cover dimensions, including extra space for the bleed. I also mark where the spine of the magazine will be, so I know not to put any important information there. I also set my workspace to CMYK and 300dpi, as this is for print, and make sure to leave space in the top right of the image for the magazine logo. Lastly, I think carefully about the different elements in the sketch and how I can use them to lead the eye to the focal point – in this case, the kids in the chair.

"MUCH OF MY WORK INVOLVES A GROUP OF KIDS EXPLORING OR HAVING FUN IN A SIMPLE STORY MOMENT"

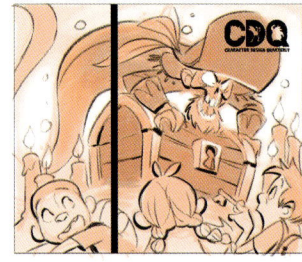
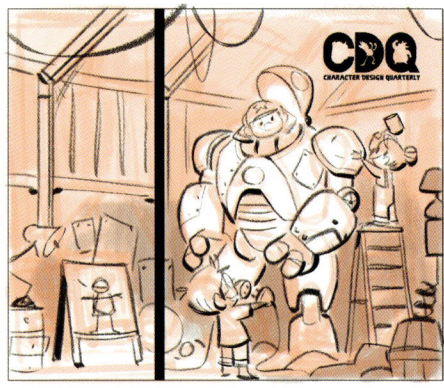
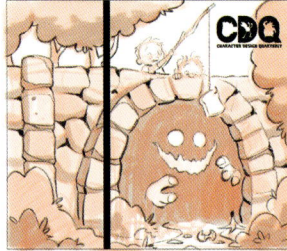
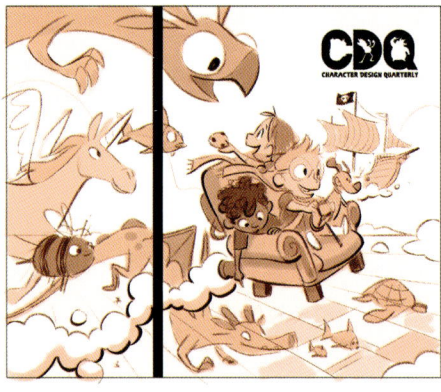
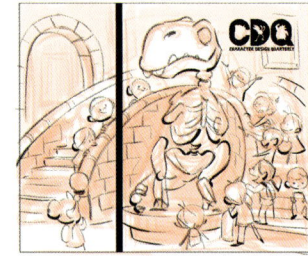

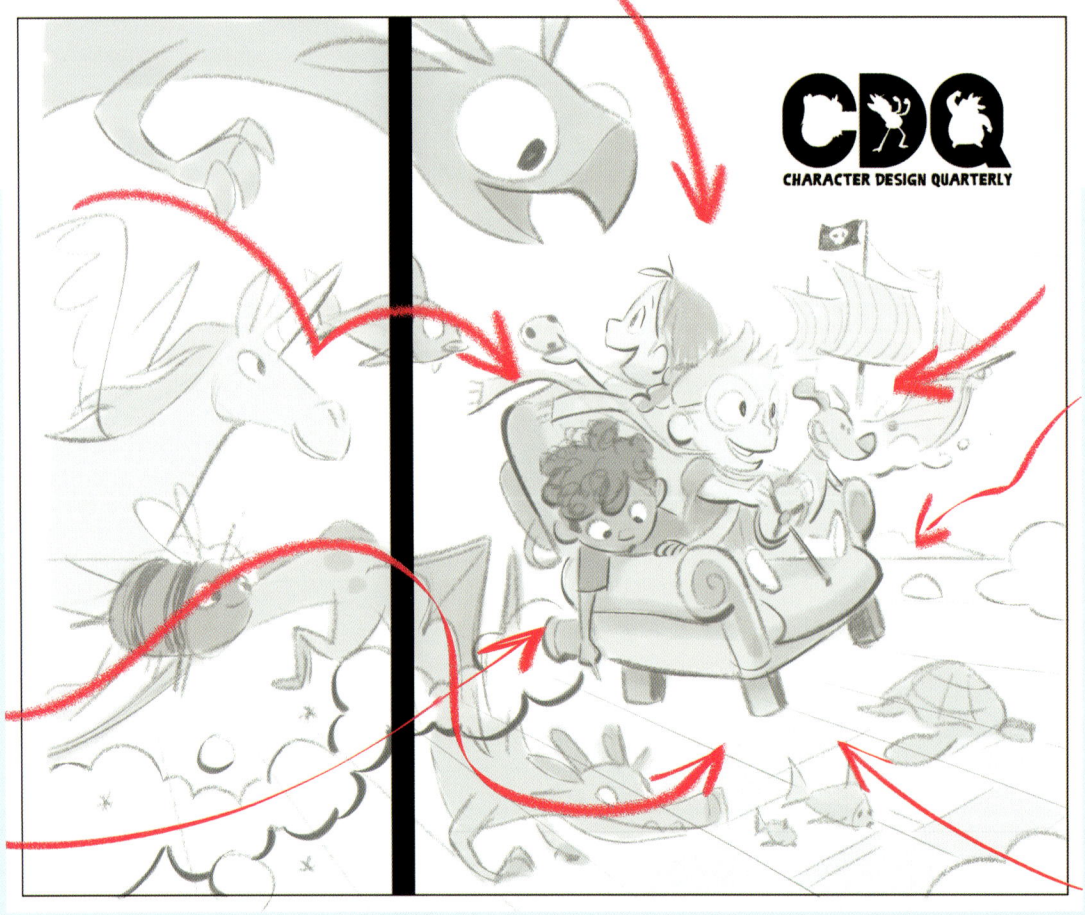

This page (top): Rough thumbnails are a great way to explore ideas without committing too much time and energy to them

This page (bottom): Preparation is key when drawing a print media illustration

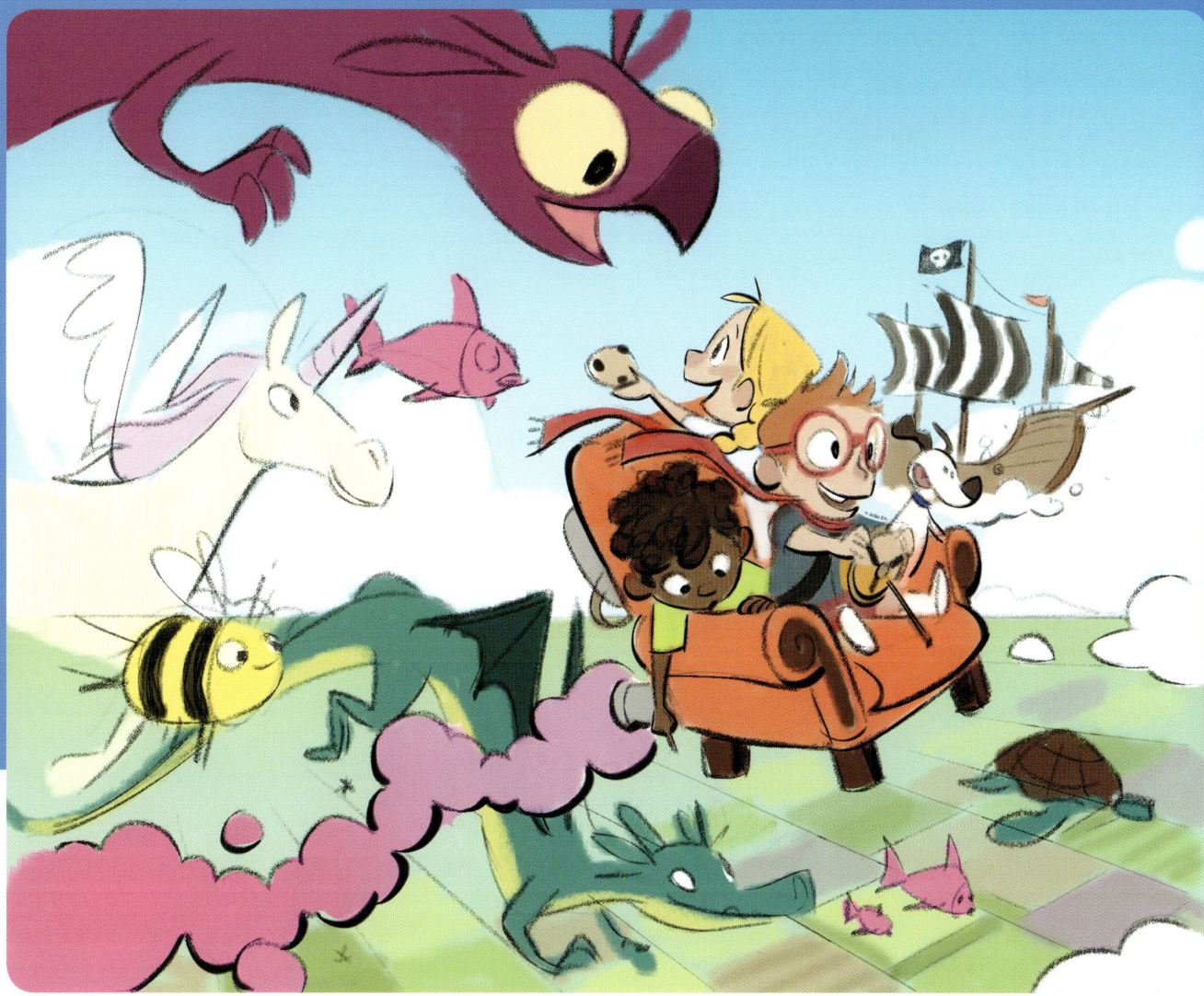

BLOCKING IN THE COLORS

My rough sketch was tight enough to work to, so I go straight to blocking in a color scheme around it. I prefer having a drawing to paint to rather than working without one – I find it easier to stay on track with the lines as a guide. I experiment based on how I want the image to look in my head: a fun, vibrant, daytime setting. The colors aren't set in stone here, I will likely push and pull them as I progress the piece. At this stage, my focus is on creating a harmonizing color palette – color isn't my strong point, so I find it helps to focus on local colors first and work from there.

ESTABLISHING THE FORMS AND LIGHTING

With a rough color direction in place, I start to paint out the lines of my sketch, and begin to establish my lighting direction. I find it best to lock this in as soon as possible so it's clear in my head as I continue painting.

I usually start with a simple Multiply later on top of my local color layer. The sketch was a good starting guide to work from, but now I need to figure out the structure and forms of the main characters, and other elements in the scene in more detail.

REFINING THE CHARACTERS AND COMPOSITION

I slowly build up the forms and lighting on the characters and background while pushing and pulling the placement of elements in the scene to work with the compositional lines I established earlier. I also start to use references to flesh out the design of the bees and the other background characters. It is also a good idea to check the grayscale value of the image every now and then to make sure there is a good tonal contrast developing.

"I START TO PAINT OUT THE LINES OF MY SKETCH, AND BEGIN TO ESTABLISH MY LIGHTING DIRECTION"

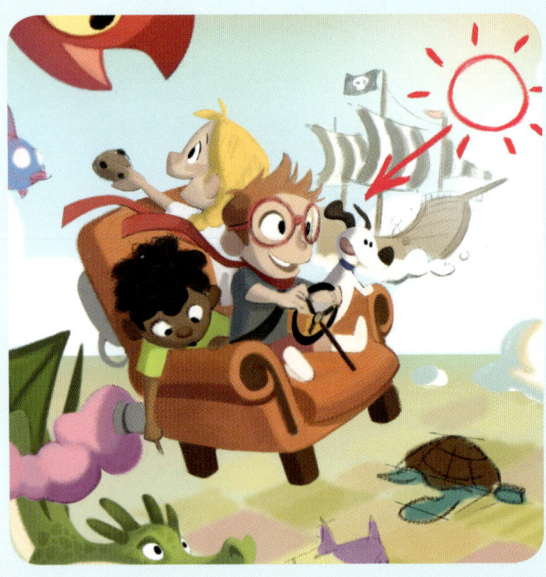

Opposite page: Using my rough sketch as a guide I start to block out the local colors of the piece

This page (top): I start to paint out the sketch lines, refining forms and bearing in mind the lighting direction

This page (bottom): Using references, I start to problem-solve the design of each of the characters

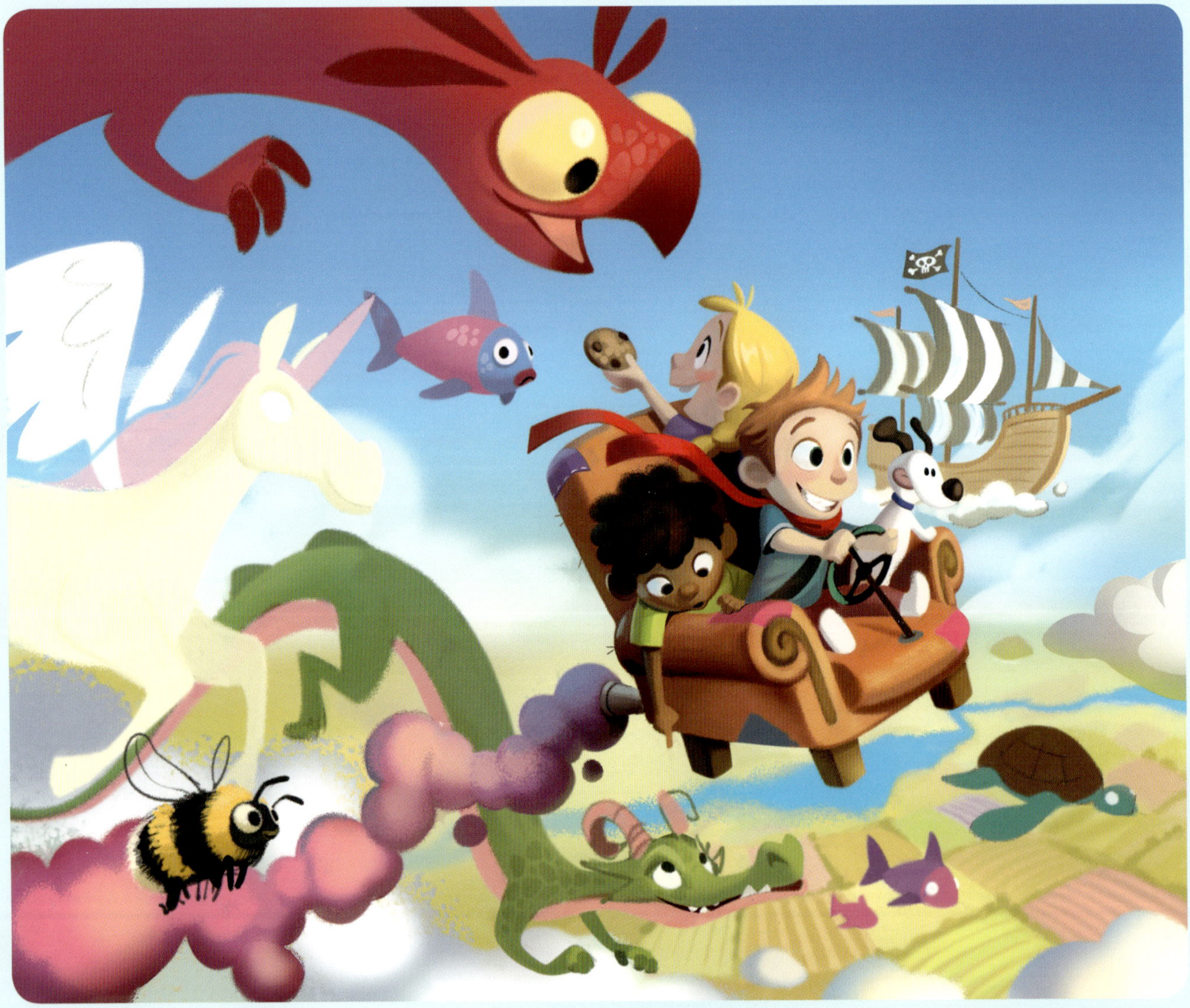

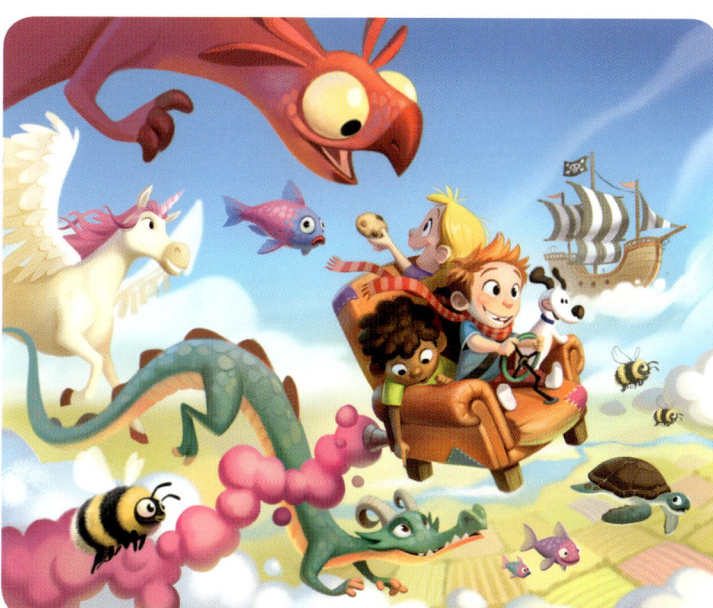

PAINT IT PERFECT

With most of the problem-solving done, the rest of the illustration process is just painting and refining the forms and lighting. I tweak the characters and composition as I go, investing most of my time rendering details and fine-tuning the composition. At this point, there are just a few extra details to add and some final tweaks before I consider it done. Personally, I am never 100% happy with work I create, but I try to stop myself being too much of a perfectionist and make peace with the art.

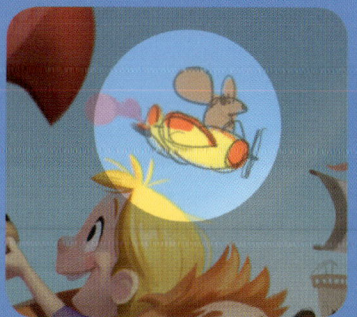

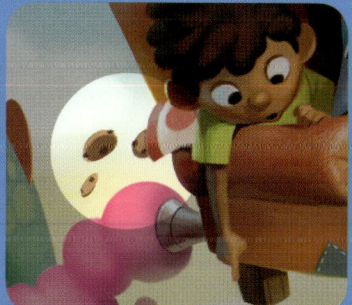

MICE MIGHT FLY

At one point I played with having a mouse flying a tiny plane in the background. While I liked the idea, I felt it was starting to crowd the image, so I removed it – sometimes, less is more. I also wanted some cookies falling out behind the sofa, but again, it cluttered the image and affected readability.

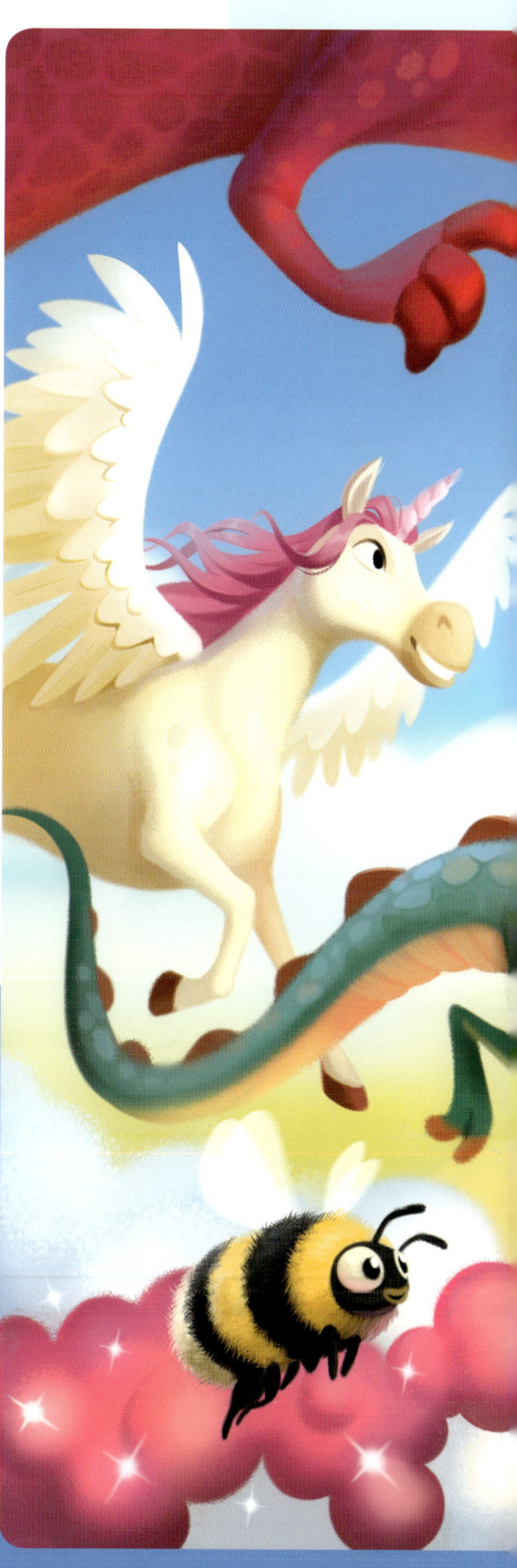

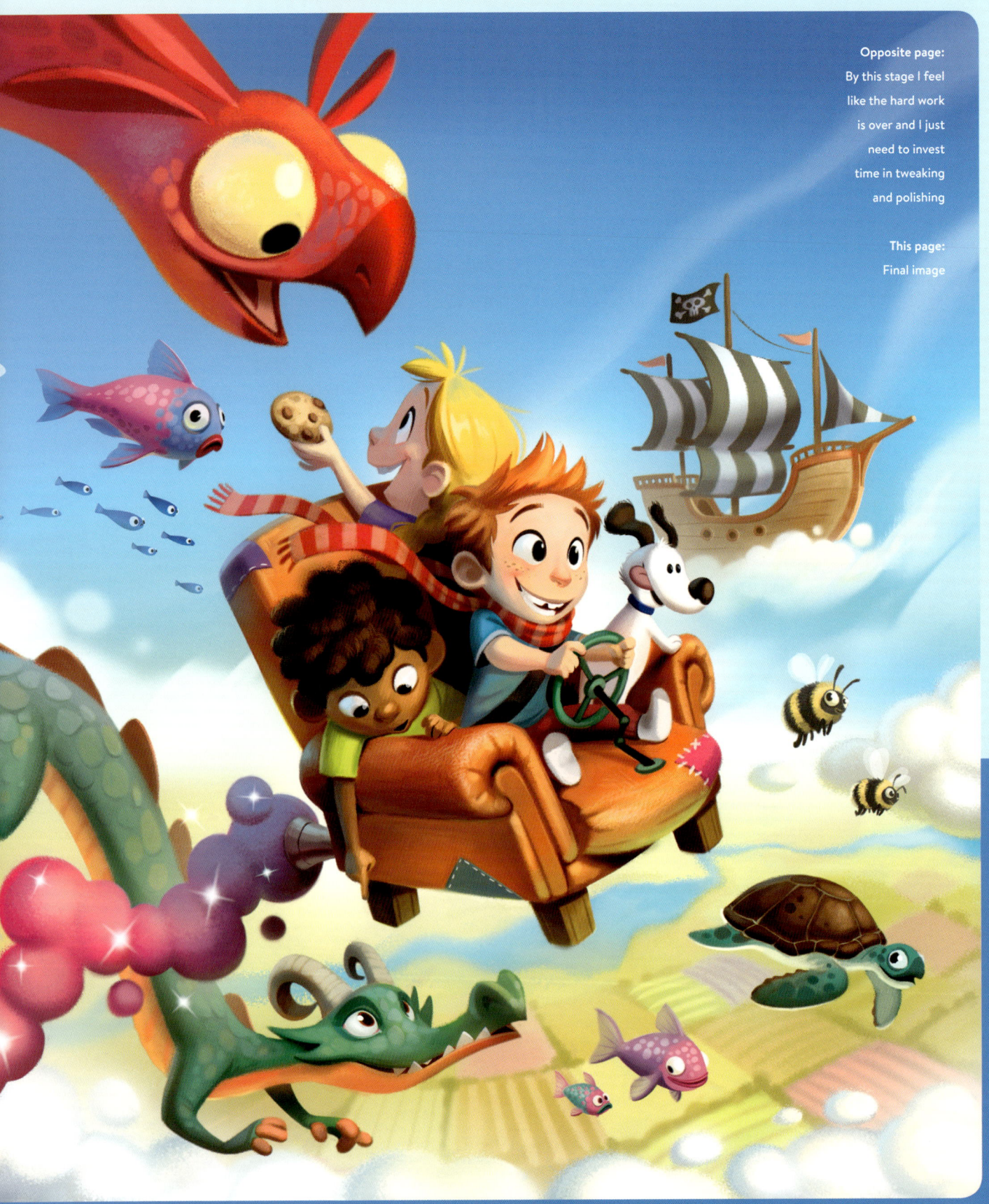

THE MANE STAGE

ANGEL REN

Character design is all about feeling the character deep down and imagining they are alive in the world and the story we are creating. Great designs will let the audience form an emotional bond with a character. For this mini tutorial, I will walk you through my creative process to design a white lion rock guitarist. I will emphasize the importance of research, as well as not being afraid to experiment and push the boundaries to help shape the character's personality.

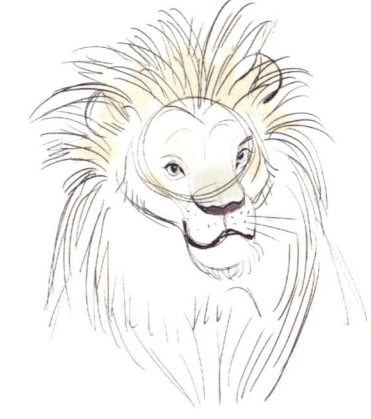
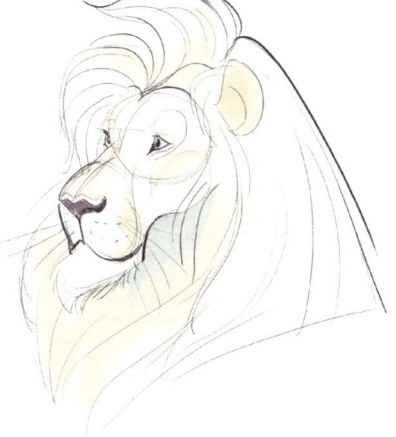

RESEARCH!

Good research will elevate your design and help you to create a believable living character. It can also give you a solid understanding of your character's structure and any unique features that different animal species or people may have.

White lions all have different mane and head shapes that suggest different personalities. Breaking down the lion's face into simplified sections will help you gain a better sense of where to push without losing the basic structure.

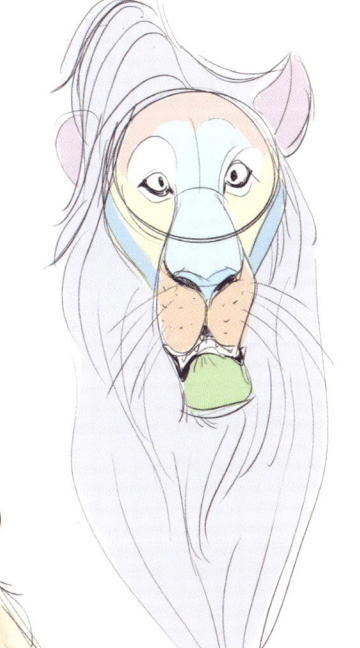
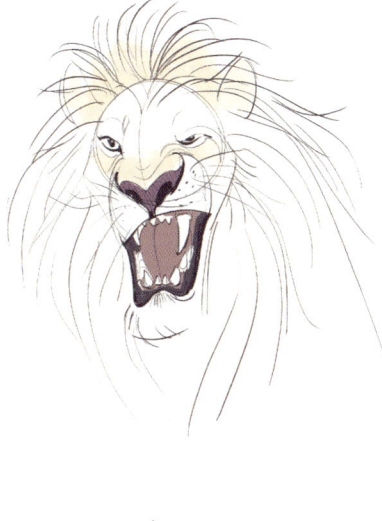

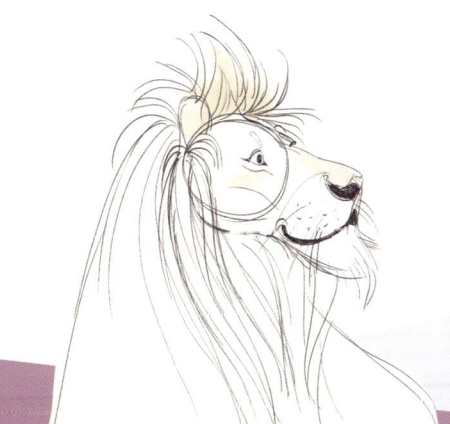

LET IT BREATHE

Before designing any character, I like to brainstorm and research real-life people, even my friends and family, who share the same personality as the character I imagine. Sometimes, you can even reference their facial features. Just sit down and watch a character on TV, or observe a friend's expressions and their body language. It's great fun to translate human emotions and body language into animal characters.

LET'S GO WILD

Let's start with the face – I find this the most fun part of designing a character! The lion's face is broken down into the mane, the ears, the forehead, the eye area, the cheekbones, the fur around the cheekbone, the nose, the mouth, and the jaw. Play around with pushing the shape and sizes of each section. Stay very loose and don't be afraid to draw out the weirdest designs that spring to mind. Think about how the mane can form into different interesting shapes – what do these shapes say about their personality? I also like to play around with soft and sharp lines that will further emphasize the lion's character.

DRESS FOR SUCCESS

Rock guitarists are often depicted wearing black leather jackets with spiky studs. This is the first idea that comes to my mind, but as designers, we should always be open to considering other possibilities – it's never too late to do more research. I choose three head designs that I like the most and blow them out based on the looks of three 1970s rock legends. Each of them has their own style of dressing on stage – I find the designs of their outfits hugely inspiring.

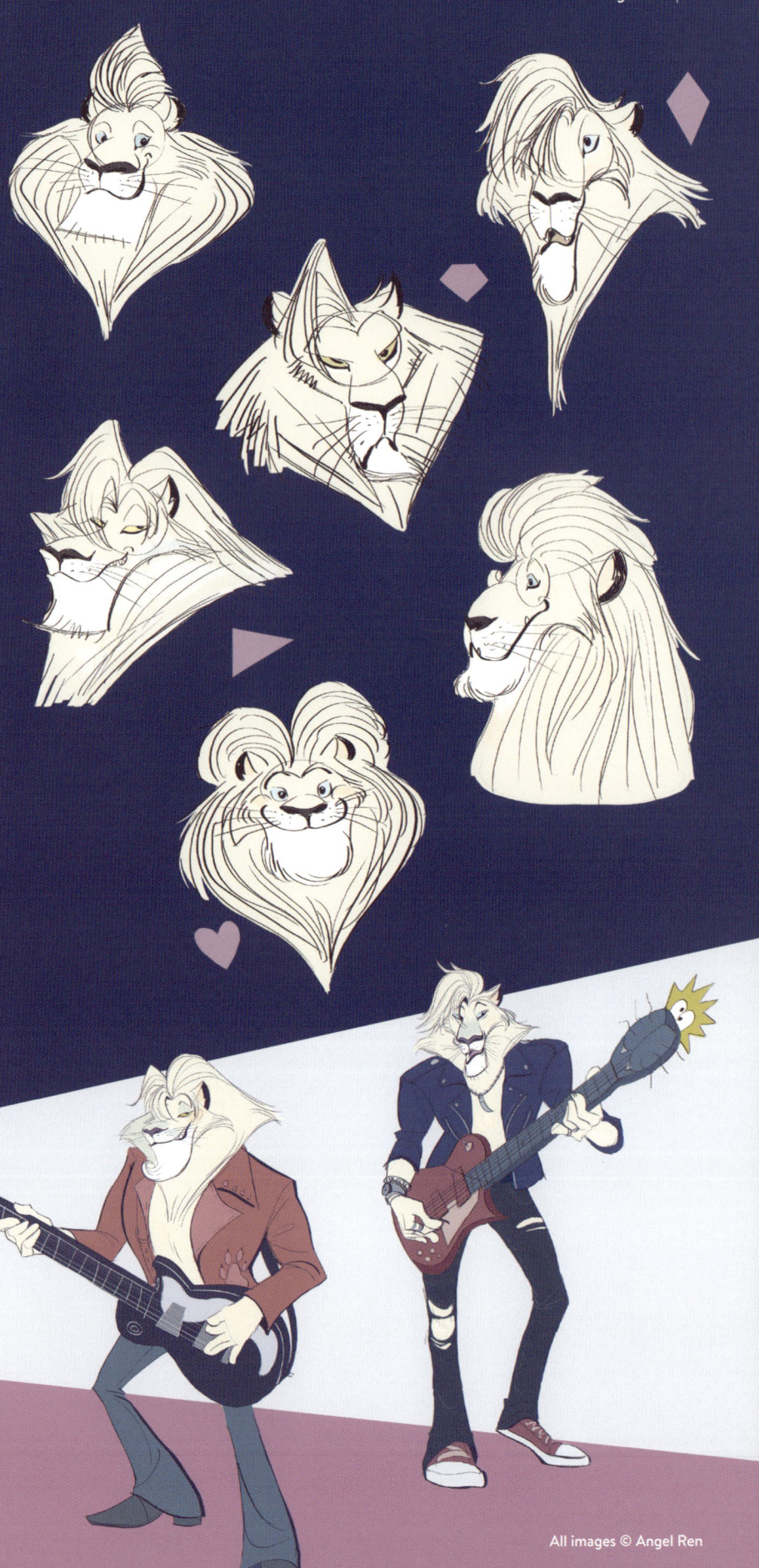

ACT THE PART

Having decided to move forward with the most charming lion design, it's time to bring him to life. Pull out a mirror or turn on your selfie camera and pretend you are your character. Since lions and humans have different facial structures, look for videos or photos of lions online and observe the funny faces they make. Always remember to maintain the consistency of your character – play around with squashing and stretching your design, but don't lose the volume.

PUSHING DYNAMICS

I finalize the design by dressing my lion in a red leather jacket. This will draw the viewers' eyes to his face and away from the guitar. Next, we need to decide on a pose. Posing will help you further understand how your character moves in a 3D space. After watching some rock band performances, I sketch down a few thumbnails of guitarists' awesome and dynamic stances. I choose two poses that I feel have a good silhouette and dynamic, and most importantly will convey the lion's charming personality.

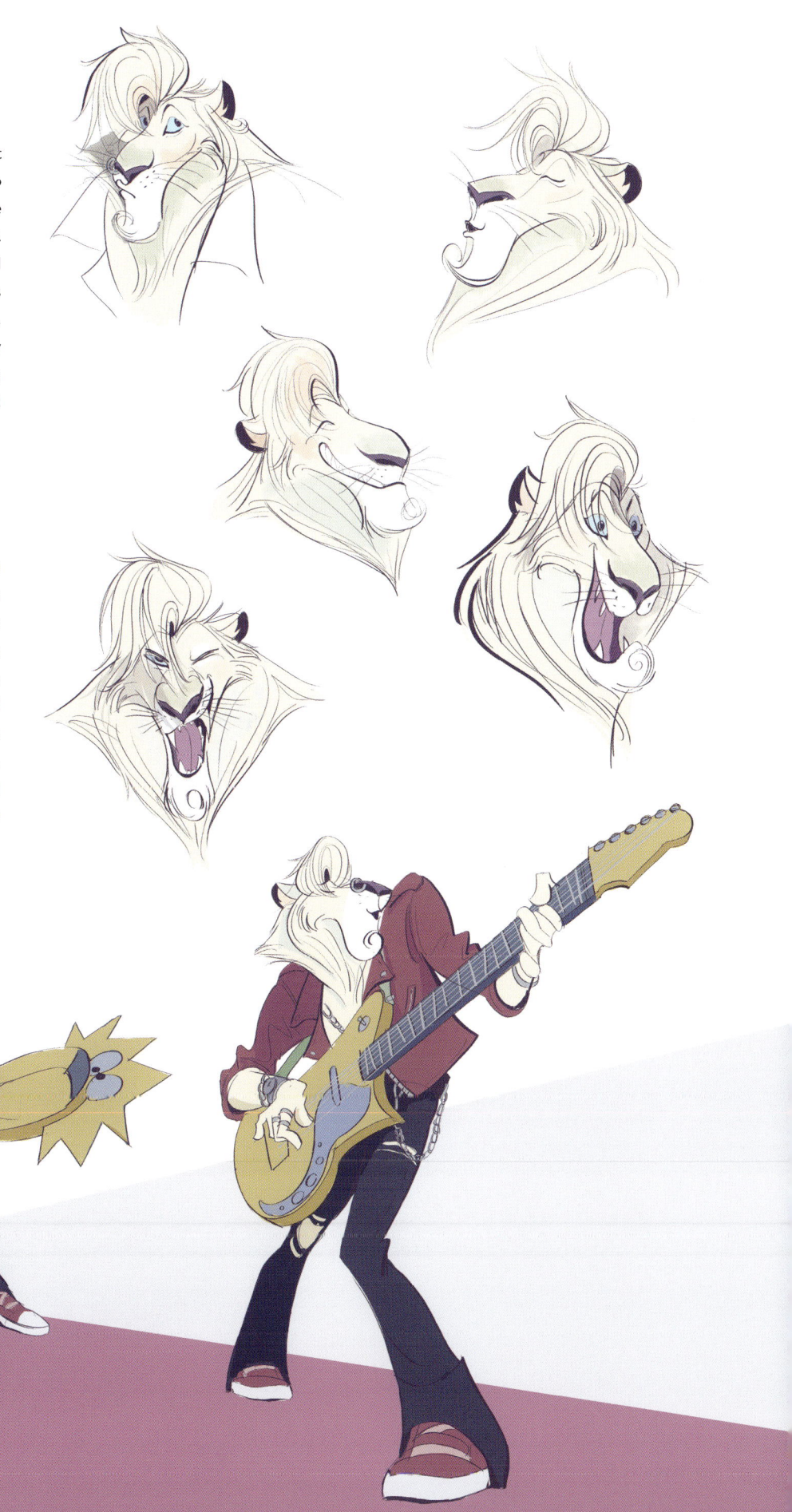

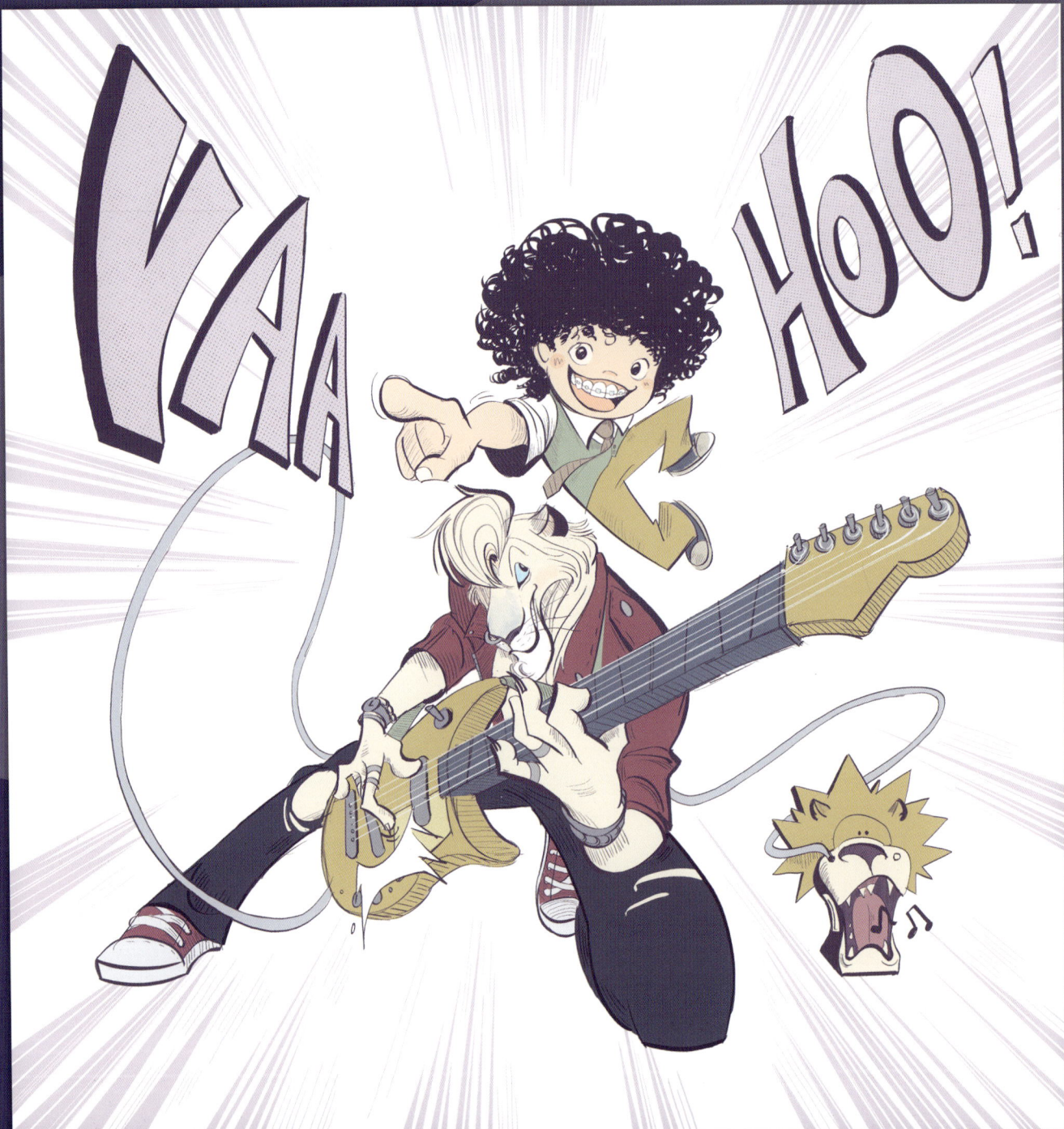

A ROARING SUCCESS

It's great to have your own unique style, but it can also be fun to experiment, explore, and try new things. In the final illustration, I want to further bring out the energy of a rock guitarist. I enjoy reading comics, and therefore I experiment with incorporating elements such as a comic-book line quality, action lines, and sound-effect words. And now, without further ado, let me introduce my white-lion guitarist, performing with his friend Roovy!

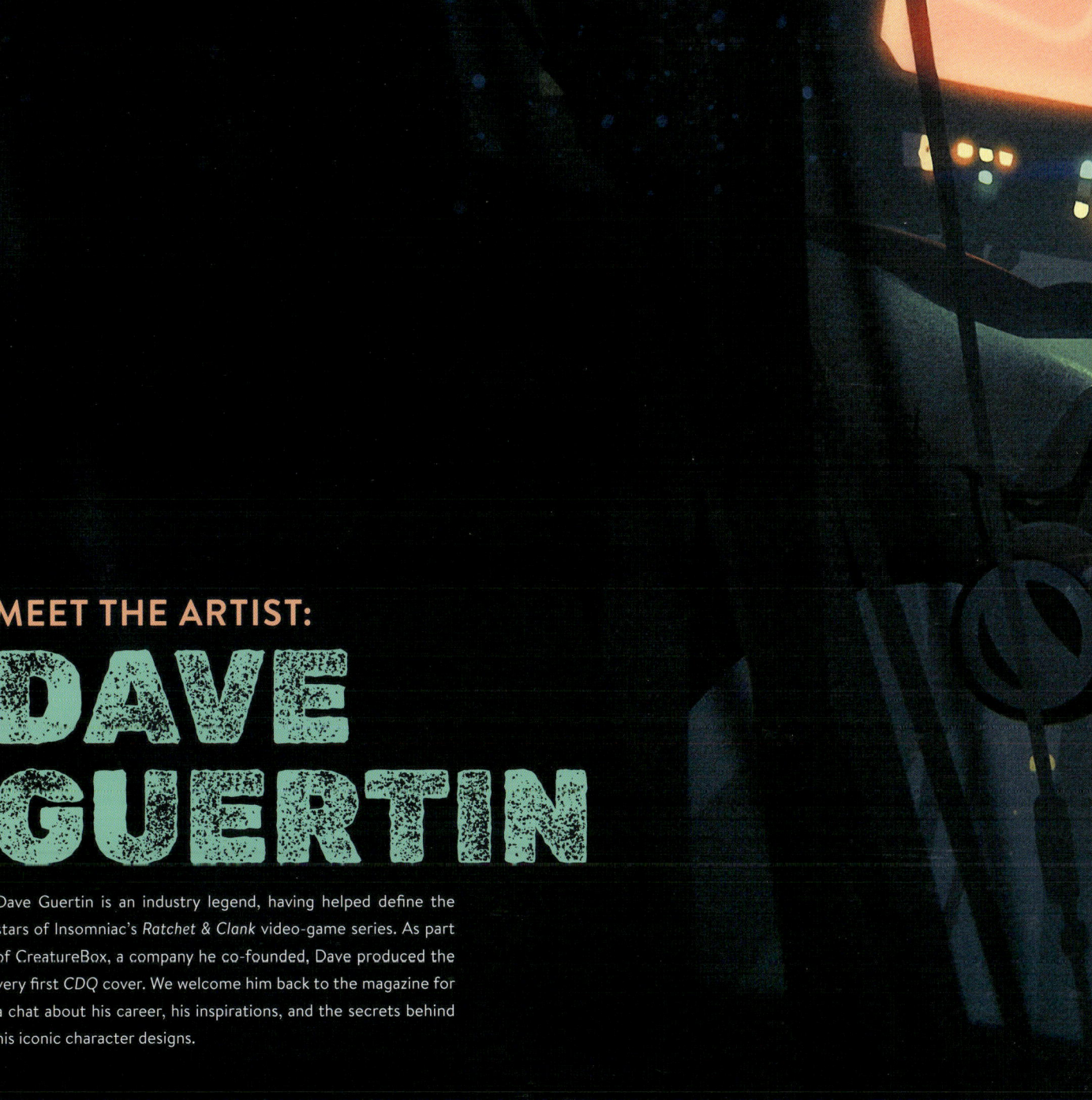

DAVE GUERTIN

Dave Guertin is an industry legend, having helped define the
stars of Insomniac's *Ratchet & Clank* video-game series. As part
of CreatureBox, a company he co-founded, Dave produced the
very first *CDQ* cover. We welcome him back to the magazine for
a chat about his career, his inspirations, and the secrets behind
his iconic character designs.

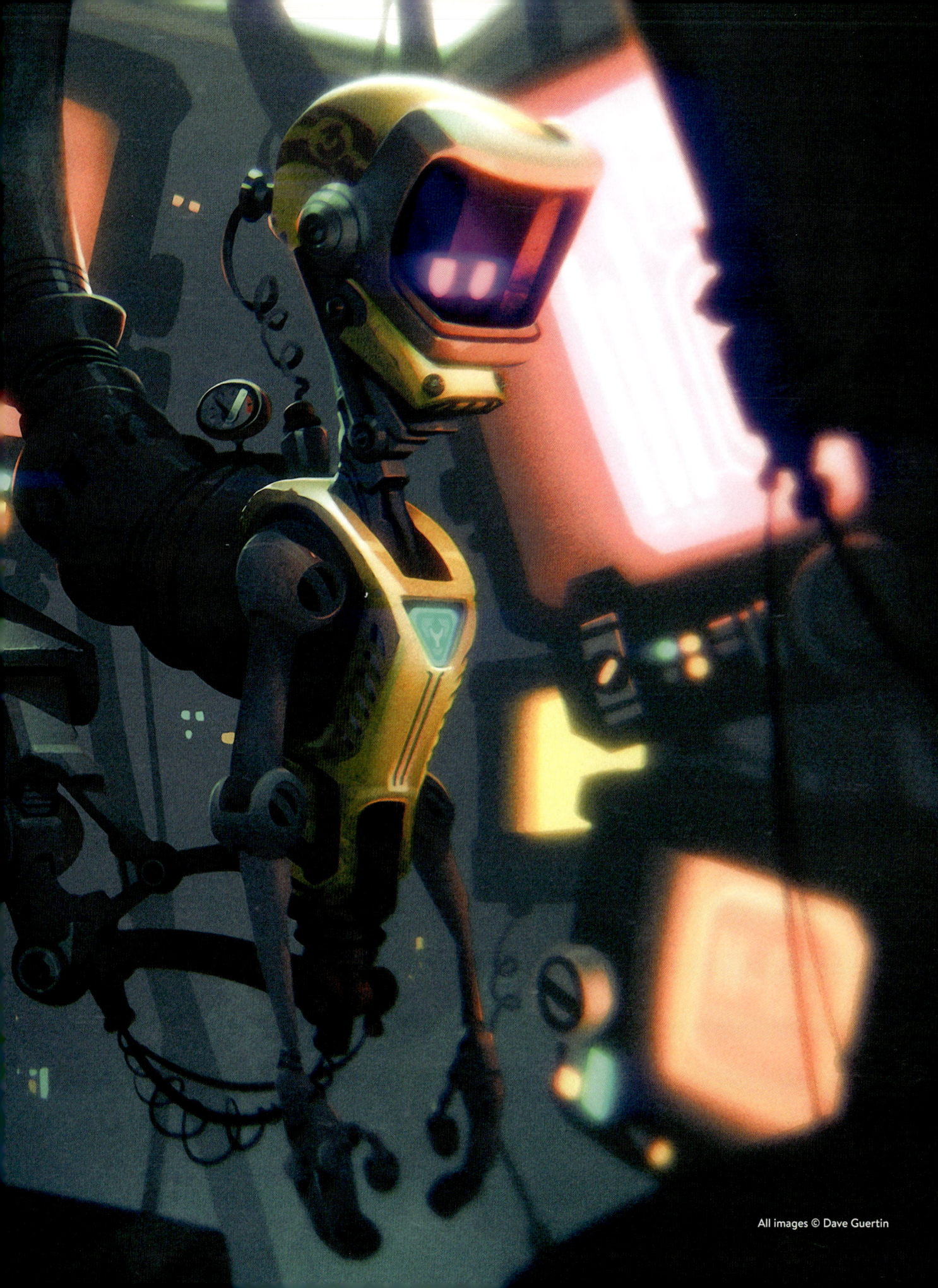

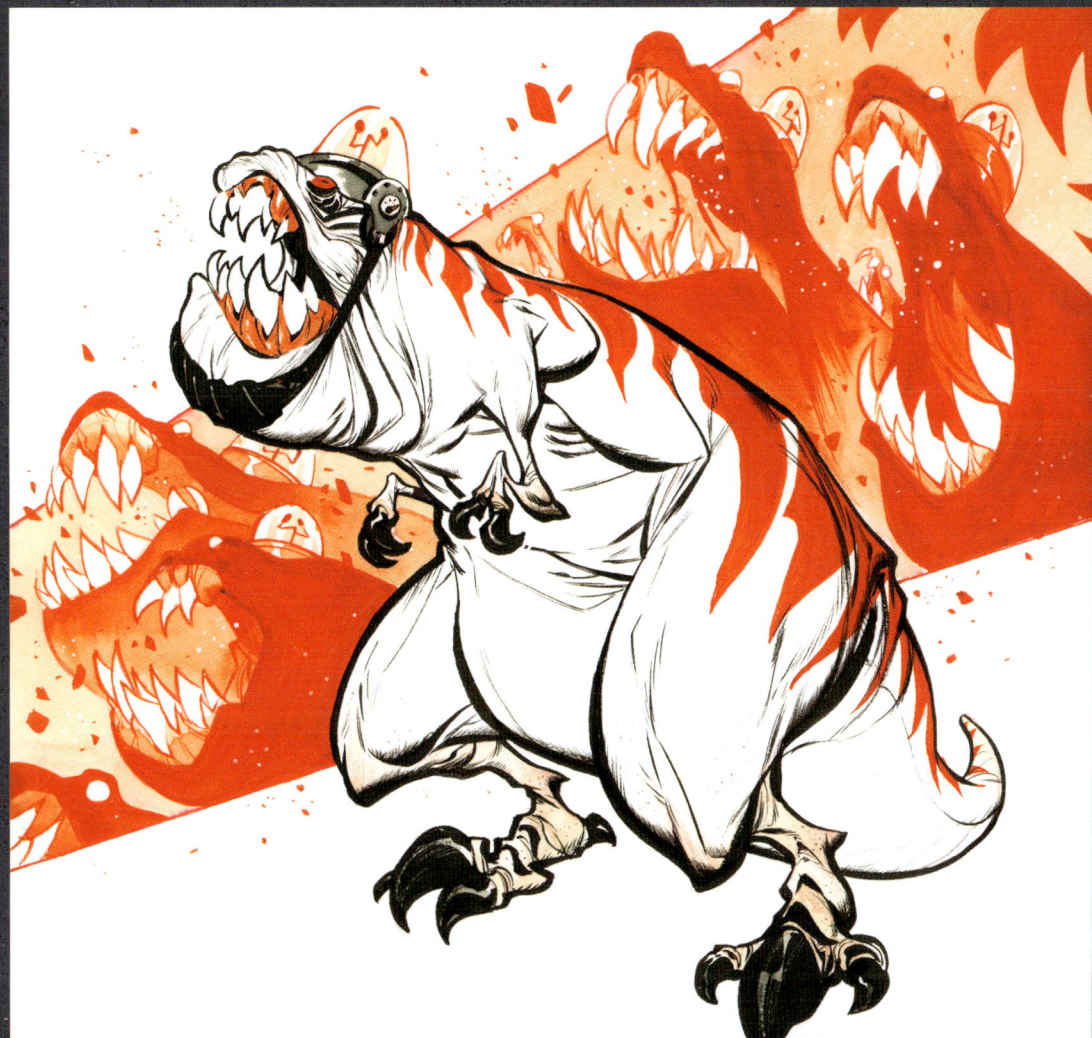

Hi Dave! It's great to have you back in CDQ! Can you start by telling our readers a little about your career to date and what you've been up to since CDQ 1?

Thanks for having me! *CDQ* continues to be such an amazing source of inspiration. Looking back, I've had the pleasure of working in the wilds of the entertainment industry for over 24 years. When I started out, I had big dreams of drawing comics for the major publishers in NYC, but the comics crash of the late 90s scuppered those plans. As I wrapped up school at the Savannah College of Art and Design, I pivoted to character design and concept art, and found myself swept up into the video-game industry. Within a couple years, through some surreal planetary alignment, I joined the pixel wizards at Insomniac Games to develop a mascot title for the PlayStation 2. Before long, *Ratchet &*

Clank were running around on screen. I had the privilege of helping to guide the character and visual development for the franchise.

While I was at Insomniac, my buddy Greg and I formed CreatureBox, where we explored IP development and self-publishing, joining forces with lots of remarkable companies across the industry. I'm not sure my 10-year-old self has fully recovered from the amazement of creating books of monsters or drawing Optimus Prime professionally.

After launching *Ratchet & Clank: Rift Apart* on PlayStation 5, I stepped away from Insomniac and jumped into freelance, while exploring a handful of personal projects. It's been an exciting time of discovery, with plenty of twists and turns, and the occasional spaceman wrestling an alien!

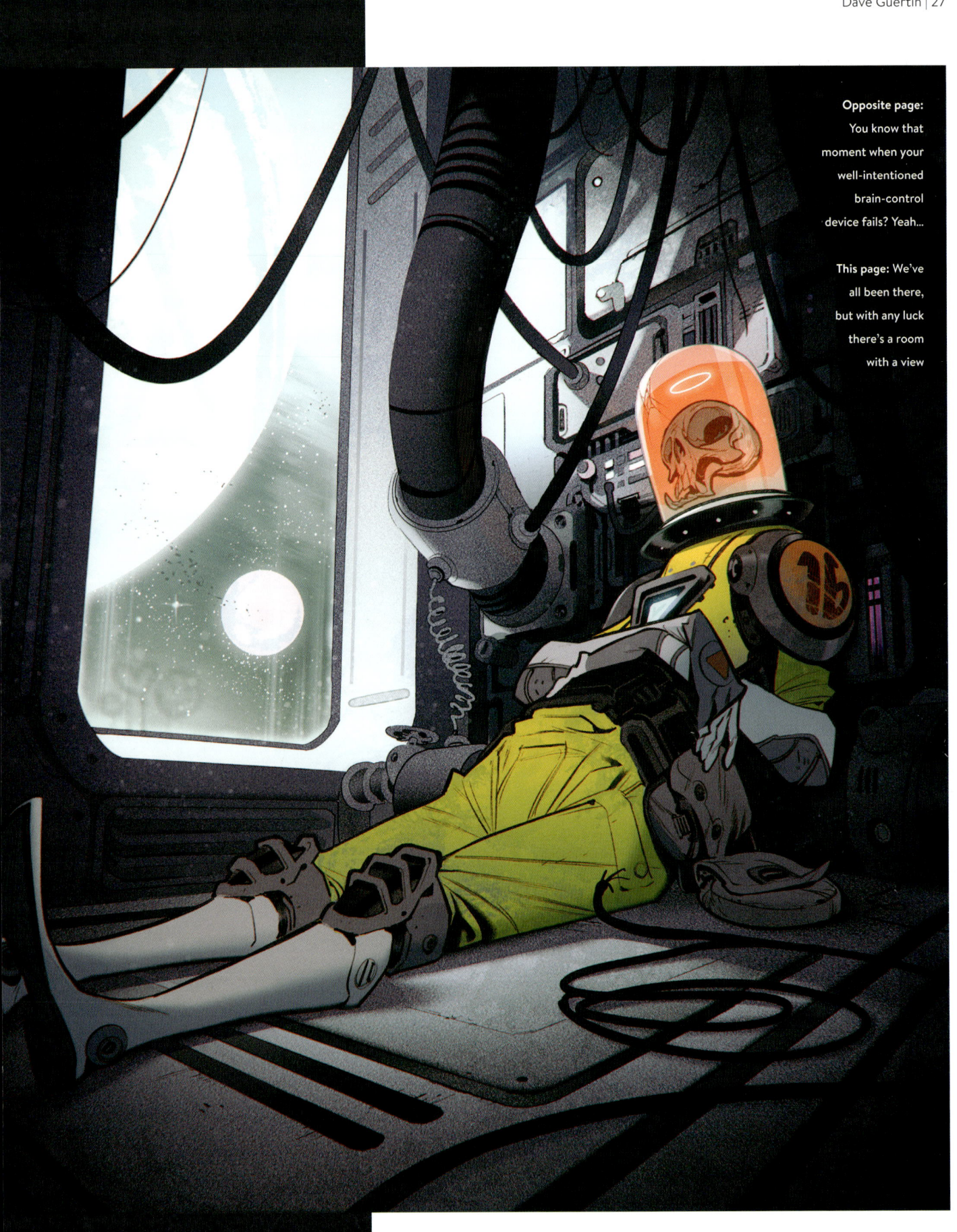

How did you keep your design ideas fresh and interesting while working in the *Ratchet & Clank* universe for so long?

I've always seen the *Ratchet & Clank* franchise as a wild sandbox with some pretty loose guardrails. As a team, we embraced the notion of "What if?" as a core pillar of the series. Clank, for example, was born from asking the gameplay designers, "What if Ratchet's gadgets were sentient?" This mindset continuously inspired vibrant, ridiculous brainstorms – almost like an island of misfit toys waiting to be brought to life.

Ratchet is also focused heavily on a sense of exploratory wonder. Traveling throughout the solar system is a pretty broad canvas – we worked to celebrate intergalactic discovery, which begged for shape variety. We wanted to surprise players, while still pulling thematically from relatable aspects of life, relationships, and obstacles. Introducing these more human elements was extremely helpful in forming a compelling cast.

Ultimately, I'm a classic sci-fi junkie. I continue to find myself immersed in Streamline Moderne architecture, 60s industrial design, and all things *Flash Gordon*.

Do you have any advice for our readers who are looking to work in video games in particular?

The great news is there's never been a better time to jump into game development. The tools professionals use every day – such as Unity, Unreal, and Blender – are completely free to play with and learn. This allows anyone with a curiosity for games to jump in and explore the endless potential of the medium.

For the budding character designers out there, never forget the importance of clarity in your drawings. Since video-game characters are often seen at many different sizes on screen, players should be able to understand your creations at a glance. Iconic shapes, paired with carefully organized details, go a long way in helping designs read as clearly as possible. And if I can ever get the flux capacitor on my time machine working, I plan on begging my younger self to draw from life more often. As designers, we're tasked with displaying a keen understanding of the familiar, while celebrating the spectacular. Nothing helps that process more than truly studying and sketching the people and places around us.

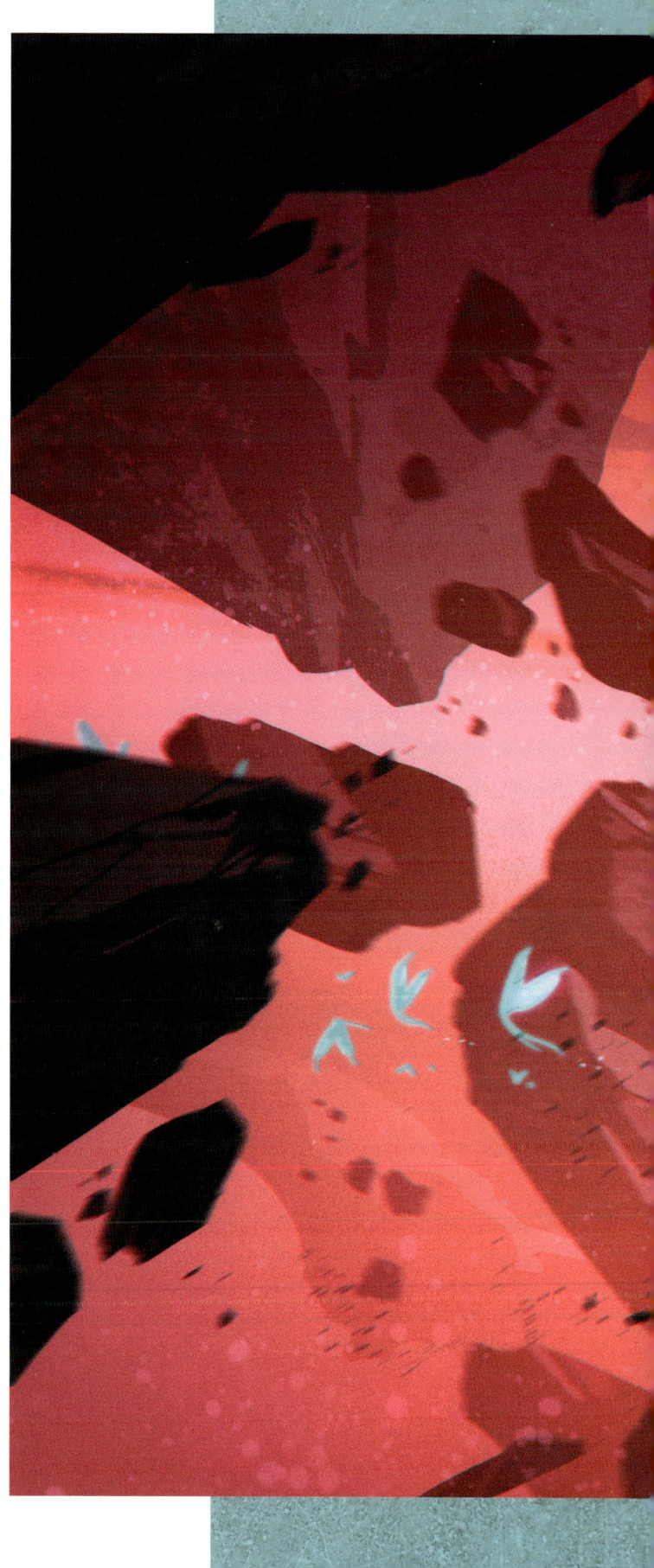

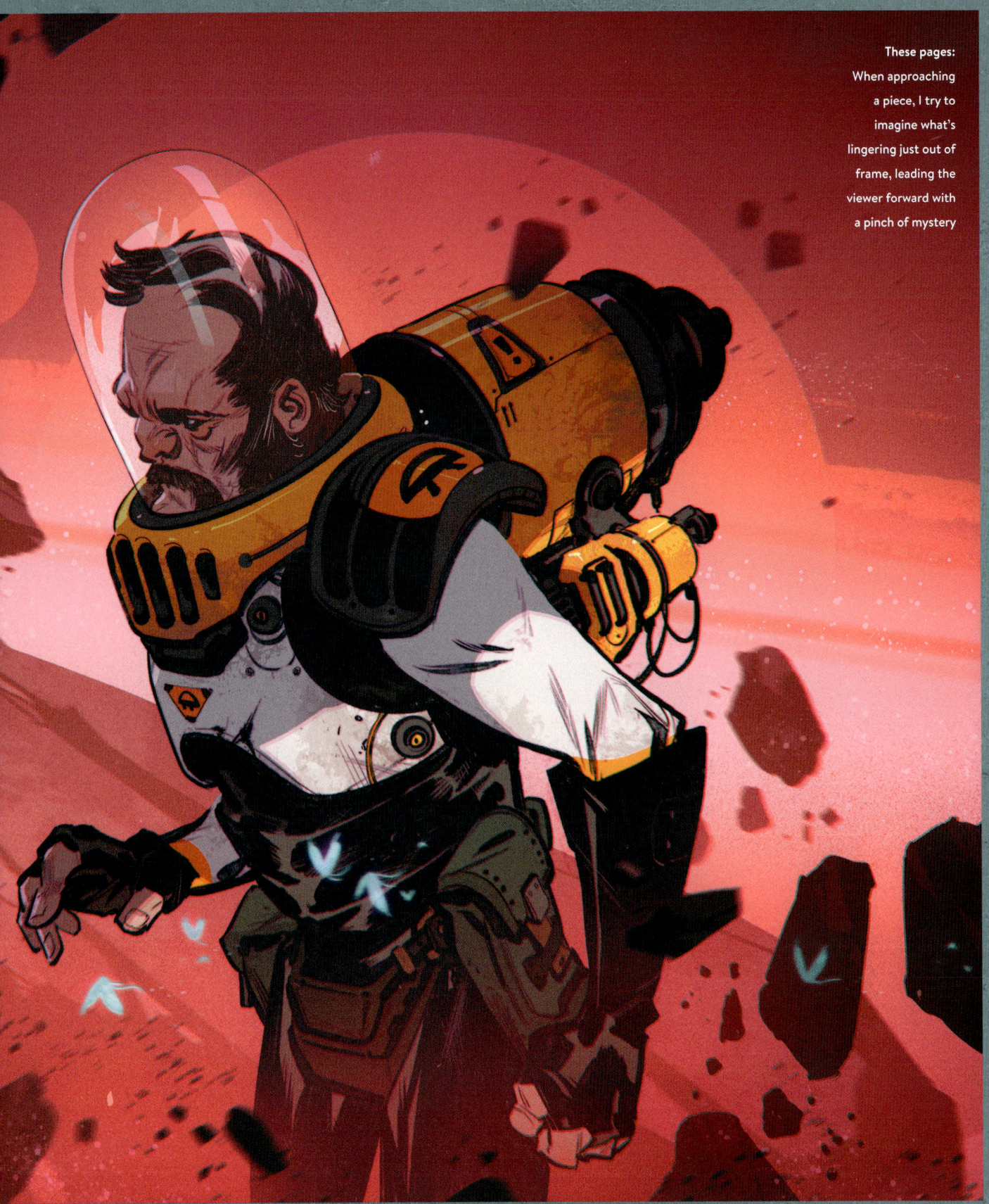

This page: I love experimenting with different designs – this is my time to ask "What if?" as I dig for new themes

Opposite page: I've always been a big fan of exploring shape and scale contrast, especially when an evil robot head gets knocked off

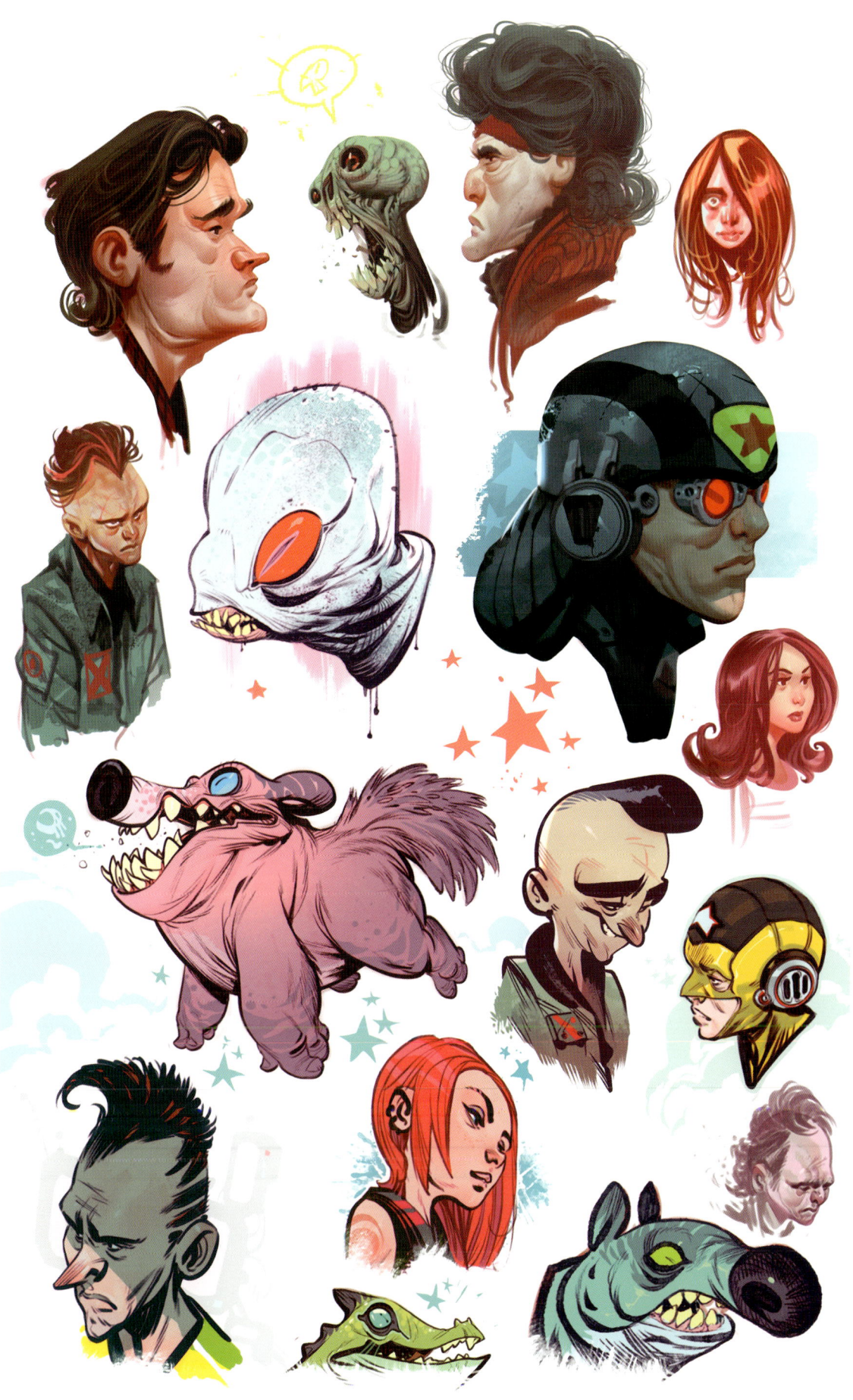

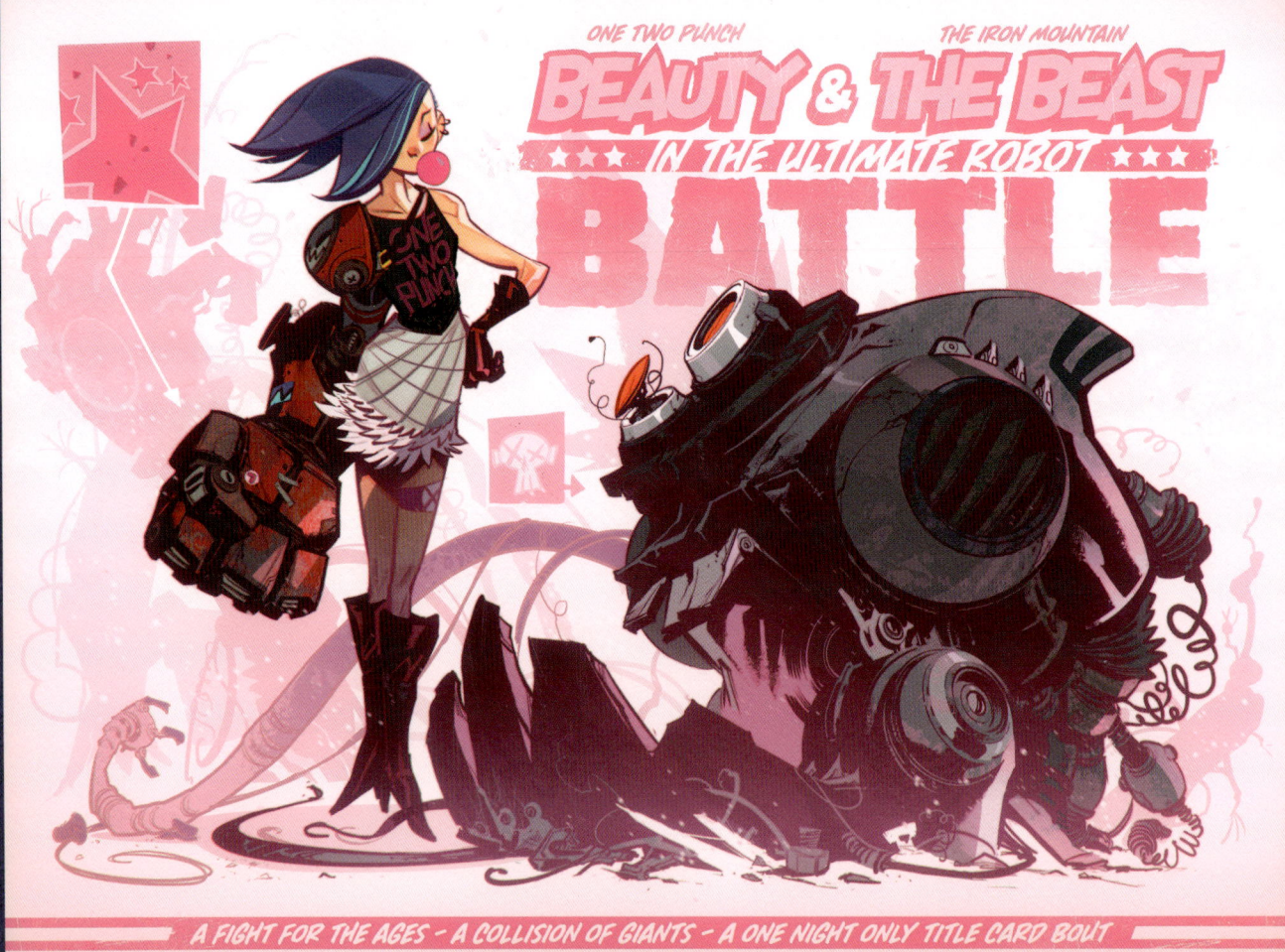

ONE TWO PUNCH

THE IRON MOUNTAIN

BEAUTY & THE BEAST

IN THE ULTIMATE ROBOT BATTLE

A FIGHT FOR THE AGES - A COLLISION OF GIANTS - A ONE NIGHT ONLY TITLE CARD BOUT

" WHEN I LOOK AT THE WORLD, I'VE ALWAYS BEEN ENAMORED WITH THE BALANCE OF CLUSTERED DETAIL AND AREAS OF REST "

Who and what have been the biggest influences on your style of character design?

Considering the constant stream of stunning work being produced, my influence list has become pretty endless. It's safe to say Bill Watterson's *Calvin & Hobbes* was my first love in cartooning. Each strip was a masterclass of charm and humor, punctuated by his revolutionary Sunday comics. I went on to discover other classic artists, including Winsor McCay, Alex Toth, Mort Drucker, and many others.

Modern masters also continue to inspire me every day. I'm blown away by everything from the graphic clarity of Mike Mignola, the hyper rendering of Travis Charest, the charm of Enrique Fernández, Andrew Robinson, and Jamie Hewlett, to the kinetic energy of James Harren and Ben Caldwell. And you can't go wrong with the timeless relatability of Cory Loftis, the impeccable weight and form of Claire Wendling, the endless immersion of Paul Felix, or the stunning vision of Syd Mead and Eyvind Earle.

When I look at the world, I've always been enamored with the balance of clustered detail and areas of rest. This rhythm reveals itself constantly from tree bark, to lizard scales, to factory machinery. There's this hidden ruleset of focus just under the surface that I try to excavate and learn from each day.

Can you talk a little more about the idea of rhythm and balance in character design? How do you apply that?

To me, compelling character design revolves around establishing core focal points: the primary area of a character that drives much of their soul. Imagine, for example, we're designing a character called Bart Kruger, the mayor of a lawless town from the Old West. Bart might be a stout fellow in a black suit, with a towering stovepipe hat and a glimmering silver bolo tie. From a design perspective, we could use the hat's tall, clean shape to drive focus downward, while the length of the tie would drive attention up toward the head. Together, these two elements would work together to frame Bart's face which would be our primary focal point. If we were then to add a furrowed brow, his expression could serve as a nice cluster of detail, balanced against the clean hat above, and the dark jacket below.

I often feel character designers deal in miles and millimeters, meaning the broad shapes and the tiny details must work hand-in-hand to maintain harmony. The trick is deciding early in the process which elements deserve the spotlight.

So much of your work feels alive and bursting with energy. Do you have any advice for making still images feel so dynamic?

When I think through the energy of a scene, I try to define the source and direction of the momentum. For characters, this tends to begin with the torso and works outward to the limbs. An arched back, compressed chest, or a twist of a stomach can all play a critical role in defining pleasing flow and dynamic lines of action. I try to keep the shapes clean, almost as if to say one thing at a time rather than a series of conflicting ideas. Glenn Keane has shared timeless teachings from Ollie Johnston where he explained, "Don't animate what the character is doing, animate what the character is thinking." I feel the same applies to all aspects of character design, essentially drawing from the inside out while allowing your character's intent to drive all the posture.

This spread: I think it's safe to assume these birds have plenty of stories to tell

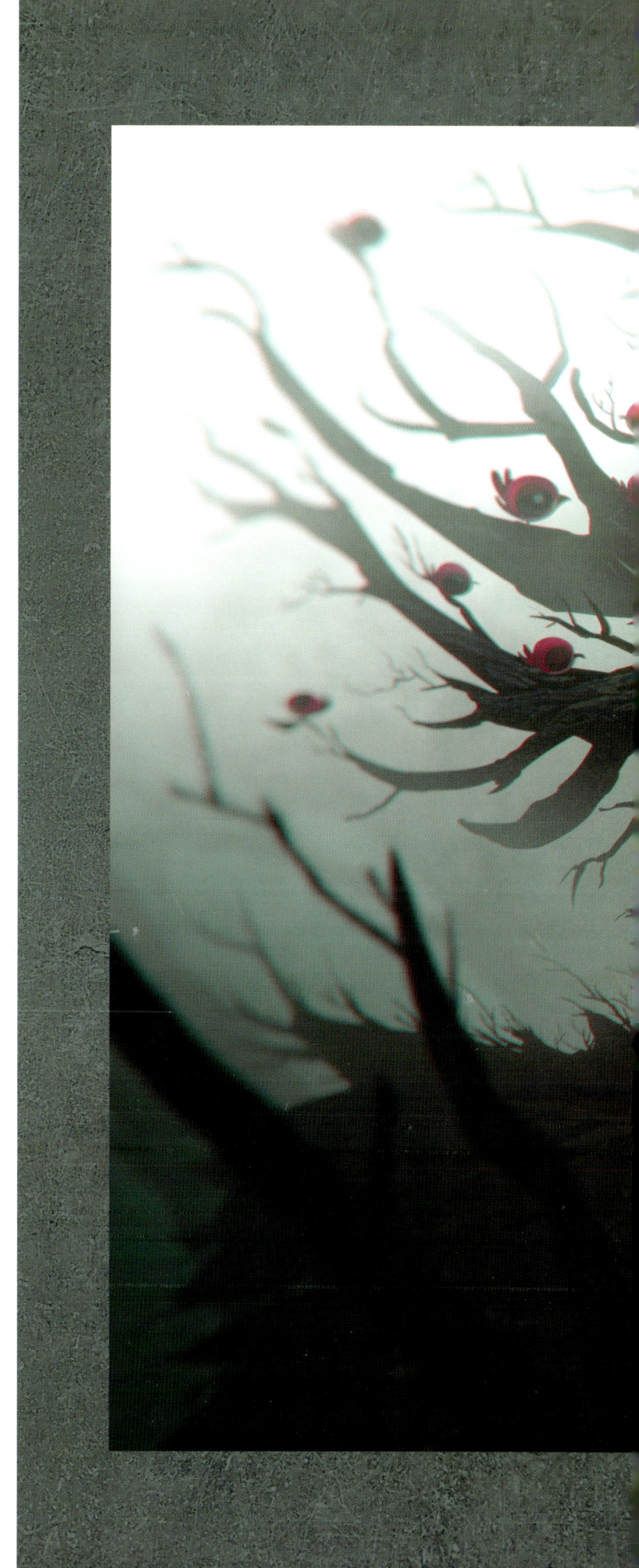

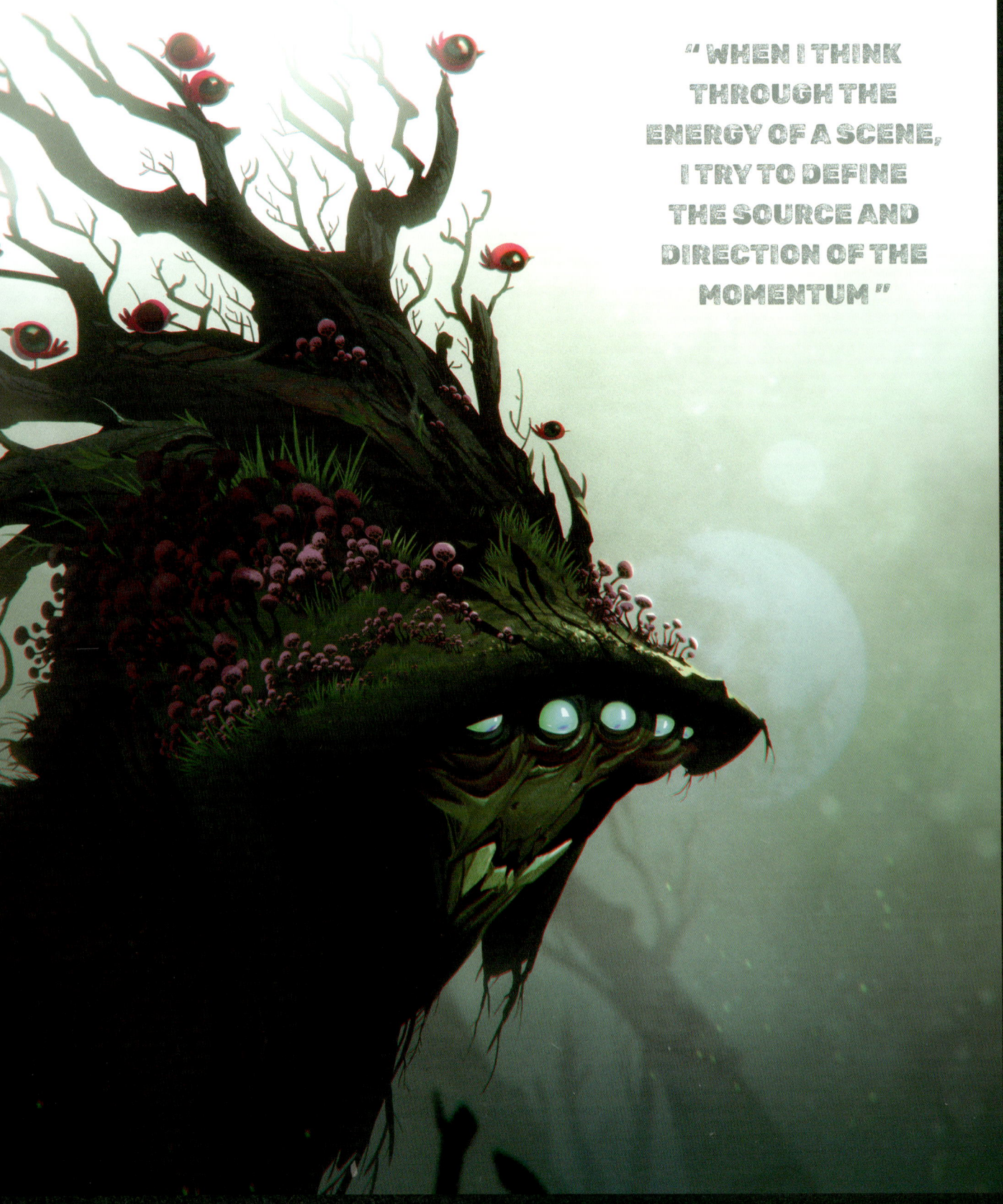

" WHEN I THINK THROUGH THE ENERGY OF A SCENE, I TRY TO DEFINE THE SOURCE AND DIRECTION OF THE MOMENTUM "

What aspect of character design do you find the most challenging and what stage comes easiest?

For me, capturing that initial iconic shape tends to be the trickiest. There's always a battle in defining the core personality of a character as efficiently as possible, all while maintaining clarity. Sometimes, I get a creeping feeling that all the shapes are taken, especially when faced with a century of design history. But similar to how most pop songs make use of the same handful of chords, when you find that unique thread it's always invigorating to realize how much variation can exist in the world. The key is staying true to what your character is trying to say.

If I've done my job in the initial shape stage, executing the actual drawing comes much easier, almost as if the character has been waiting to reveal themselves. I tend to scold them for not showing up sooner.

Do you have an example of a character design you struggled with, but ended up looking great?

Most designs like to put up a fight, but lead characters with large amounts of screen time usually require the most focus. In the case of *Ratchet & Clank: Rift Apart* for the PS5, we introduced Rivet, a new mascot hero. While working through her design, I had to balance several spinning plates, making sure she visually plugged into an existing cast of characters while still maintaining her own voice.

I began the process with a blue-sky phase of creating several designs highlighting various archetypes. Adventurers, thieves, androids, and freedom fighters all made their way to the page and helped spark broader discussions and experiments within the team. Bit by bit – through a host of brainstorms, drawings, and rough models – she began to take shape. There were plenty of roadblocks, though the crucial ingredient was working together to iterate across departments, allowing her personality and primary details to rise to the surface. Without a doubt, character design throughout production is a team sport.

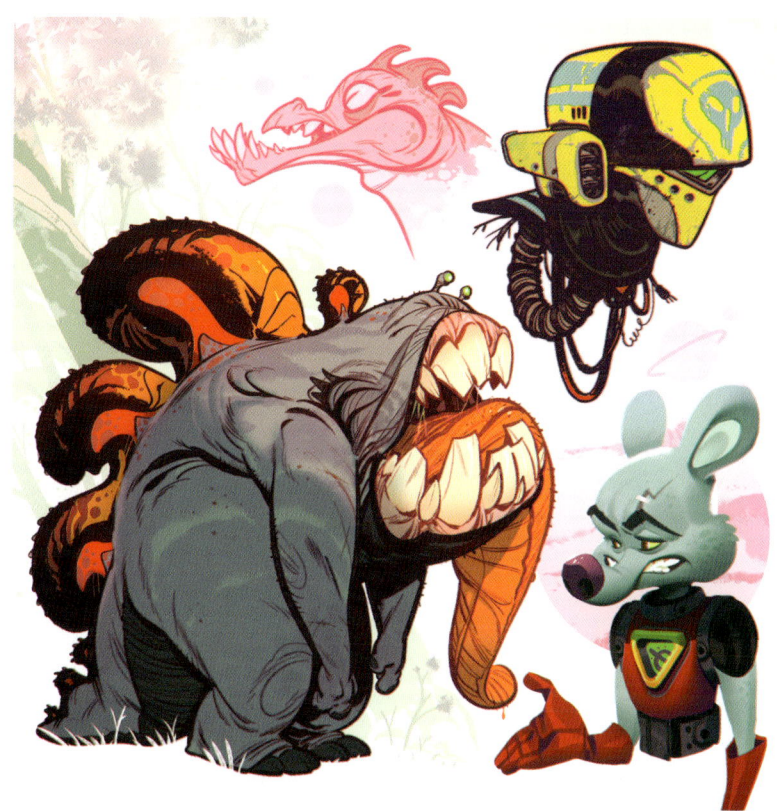

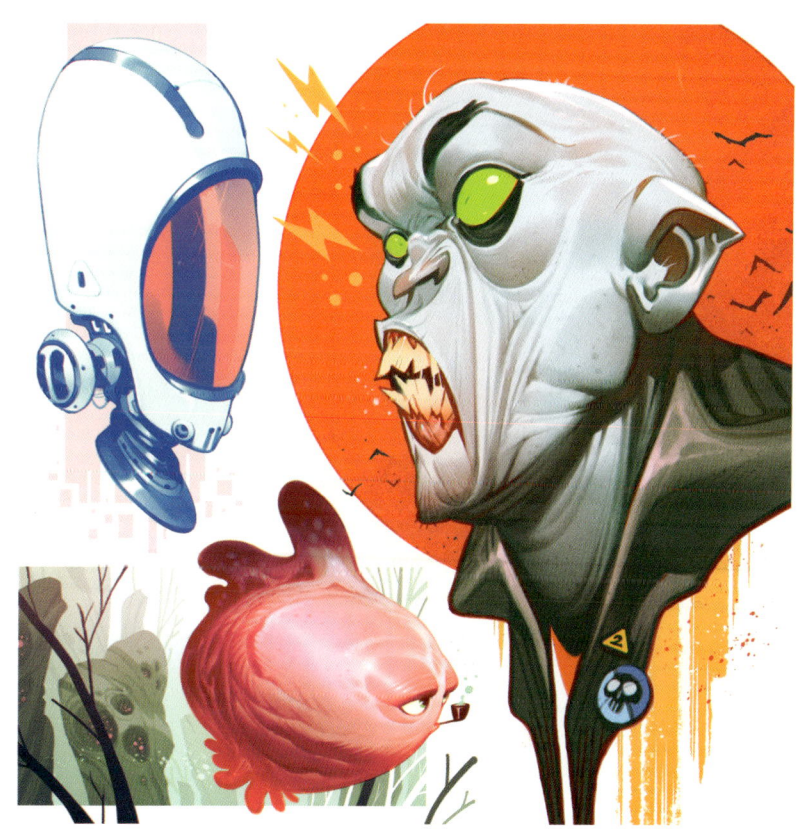

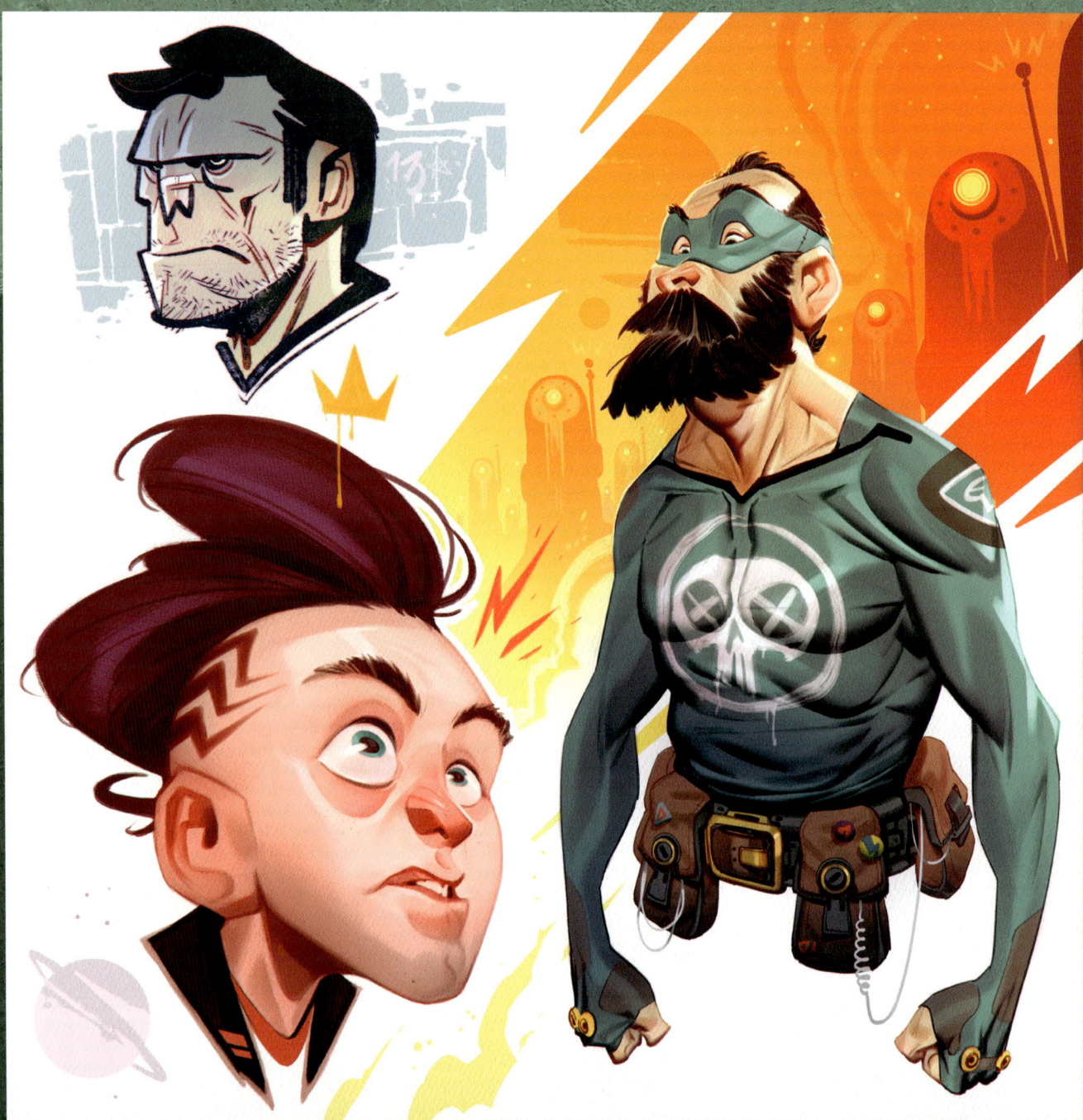

Thanks for talking to us Dave! Are there any upcoming projects we should be looking out for?

Thanks again for having me – this has been a blast. While I don't have a specific project to announce just yet, I can say that alongside freelance I'm finally scratching that itch for comics and storytelling. My website (daveguertin.com) and Instagram (@daveguertin) will be the best places to catch upcoming details. And to anyone swinging away at a drawing table today, have fun! The world is a better place with your work in it.

Opposite page (top): Okay, I'll confess – I have a thing for drawing teeth. I'm working through it, I promise...

Opposite page (bottom): Digital sketchbook pages help me play out story threads while planning larger narratives

This page: When approaching characters, I always keep an eye on how their palette interacts with the environment

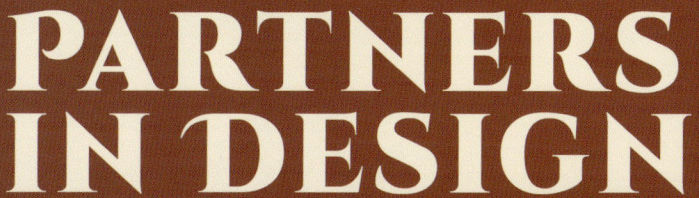

PARTNERS IN DESIGN

KAINING WANG

In this tutorial, we will take a look at how to create two characters that work together as a team, for use in an ongoing narrative. We'll work through the whole process, from how to come up with fresh ideas, to sketching early versions of the design, and finally completing a finished character or two!

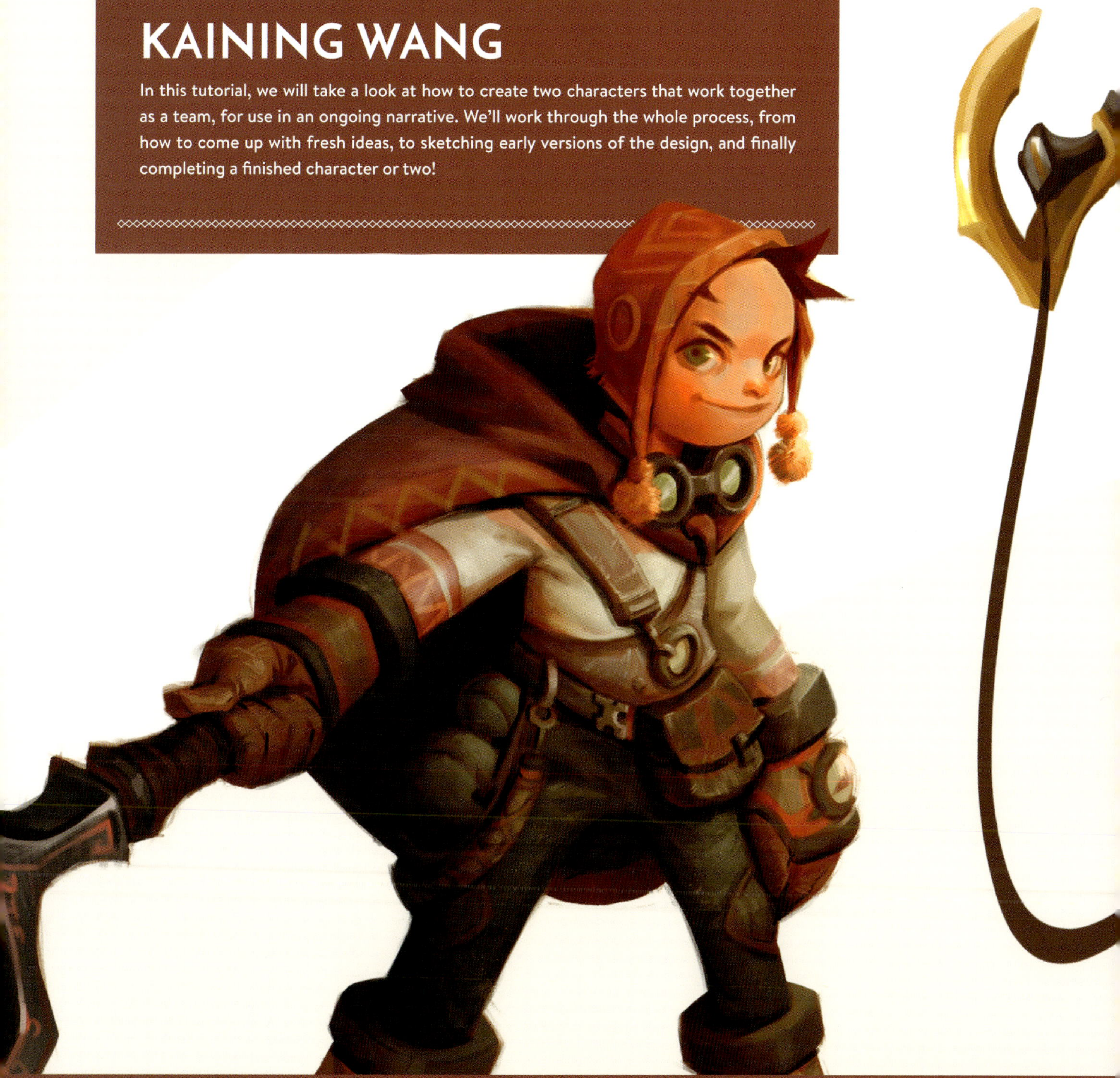

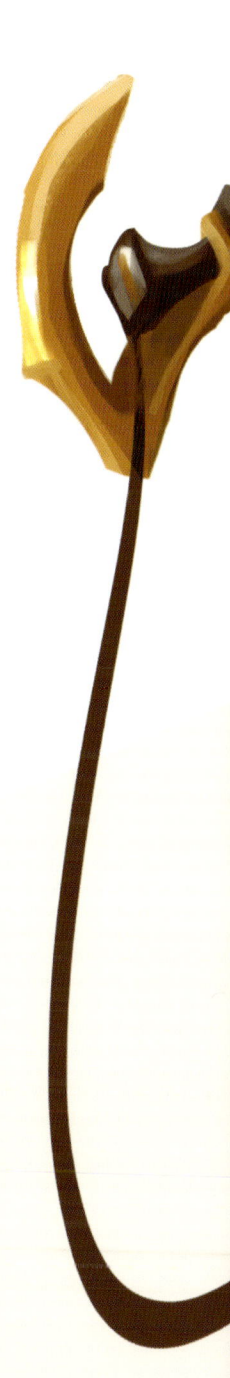

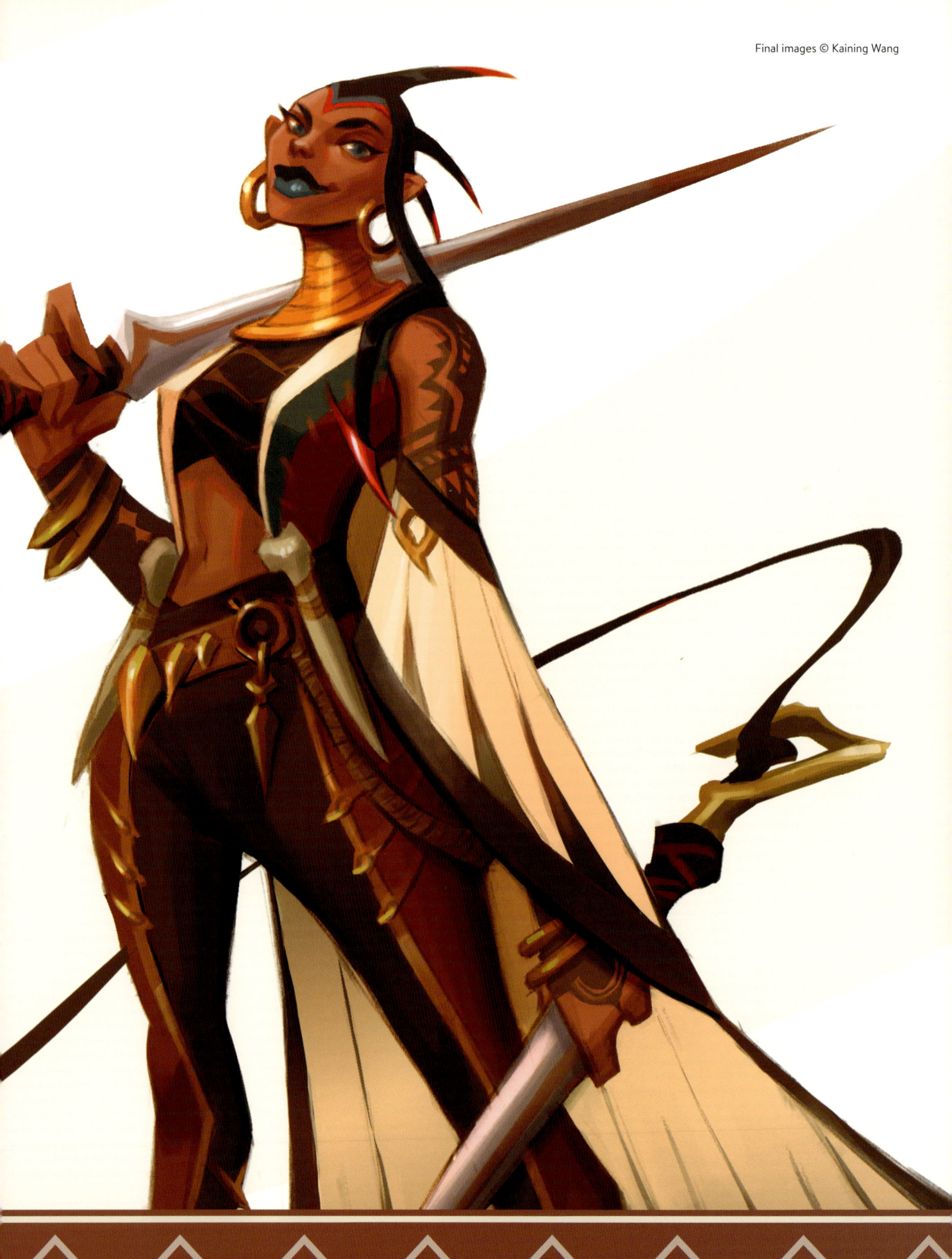

Final images © Kaining Wang

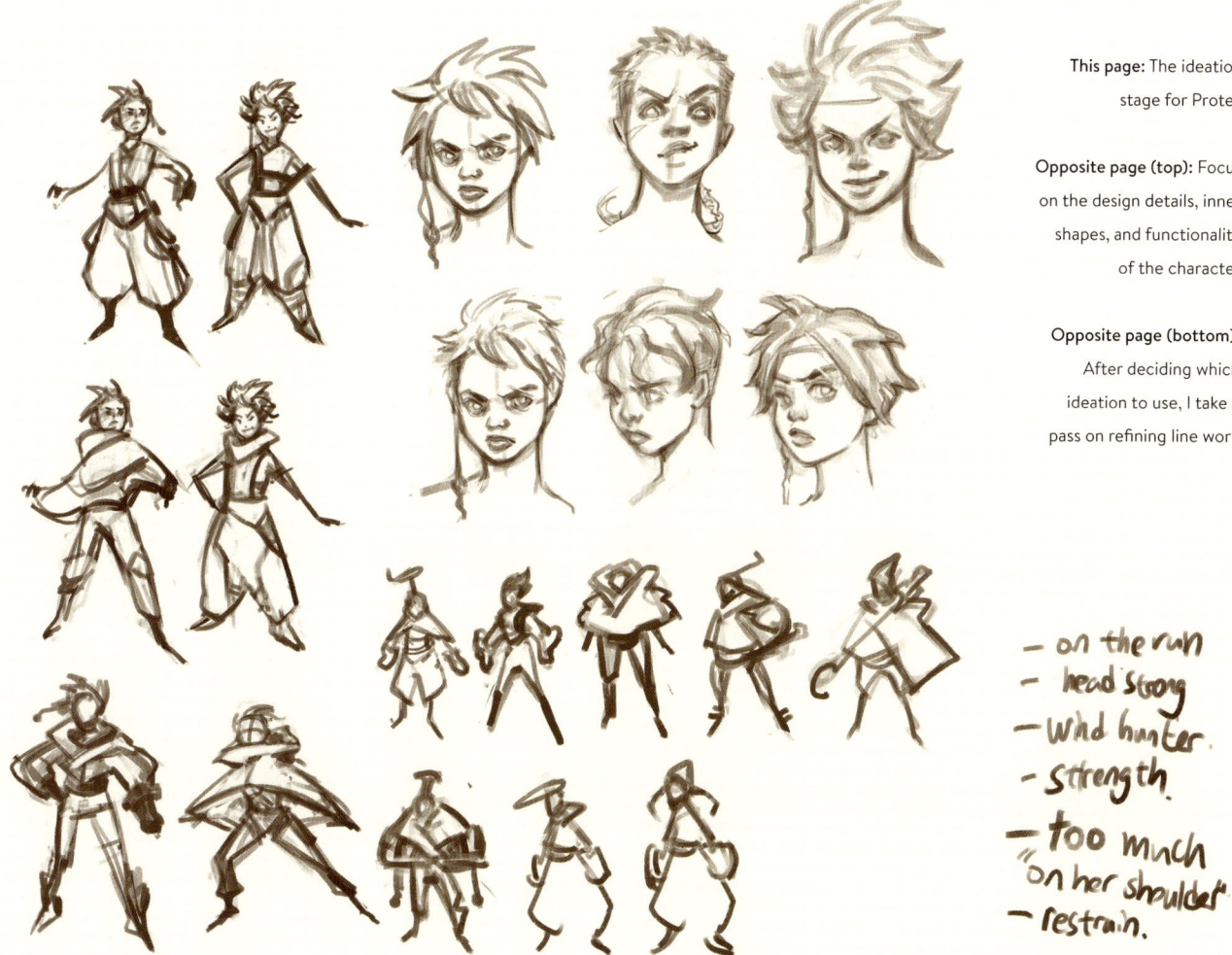

This page: The ideation stage for Protea

Opposite page (top): Focus on the design details, inner shapes, and functionality of the character

Opposite page (bottom): After deciding which ideation to use, I take a pass on refining line work

- on the run
- head strong
- wild hunter
- strength
- too much "on her shoulder"
- restrain

START WITH A SKETCH

To start brainstorming character ideas, have a think about some keywords that describe their personality, profession, and design elements. For my first character, Protea, I've chosen a pilot suit, climbing tool, and Incan culture as the fundamental words to describe the design. She'll have a stubborn and rebellious personality, while also loving to go on an adventure. I gather references that relate to all these keywords. Now I can start some basic sketches, working out how Protea will act and pose.

DEVELOPING IDEAS

Next, I further develop and refine the ideation sketches, focusing on figuring out the silhouette and inner shape. Try to make the silhouette as simple as possible so that it's more readable at a distance. Sketch out any weapons or other props, and draw different poses to show off their personality.

STRAIGHT DOWN THE LINE

After doing multiple ideations, I choose one design as the final look and refine the linework. I still keep the drawing loose at this stage, while trying to unify the shape language. For Protea, I choose a circle as her main shape to show her as a good but stubborn character. I add a large cape to suggest she is hiding something, and multiple layers of clothes to show she is burdened with a lot of responsibility. When designing characters, consider every choice you make – what does each shape represent, what story do they tell, and what function do they convey?

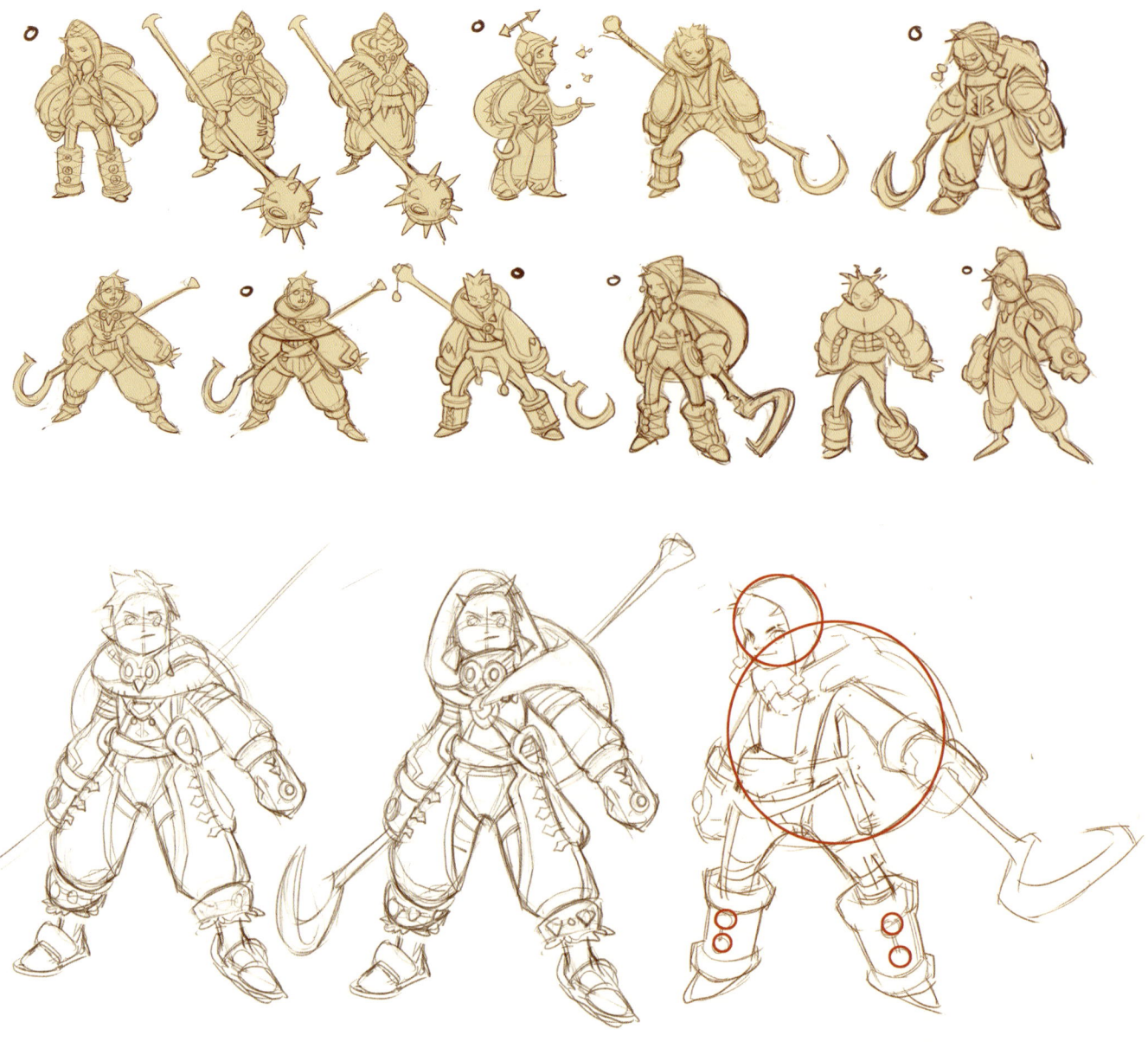

SHAPE LANGUAGE

You should always focus on the silhouette first and then the inner shape. Make sure there is contrast between the size of the shapes: small, medium, and large. Using various sizes will give the character a better balance and flow. Work out where their anchor point will be and the kind of movements the character will make. For instance, if you use a large shape for the feet, then the character will look grounded and sturdy. When they take a punch, they would brace against the impact using their big feet!

ADDING COLOR

Now that the linework is looking clean, the next step is to block in a rough color pass. Usually, it would be better to try different options and different value arrangements, and see which one works. When thinking about the color palette for a character, take into consideration their origin, what their job may be, and what sort of personality they have. In this case, Protea comes from a highland area where earth colors are the main palette. I also add warmer red tones that match her somewhat explosive personality.

I arrange and clean up the inner shapes for the character. Instead of continuously using circles for the shape language, I use triangles inside her silhouette to show she has a rebellious streak.

LIGHT AND SHADOW

With flat color, it's usually easier to refine the rendering with lighting and shadows. I keep the light from looking too exaggerated so the character's design and functionality are easily readable. While completing the final rendering, switch back and forth between monochrome and color modes to see if your value structure is still the same. For Protea, since the palette is mostly earthy tones, I keep her value structure mostly black and gray, with a little bit of white underneath.

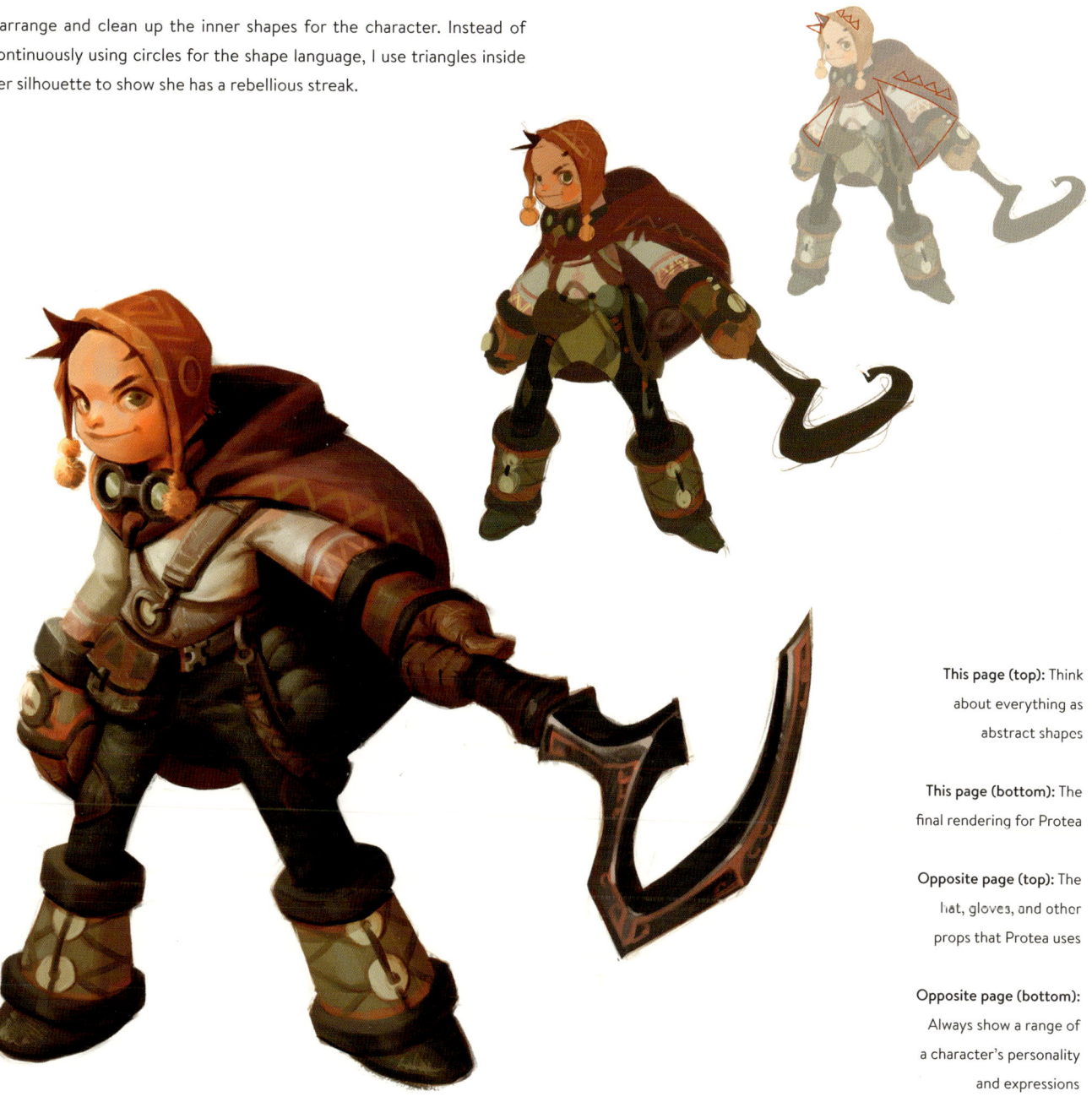

This page (top): Think about everything as abstract shapes

This page (bottom): The final rendering for Protea

Opposite page (top): The hat, gloves, and other props that Protea uses

Opposite page (bottom): Always show a range of a character's personality and expressions

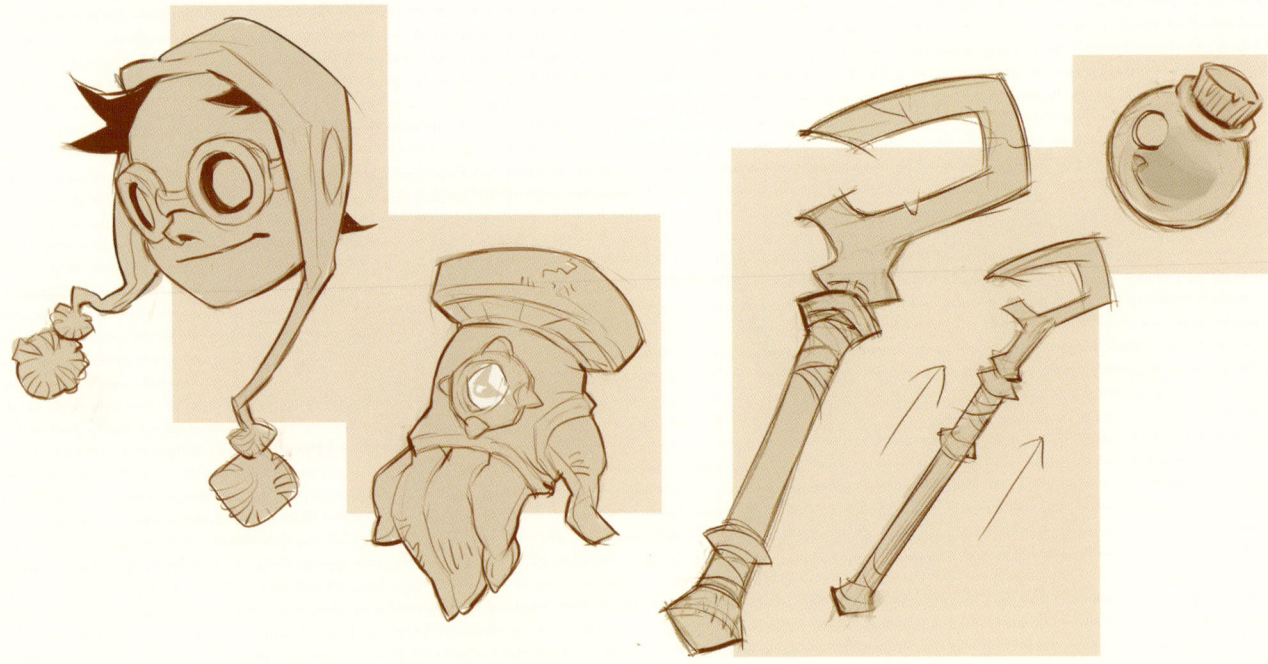

PROP PARADE

When creating any character, drawing details separately is a great way to help others better understand who your character is. In this case, I call out the gloves, weapons, and other accessories from Protea's design. Even when drawing detailed props, aim to explain who the character is as clear and simply as possible.

EXPLORING EMOTIONS

When creating characters, especially for animation, it is always good to show a range of expressions, such as sad, angry, and happy. Not only does this help others get to know the character better, but it will also help the animators define the range of movement they can use.

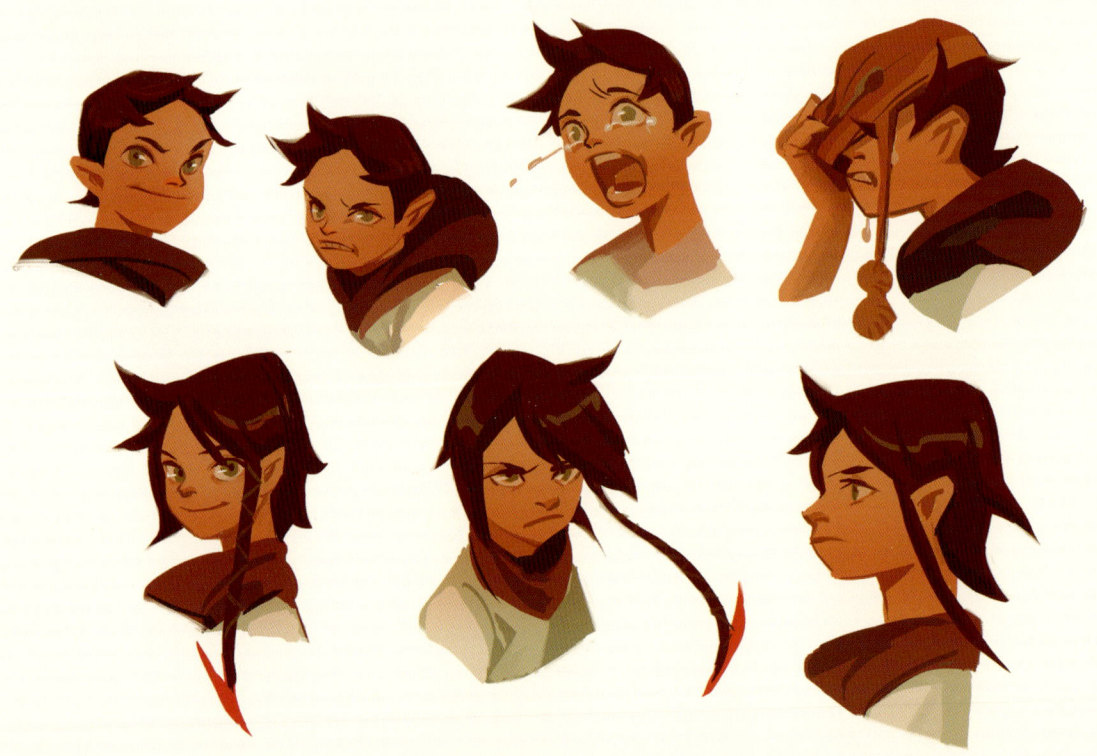

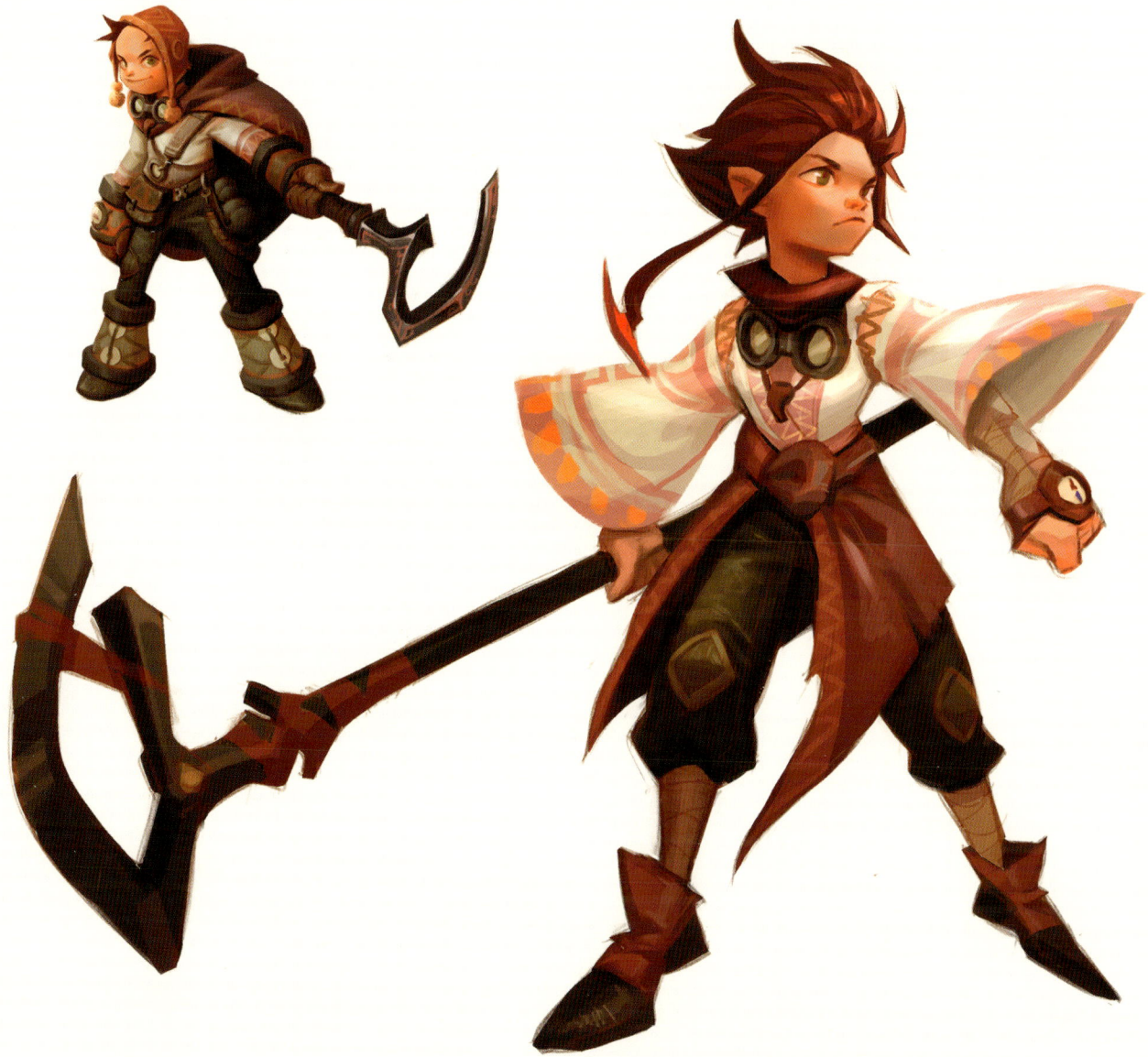

BEFORE AND AFTER

From a narrative perspective, there will always be changes to a character as the story evolves – their design should reflect the contrast between the "before" and "after" version. Use every aspect of the design to show this change – shape language, pose, value structure, and color palette. In this case, Protea's main shape language is now a triangle instead of a circle. Her pose is more open, too, indicating a change in her personality. It can also be useful to add details that create a link between this character and other related characters. Protea has the same hair band and jewelry as Azalea, indicating that a bond has formed between the two.

CONTRASTING CHARACTERS

When designing two characters that are part of a team, you should always try to show the contrast between them. For example, one may be big and the other small. My second character, Azalea, is a very skillful hunter, and her look is elegant and confident, in contrast to the scrappier look of Protea. She is older and more experienced than her counterpart. On your first pass at the second character in a pair, try to nail down how they will differ, and how they will relate to the first.

Opposite page: This is how Protea will look at the end of her story

This page: The first pass ideation for Azalea

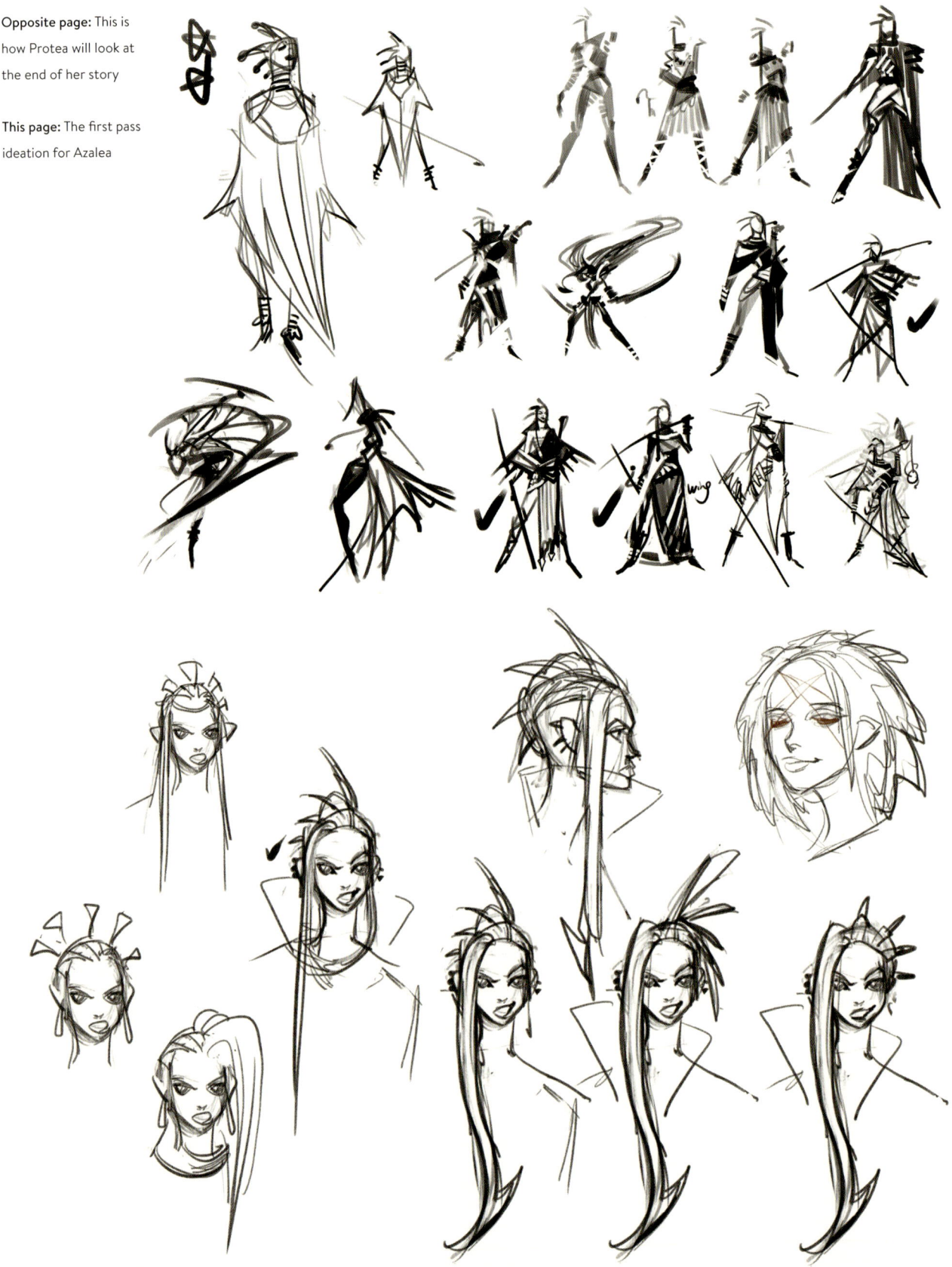

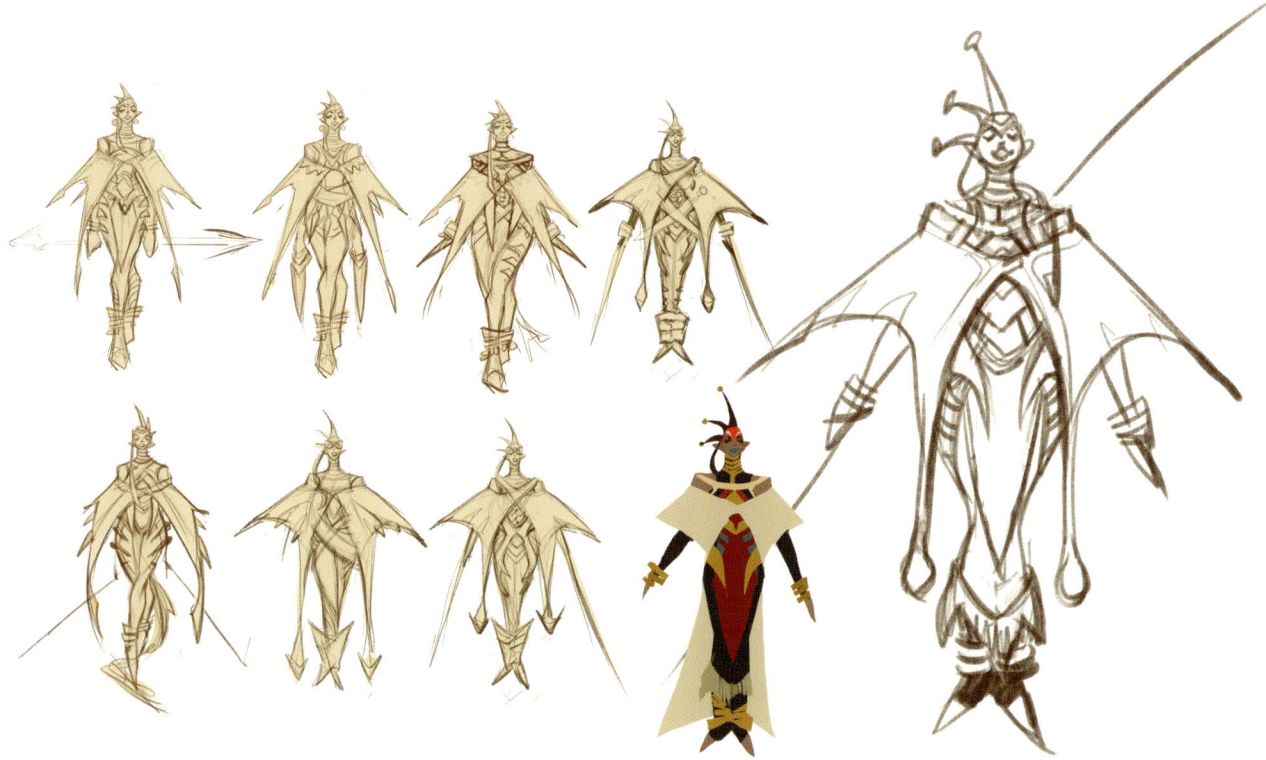

SORTING THE SHADOWS

As with the ideation process for Protea, at this stage I try to figure out the inner shape and clothes structure for Azalea. I make sure the shape language is completely different. Always aim to push the differences in the silhouette of each character so they can easily be distinguished, even from far away. Protea was predominantly built from circles, so Azalea's shape language is triangles.

POSE AND FLOW

Getting posing right is an important part of any character design. Poses can convey the attitude, personality, functionality, and even the back-story of your character. A good pose usually has a very clear direction, and a clear first, second, and third read. You should always keep in mind what you want to show and exaggerate in your design. An easy way to signpost which part of your design is most important is to angle all other shapes to point toward it.

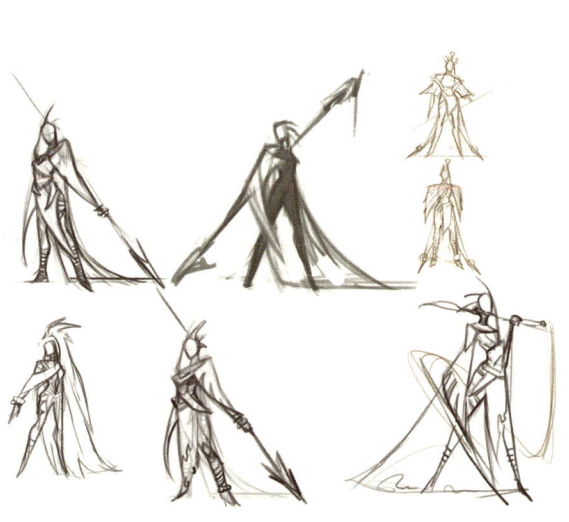

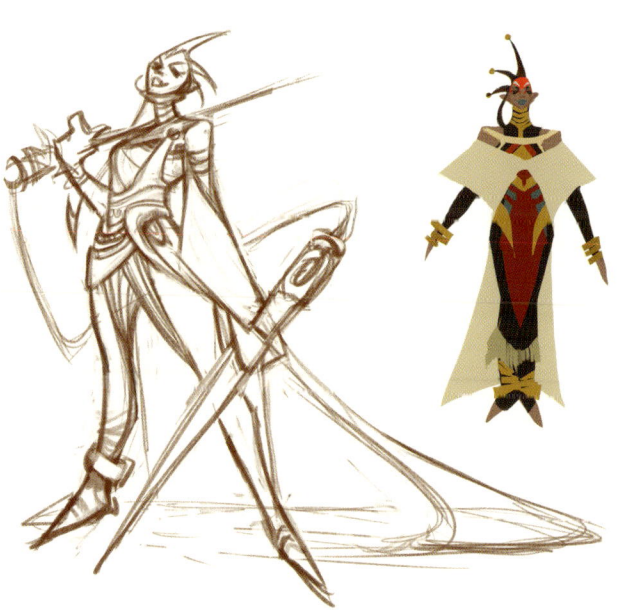

COMBINING COLORS

After deciding which pose to use, you should start with a color rough for the character, which will usually be flat, with no light source. All you should think about is the shape comparison, color combination, and value structure. Define the flow of the character and how the viewer's eye will travel across the design.

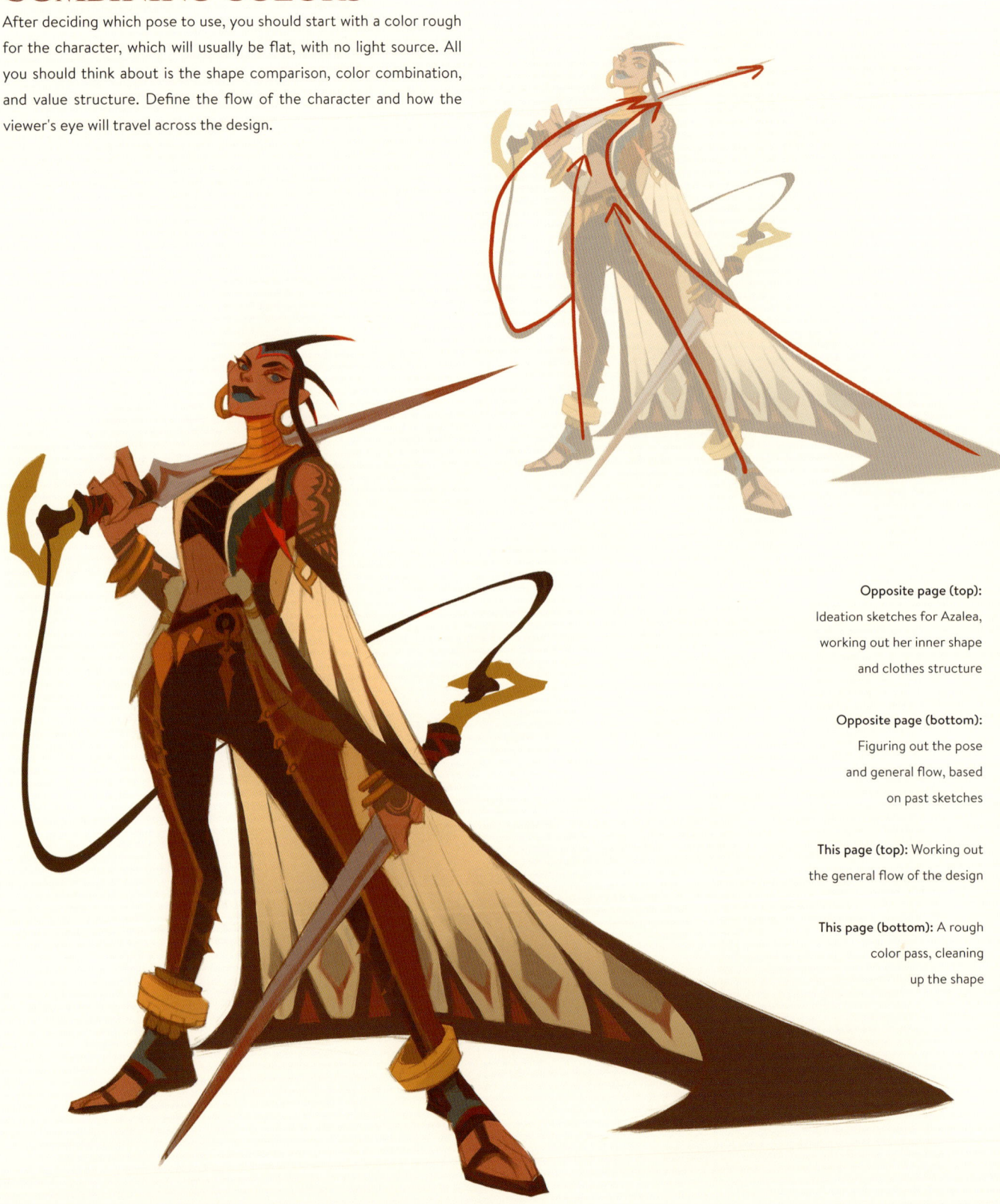

Opposite page (top): Ideation sketches for Azalea, working out her inner shape and clothes structure

Opposite page (bottom): Figuring out the pose and general flow, based on past sketches

This page (top): Working out the general flow of the design

This page (bottom): A rough color pass, cleaning up the shape

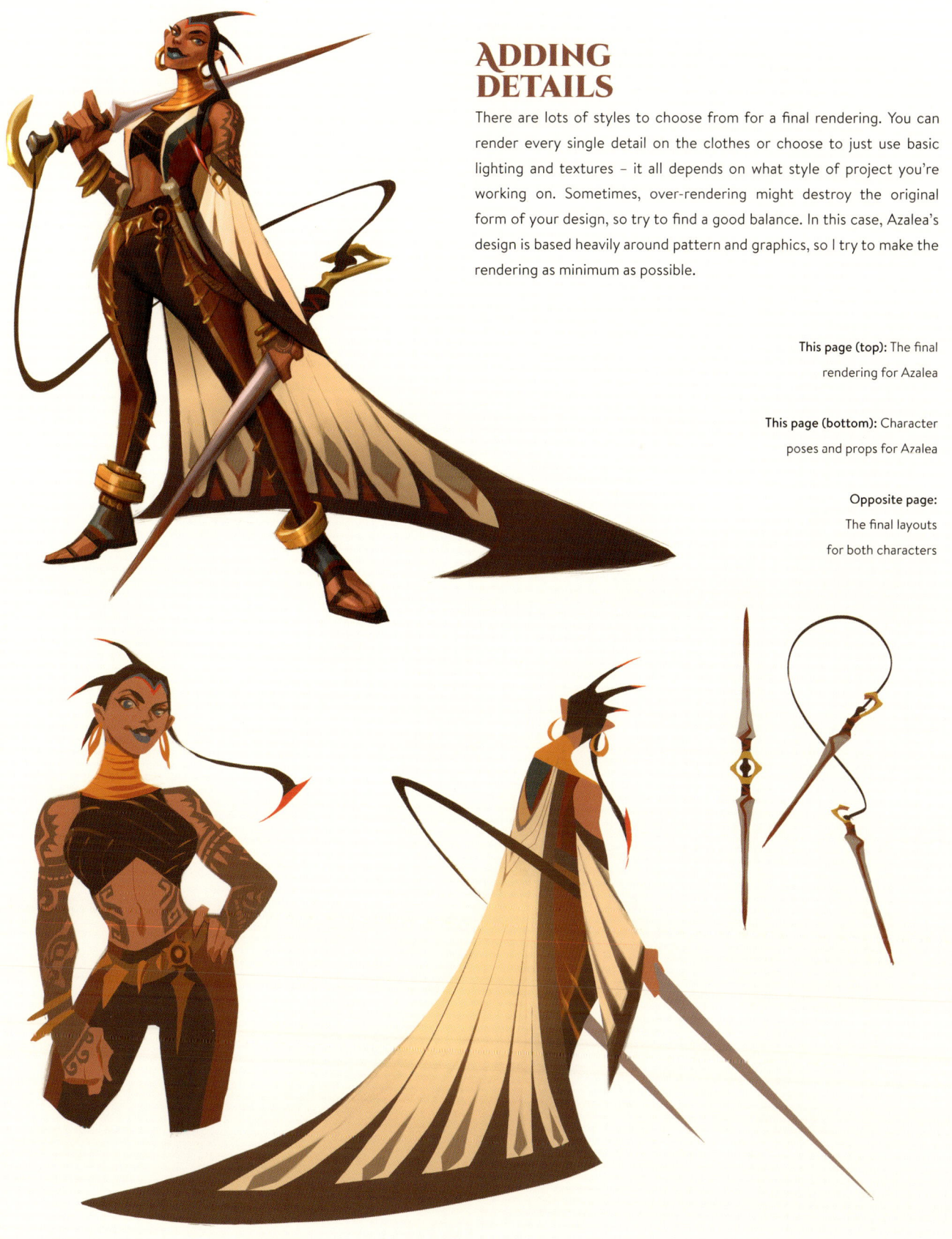

ADDING DETAILS

There are lots of styles to choose from for a final rendering. You can render every single detail on the clothes or choose to just use basic lighting and textures – it all depends on what style of project you're working on. Sometimes, over-rendering might destroy the original form of your design, so try to find a good balance. In this case, Azalea's design is based heavily around pattern and graphics, so I try to make the rendering as minimum as possible.

This page (top): The final rendering for Azalea

This page (bottom): Character poses and props for Azalea

Opposite page: The final layouts for both characters

A DIFFERENT POINT OF VIEW

Besides the front of the character, sometimes it can be helpful to show the reverse of the character as well – if you are working as part of a pipeline, the modeler will then know exactly how your character's structure should work. I also recommend showing some interaction between the two characters you've designed, so the rest of your team can get a sense of the dynamics between the two.

THE FINAL LAYOUT

Layouts are super important for showcasing your work. A good layout is easy to read, informative, and tells a story within itself. Think of a layout the same way as when arranging character's shape language – you should lead the viewer's eyes across the page, creating a flow of ordered information.

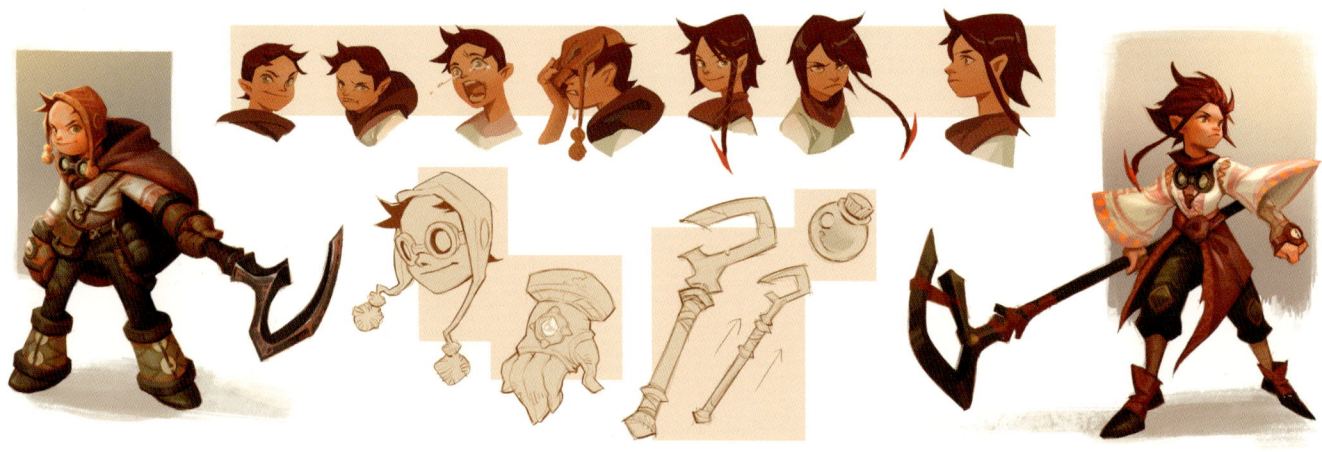

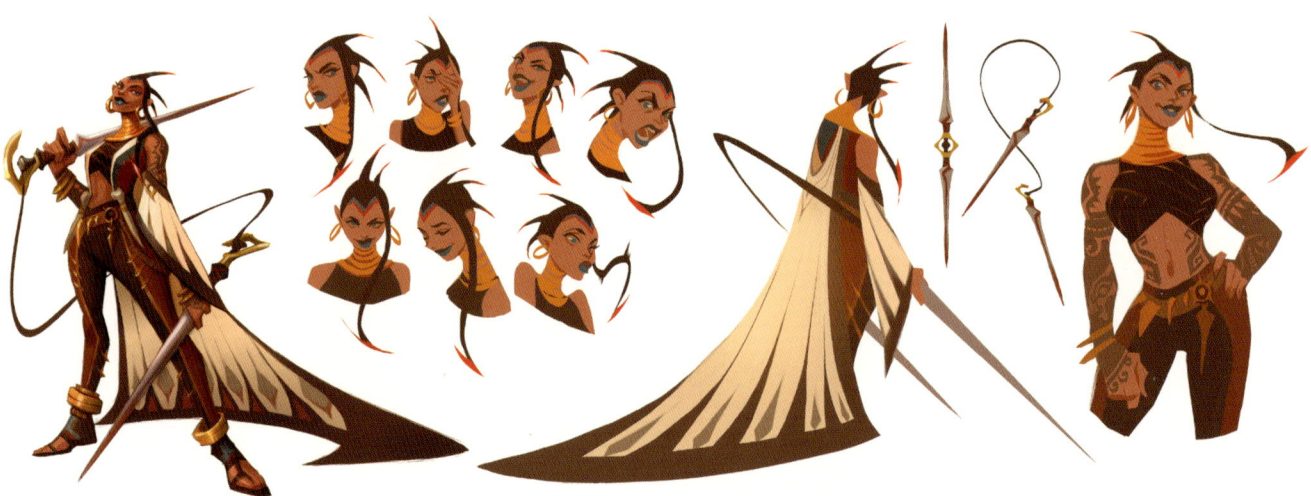

Final images © Kaining Wang

A COLORFUL ENCOUNTER

NATHANNA ÉRICA

Having been born in such a colorful country as Brazil, my main sources of inspiration come from nature – its unique hues and beautiful textures. When I first started working with paper, I discovered that with this medium (which quickly became my favorite) I could develop my art further in terms of color, texture, and movement. For me, these three elements are essential to every piece I create, be it paper-crafting or a digital painting. On the following pages, I'll be showing you how to make the most of your color palette and create some dazzling designs. These techniques can be used traditionally and digitally, so get your real brushes or digital ones ready and let's begin!

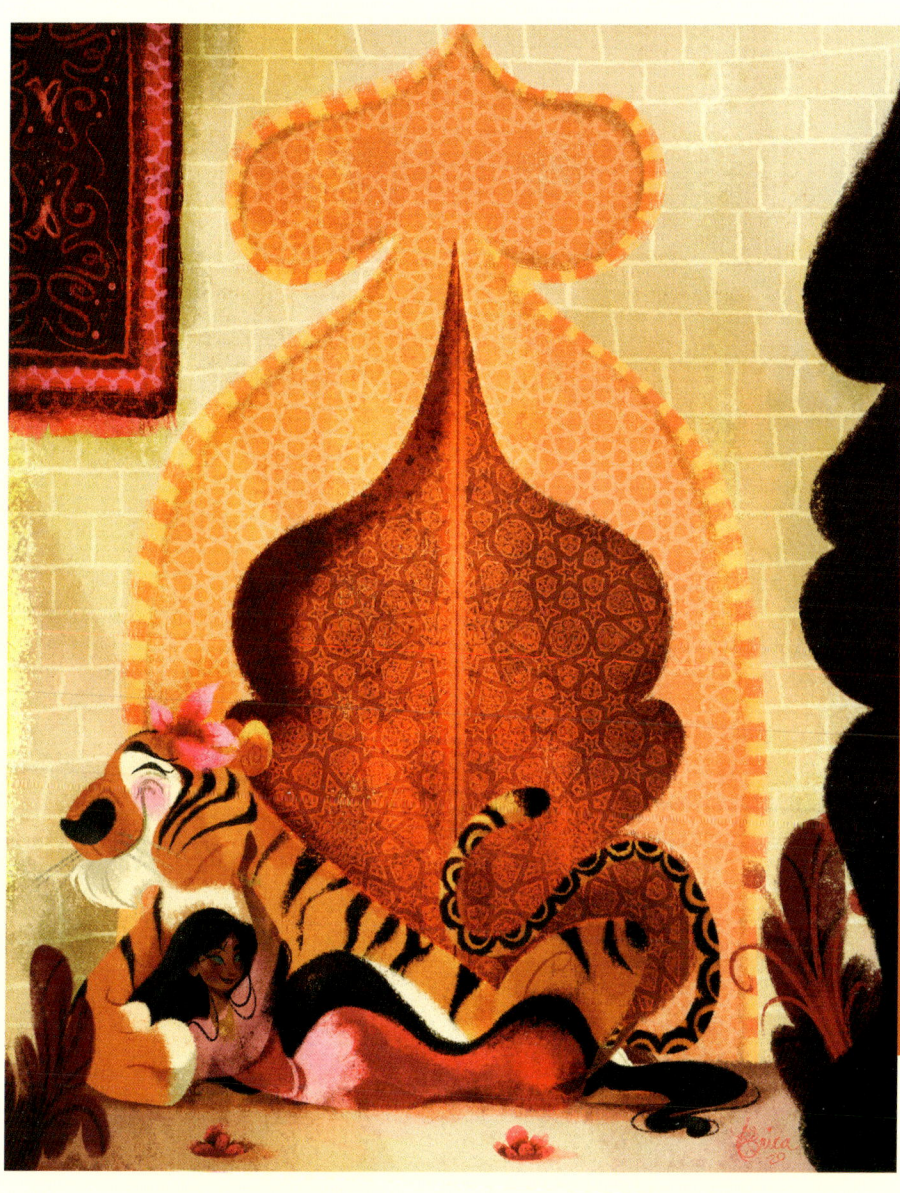

SETTING THE SCENE

The first step in finding the ideal color palette is thinking about where your scene takes place. Even if you plan to create a character without any background, the environment where you imagine the character will be is a crucial part of choosing your colors. I'm often drawn to scenes filled with mystery and fantasy, and that determines my preference for bright, vibrant colors.

THE WHEEL TURNS

With a more defined idea of our scene, let's talk about an essential tool for understanding color and how it works: the color wheel. First developed by Sir Isaac Newton, a color wheel is a visual chart that represents how colors interact with each other. Using the wheel, it's possible to distinguish a variety of color schemes: monochromatic, analogous, complementary, triadic, and so on. Complementary colors are usually very pleasing to the eye. They are located on opposite sides of the color wheel, which makes for a contrasting and balanced combination.

ANALOGOUS SCHEME (NEIGHBORING COLORS)

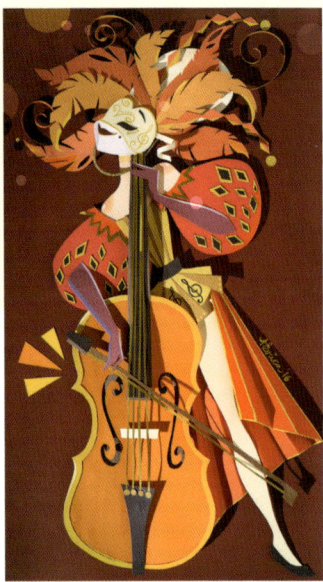

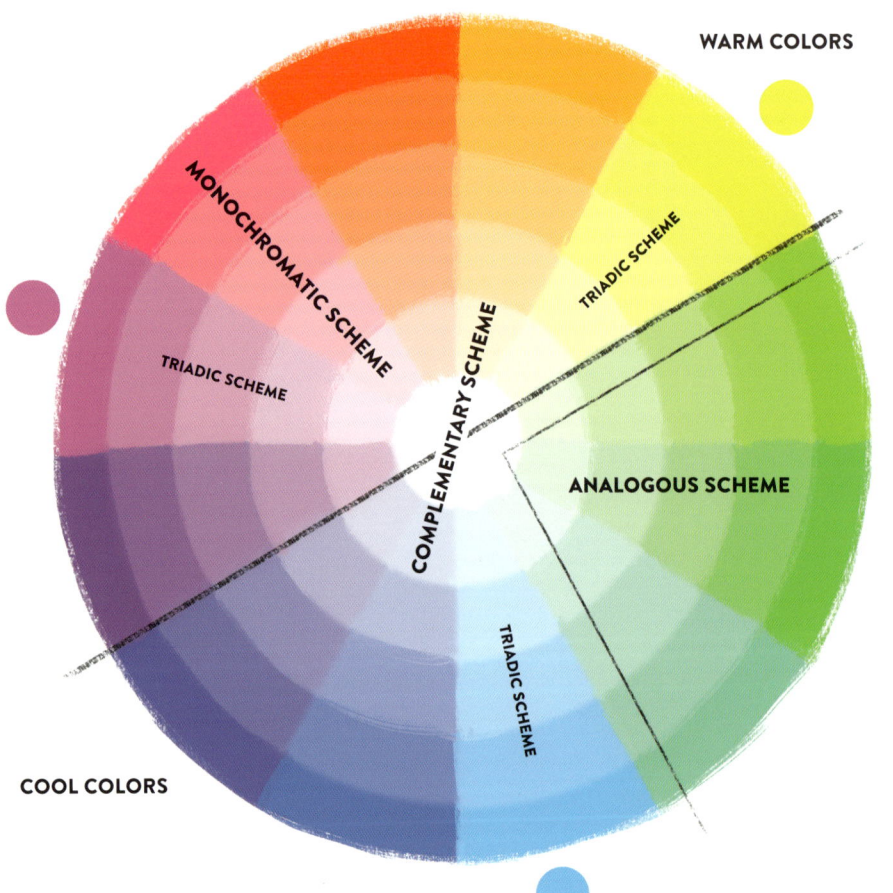

WARM COLORS

MONOCHROMATIC SCHEME

TRIADIC SCHEME

TRIADIC SCHEME

COMPLEMENTARY SCHEME

ANALOGOUS SCHEME

TRIADIC SCHEME

COOL COLORS

COMPLEMENTARY SCHEME (COLORS DIRECTLY ACROSS FROM EACH OTHER)

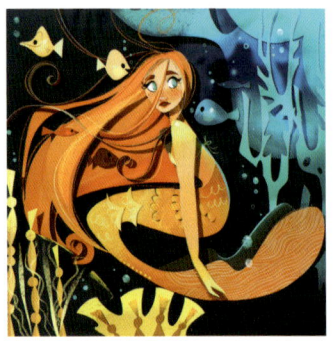

MONOCHROMATIC SCHEME (VARIATIONS OF THE SAME COLOR)

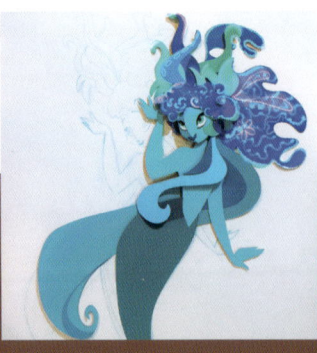

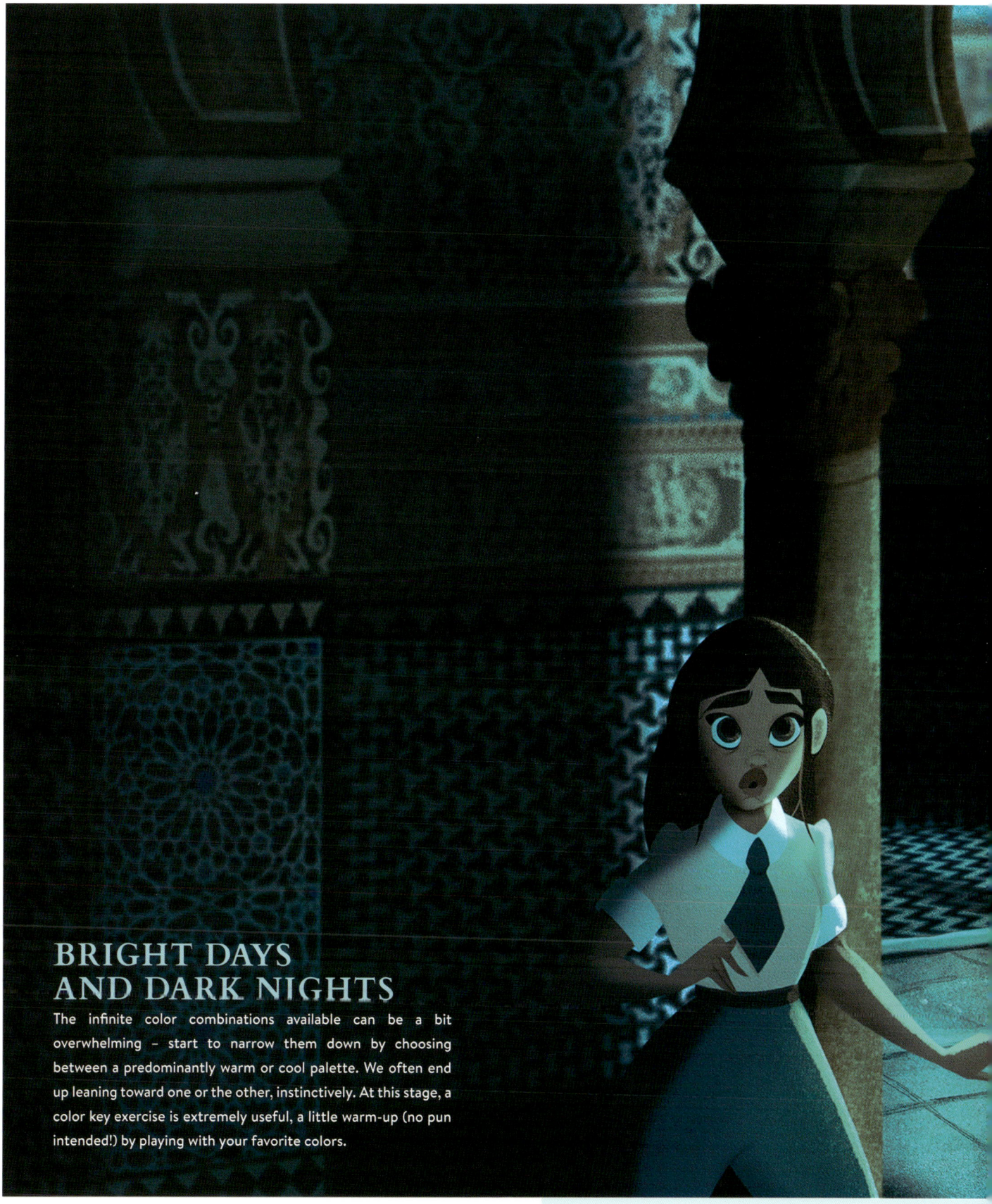

BRIGHT DAYS
AND DARK NIGHTS

The infinite color combinations available can be a bit overwhelming – start to narrow them down by choosing between a predominantly warm or cool palette. We often end up leaning toward one or the other, instinctively. At this stage, a color key exercise is extremely useful, a little warm-up (no pun intended!) by playing with your favorite colors.

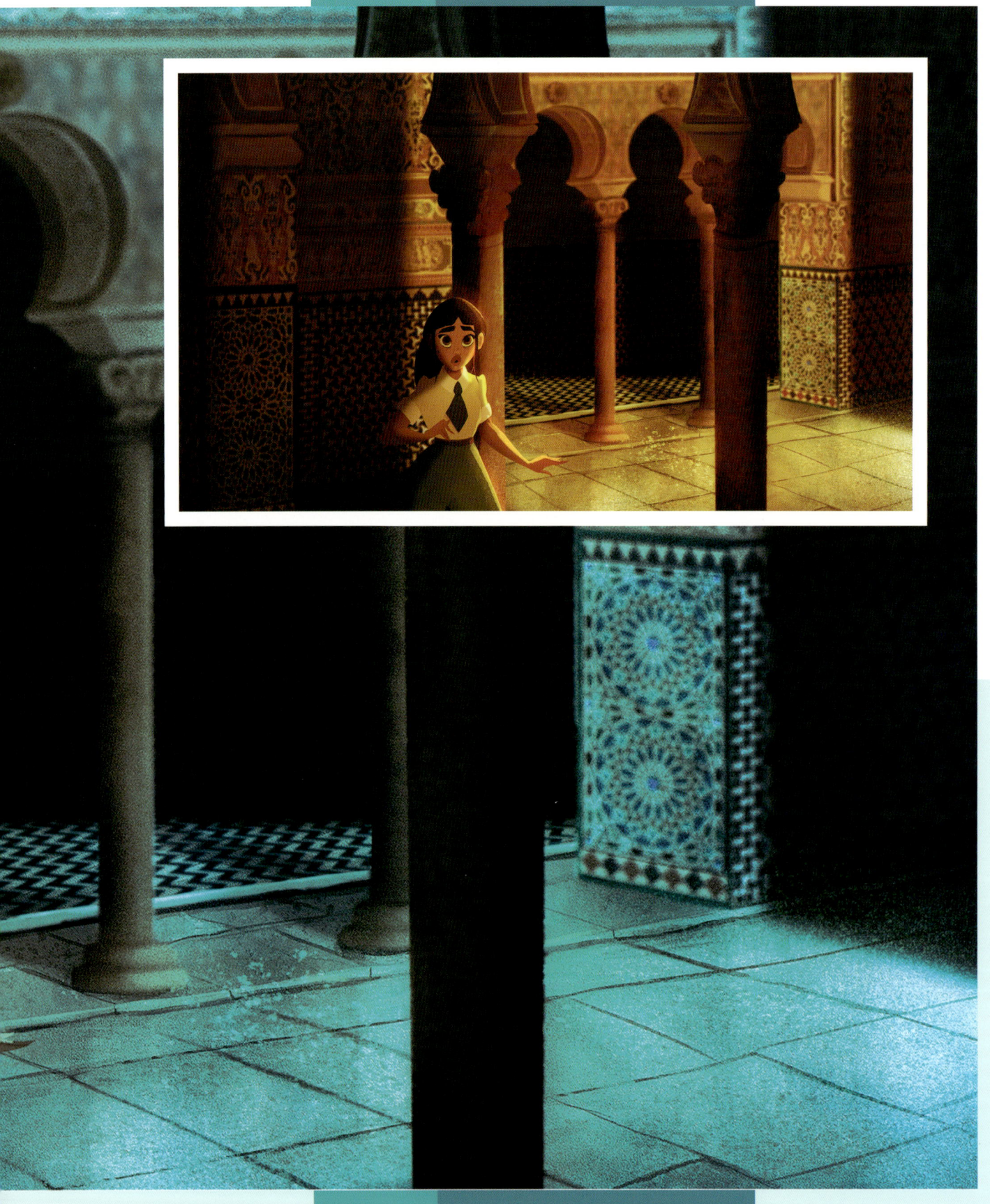

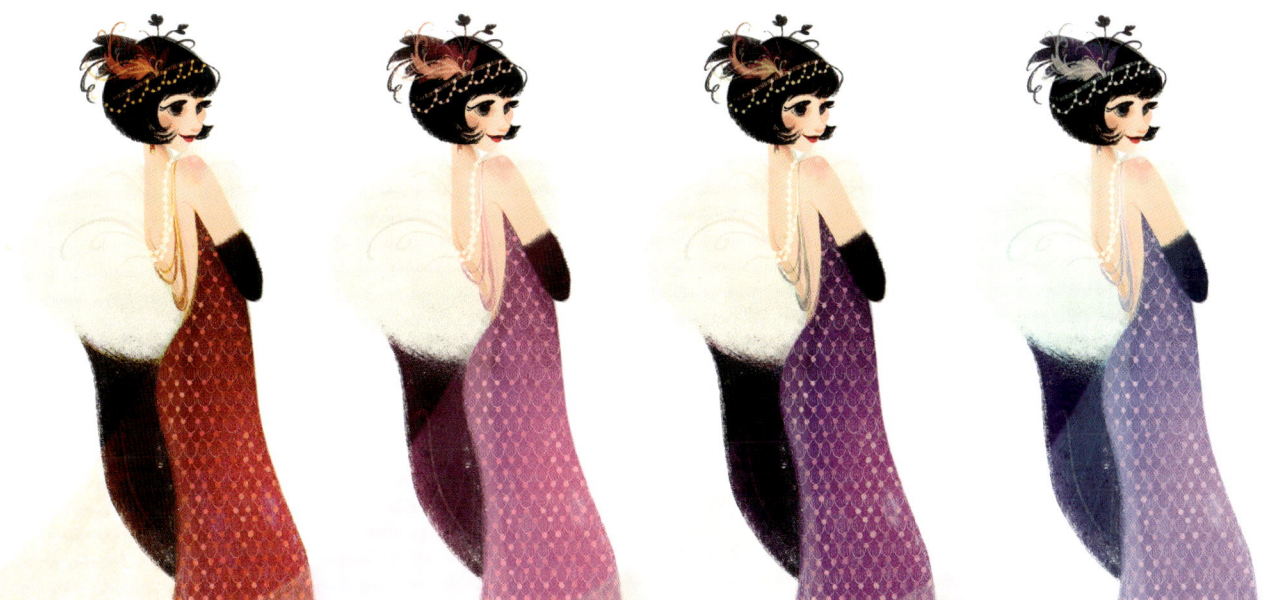

COLORFUL CHARACTERS

Now, let's apply some of these lessons about color to a character design: a flapper from one of my favorite eras, the 1920s. To decide on a color palette, we need to choose our setting – do we want to place our character in a mysterious, moonlit night? Or maybe a brightly lit environment? Once you have an idea of the scene where you envision your character, you can start to play with color combinations.

ADDING TEXTURE

I decide to go with a warm palette, with lots of violets and reds, evoking the beauty and the boldness of the 1920s. I love texture, so I add pearls and sequins to her dress, to make the final painting even more visually appealing. When in doubt, always add these sorts of elements to your designs. Textures give your viewers the impression that they can truly feel the artwork.

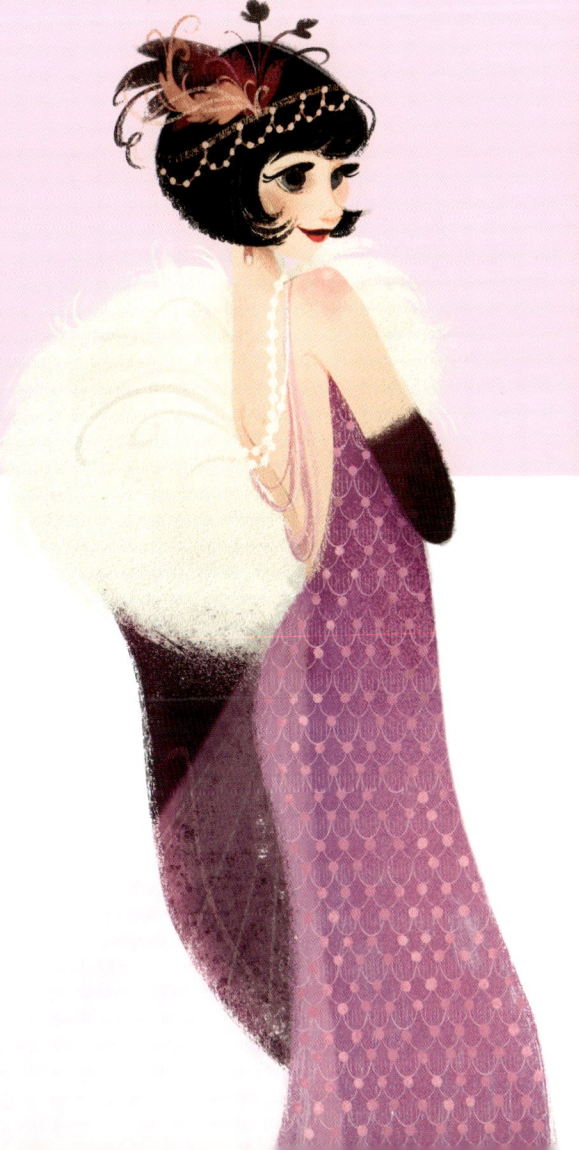

COLOR IS EVERYWHERE

The way you approach color will always be very subjective. After all, color has everything to do with human perception. Color theory provides essential concepts and definitions when it comes to the way that colors interact with each other, and it offers a way for finding their best arrangement and a sense of order and balance. But sometimes you'll find a combination that may escape the formulas of color theory – the natural world doesn't often obey these rules, for instance. This is when you need to use your instincts to find equilibrium in a seemingly chaotic palette. If you're like me and can see color everywhere, even in numbers and days of the week (honestly!), choosing a palette will become almost second nature. This may seem overwhelming at first, but once you begin to understand that there's plenty of logic in how colors work, and how they can evoke vastly different moods just by a slight change of tint or shade, you'll be able to create truly head-turning designs.

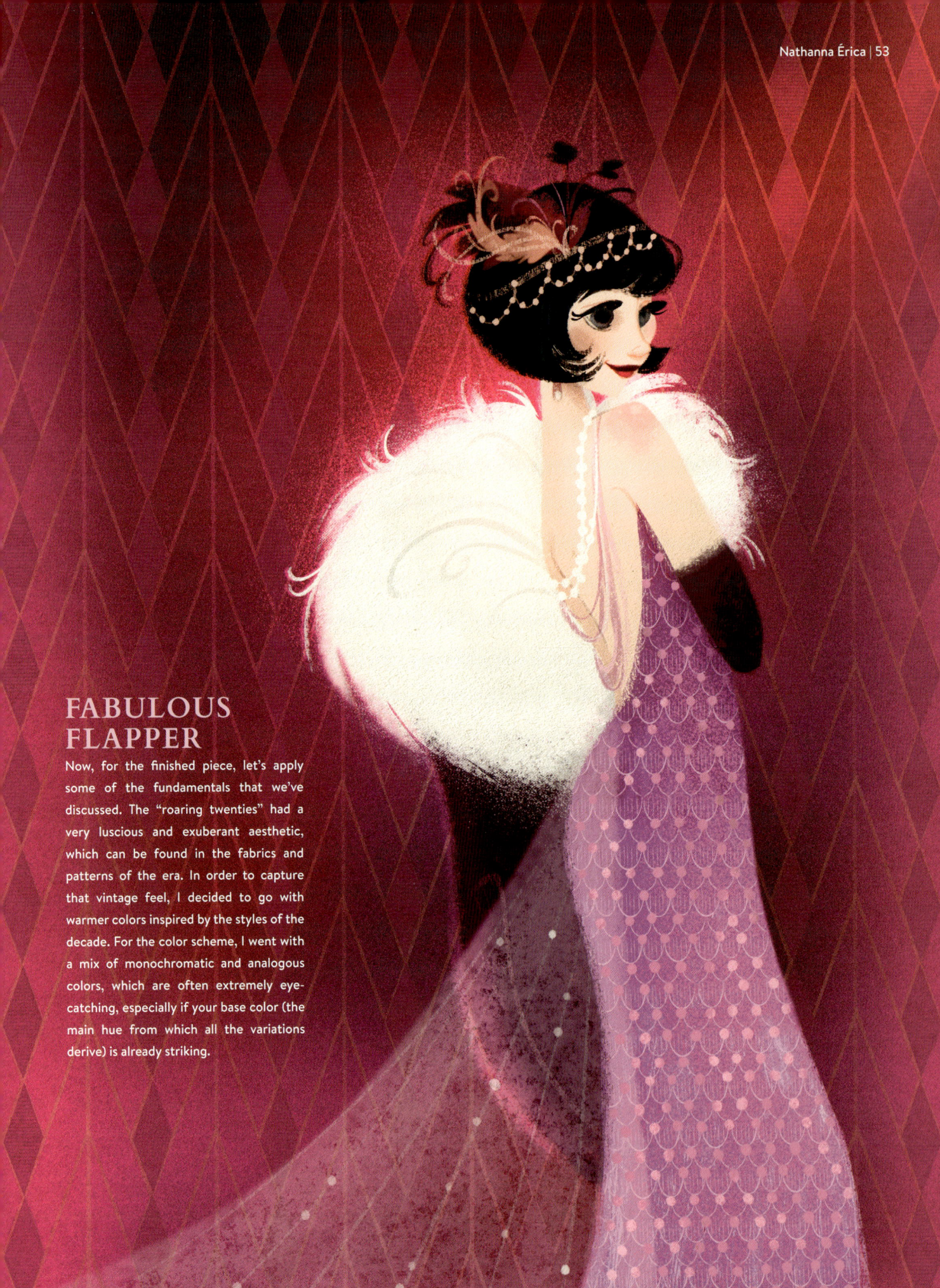

FABULOUS FLAPPER

Now, for the finished piece, let's apply some of the fundamentals that we've discussed. The "roaring twenties" had a very luscious and exuberant aesthetic, which can be found in the fabrics and patterns of the era. In order to capture that vintage feel, I decided to go with warmer colors inspired by the styles of the decade. For the color scheme, I went with a mix of monochromatic and analogous colors, which are often extremely eye-catching, especially if your base color (the main hue from which all the variations derive) is already striking.

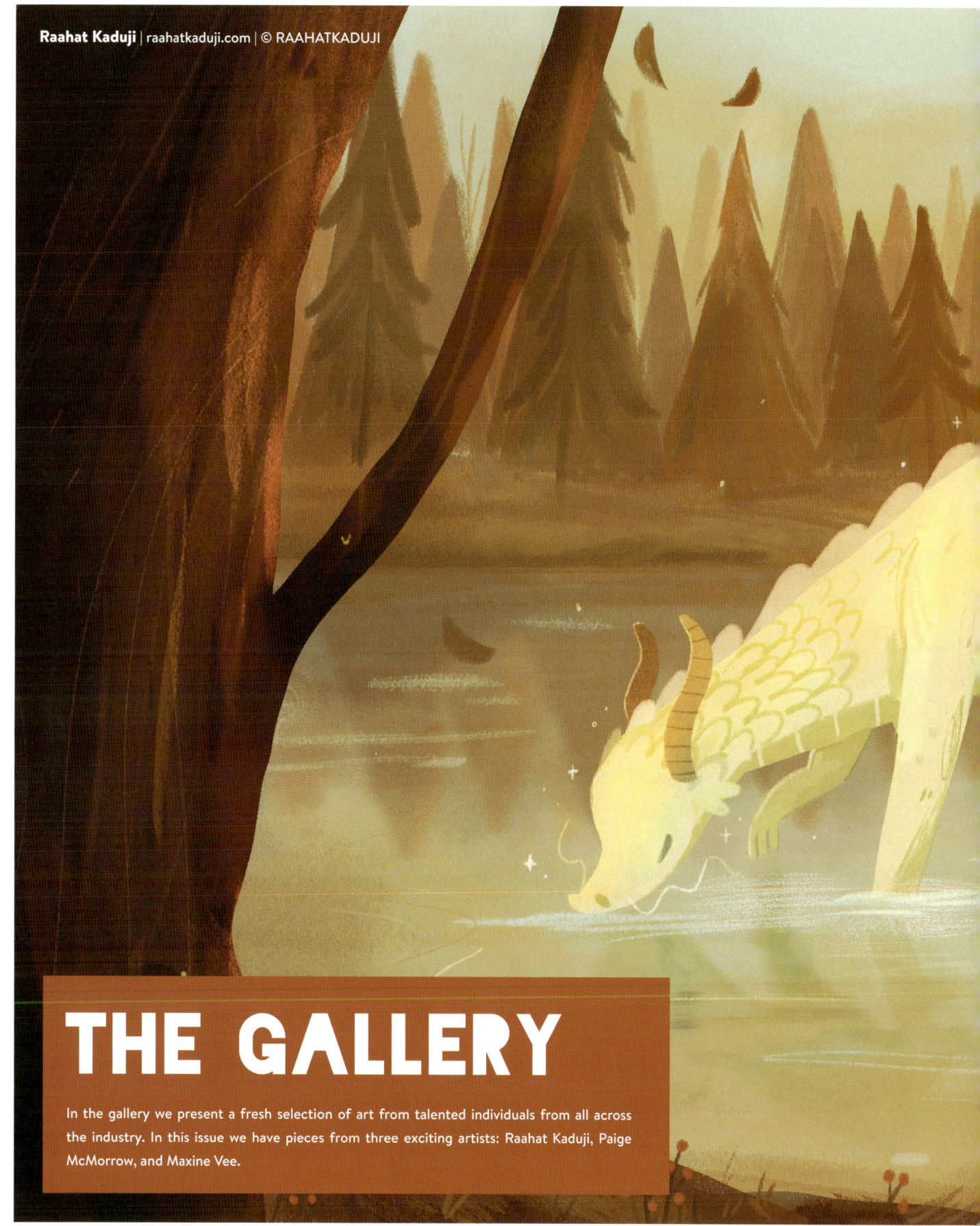

Raahat Kaduji | raahatkaduji.com | © RAAHATKADUJI

THE GALLERY

In the gallery we present a fresh selection of art from talented individuals from all across the industry. In this issue we have pieces from three exciting artists: Raahat Kaduji, Paige McMorrow, and Maxine Vee.

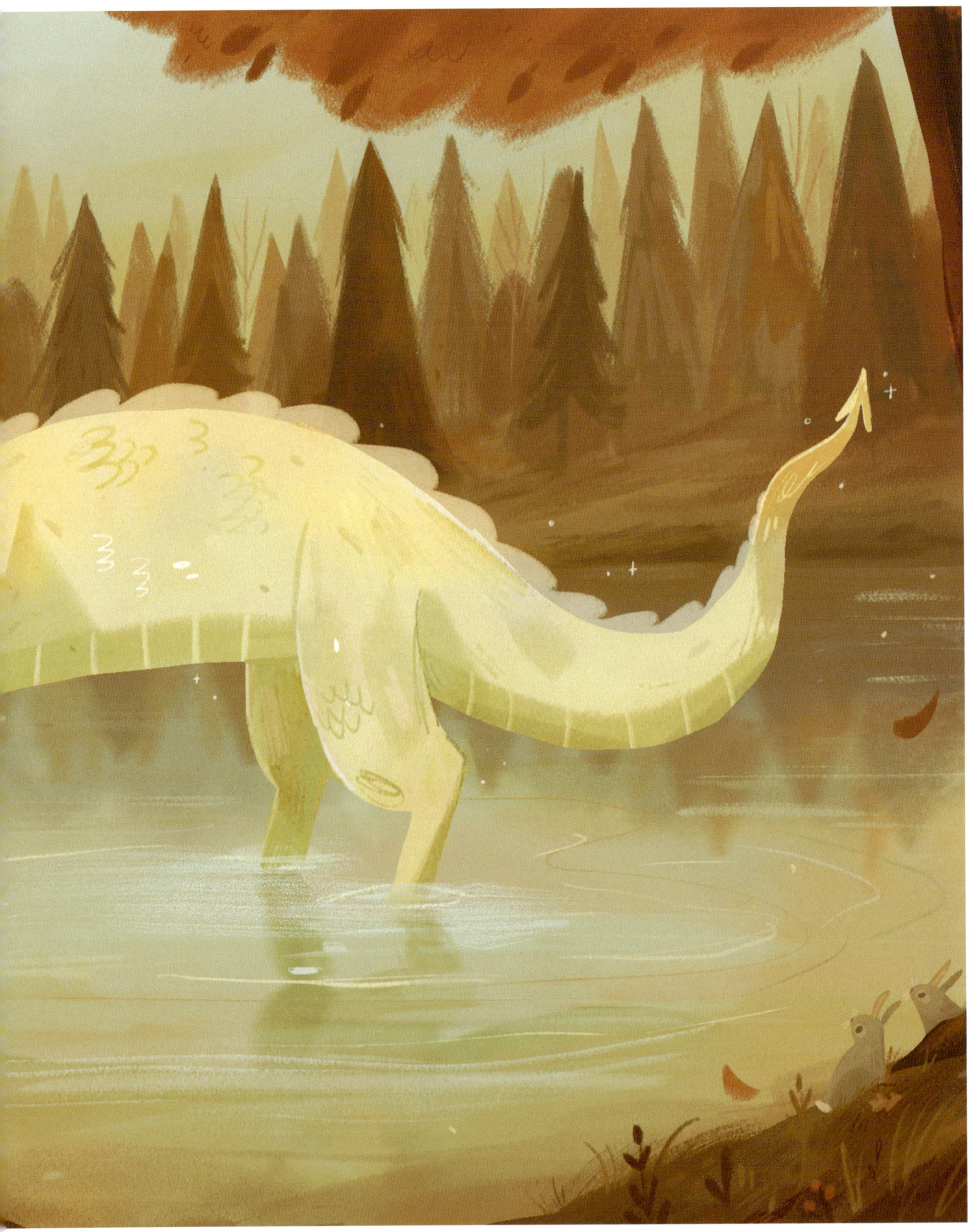

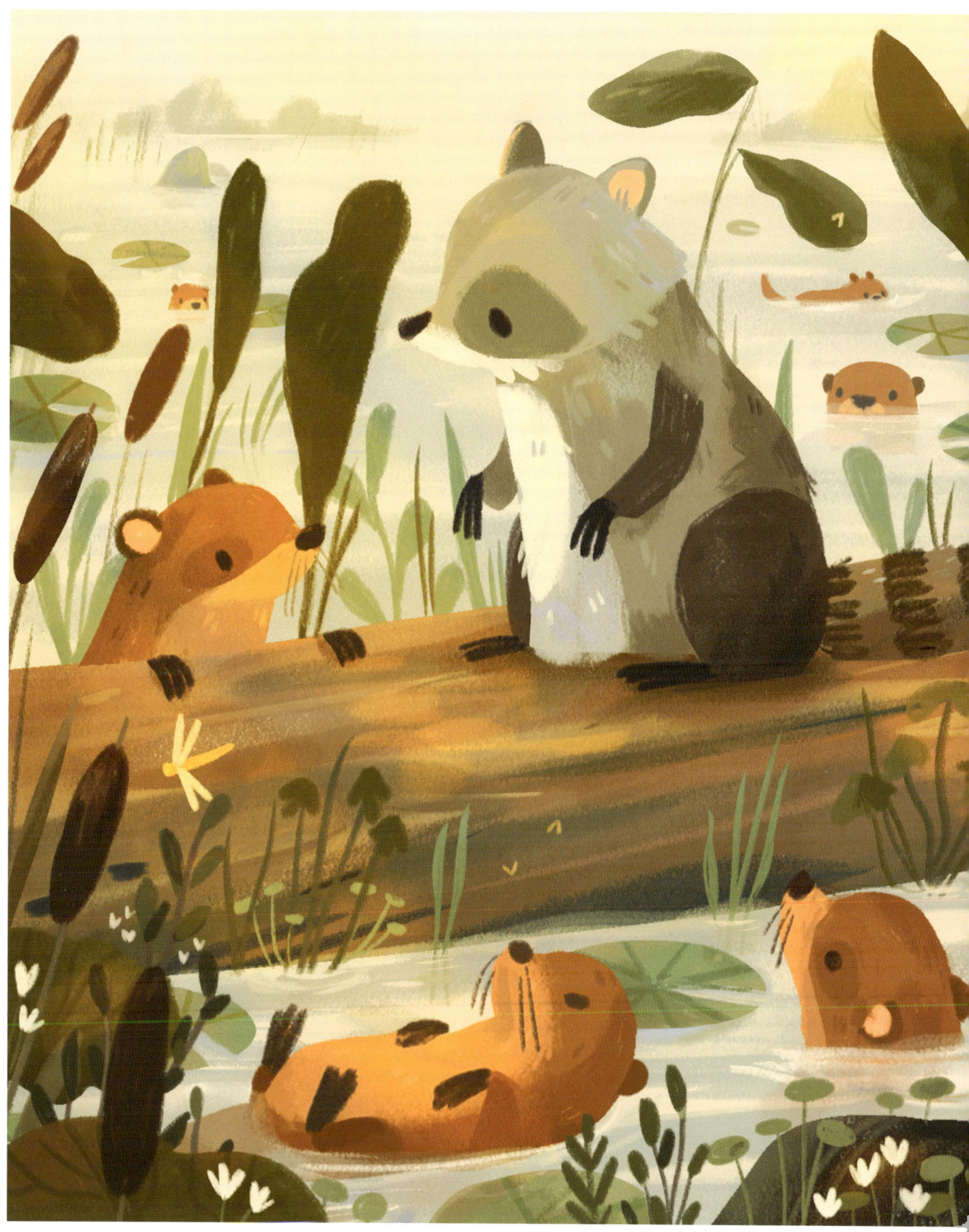

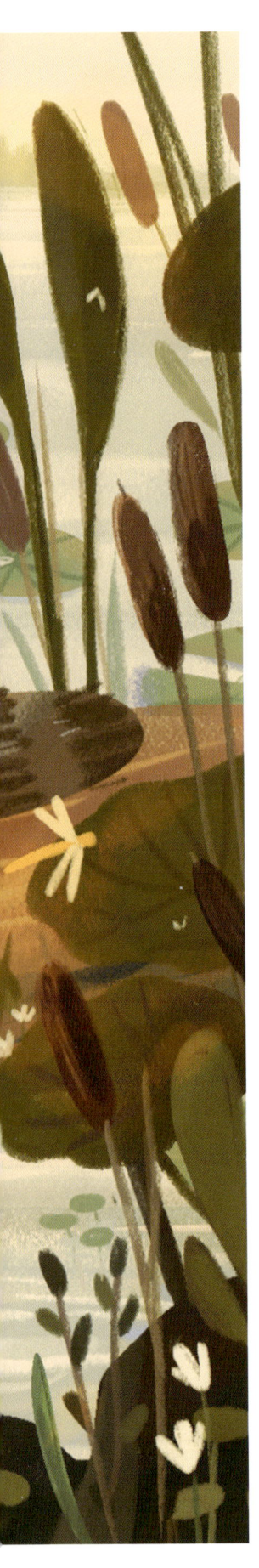

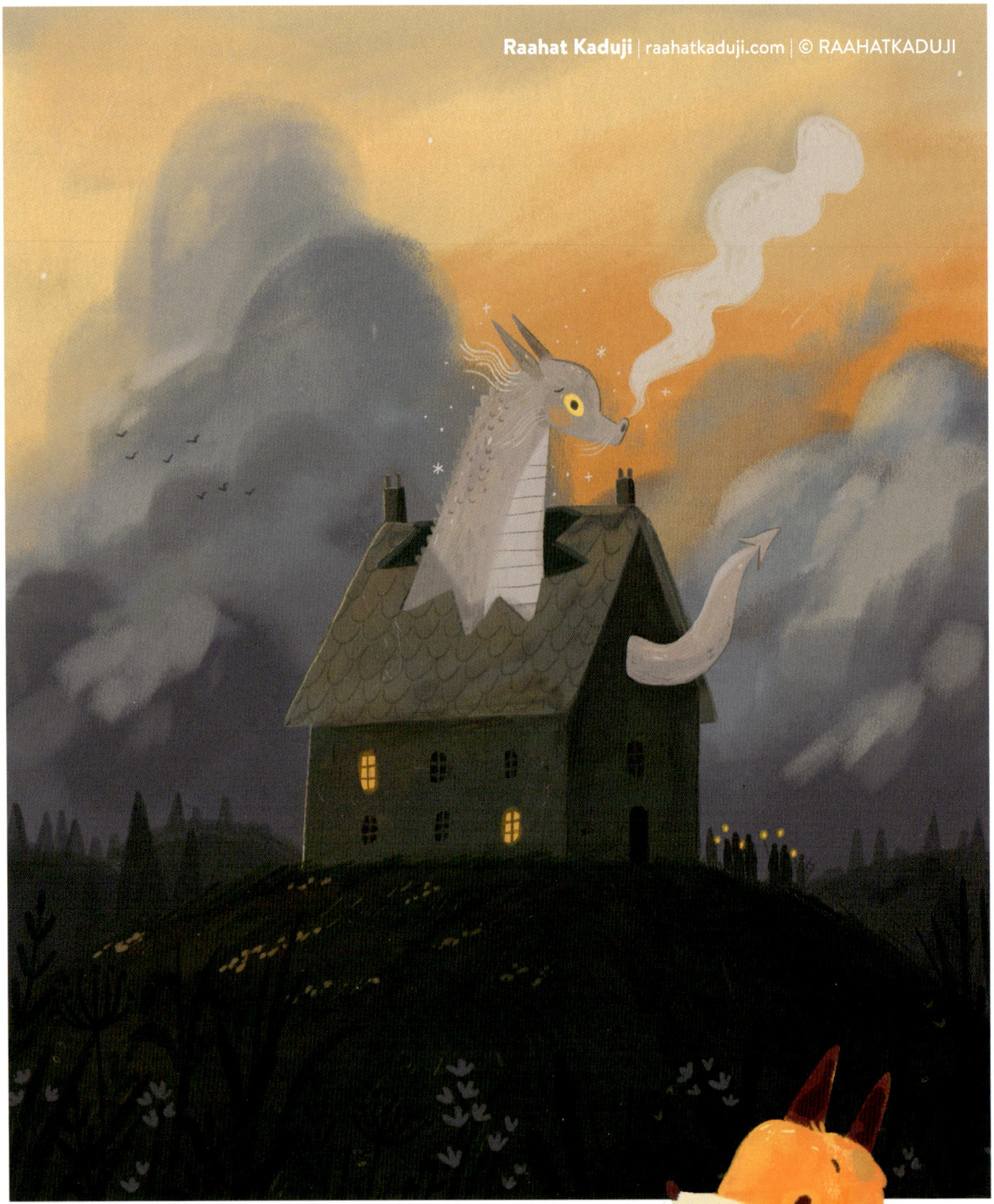

Raahat Kaduji | raahatkaduji.com | © RAAHATKADUJI

RAAHAT KADUJI IS A BRITISH-INDIAN ILLUSTRATOR AND AUTHOR BASED IN OXFORDSHIRE, ENGLAND. SHE LOVES DREAMING UP WORLDS AND CHARACTERS THAT EVOKE A SENSE OF COMFORT WITH A TOUCH OF ADVENTURE. HER DEBUT PICTURE BOOK, *I'M NOT SCARY*, WAS PUBLISHED BY ALISON GREEN BOOKS OF SCHOLASTIC UK IN 2022.

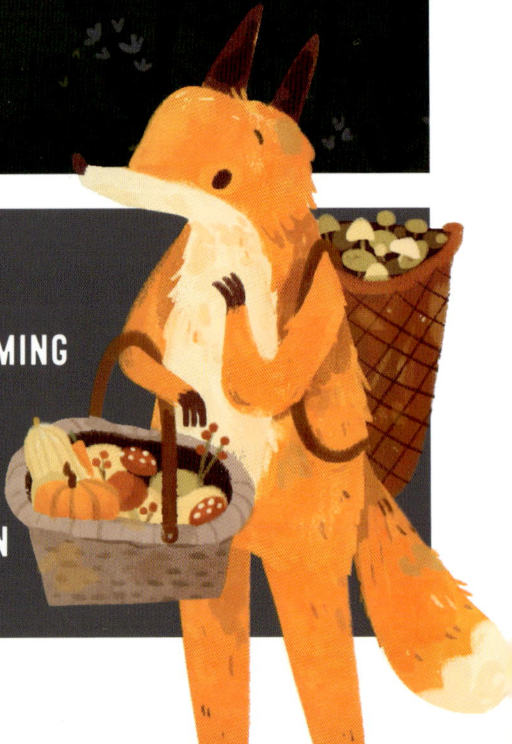

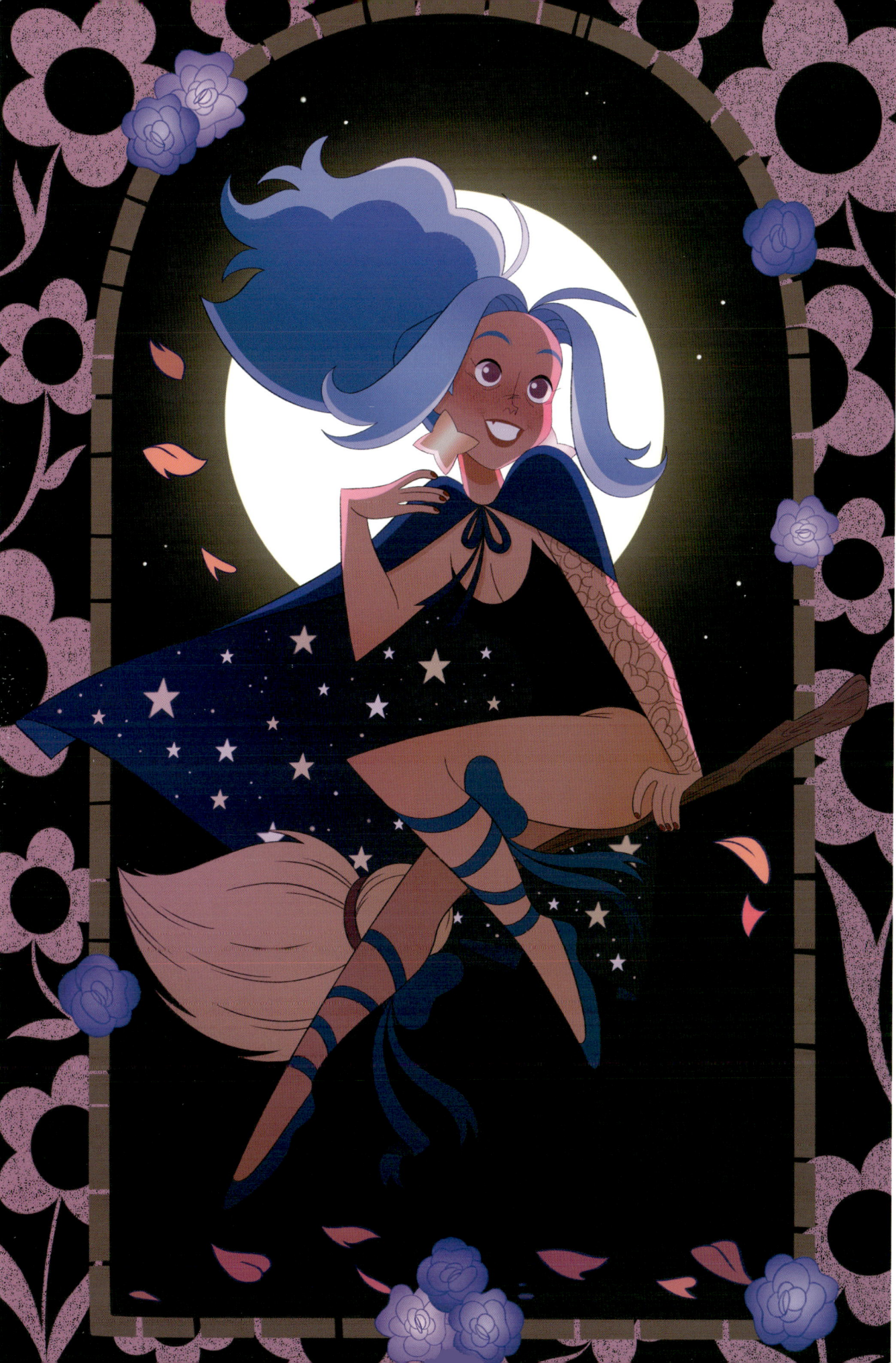

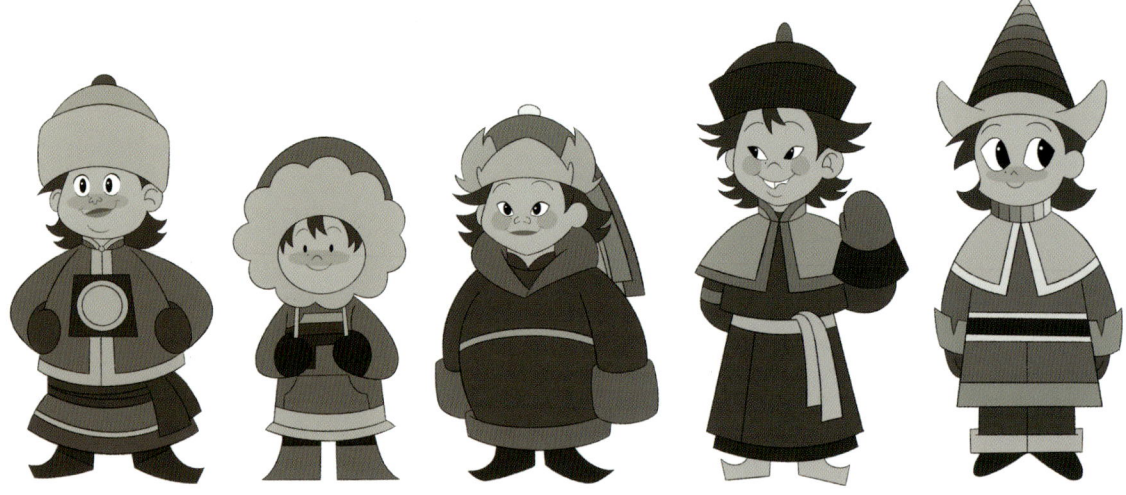

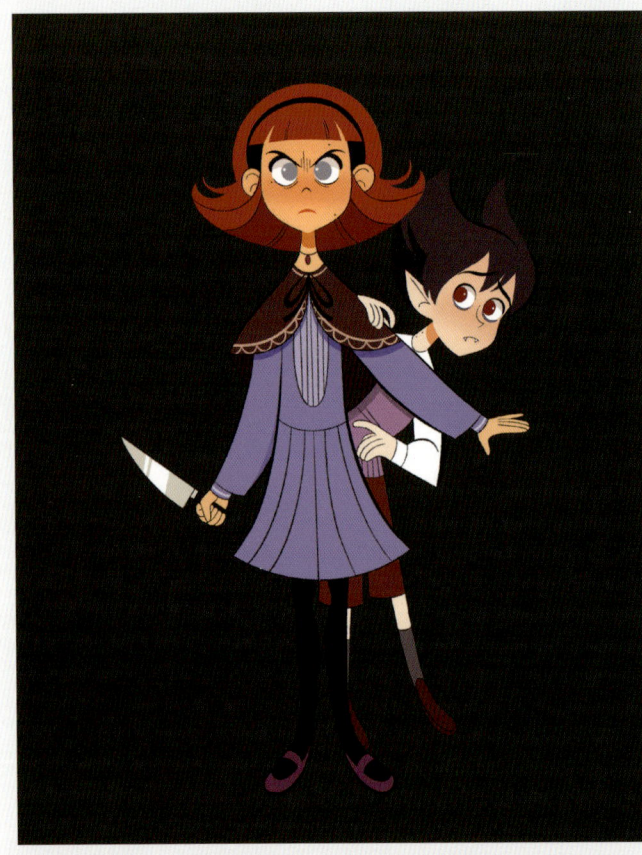

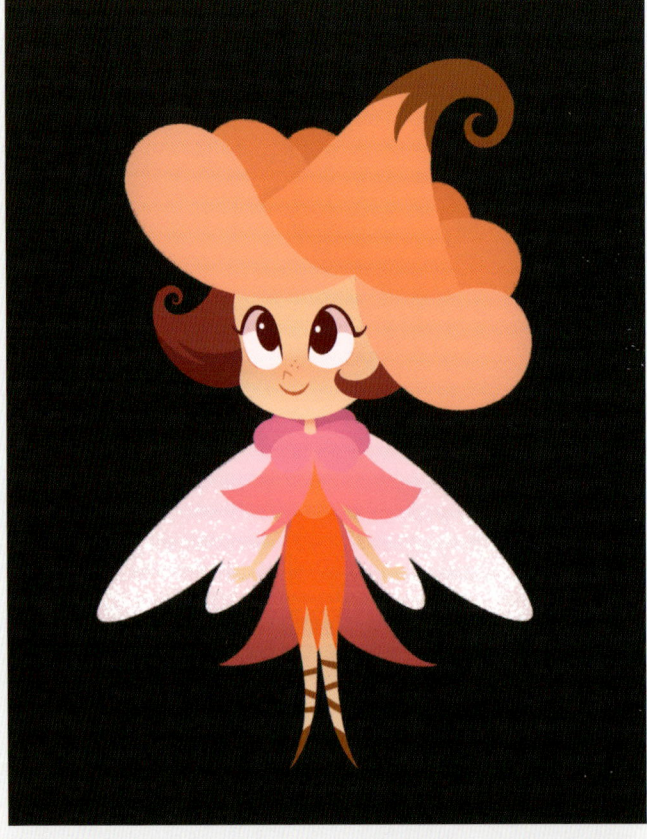

PAIGE MCMORROW LOVES ALL THINGS BRIGHT AND COLORFUL, AND FREQUENTLY INCORPORATES THESE ASPECTS INTO HER WORK. SHE HAS A PASSION FOR CREATING DIVERSE CHARACTERS THAT ARE FULL OF PERSONALITY AND LIFE, AND FINDS MUCH OF HER INSPIRATION WITHIN VINTAGE FASHION ILLUSTRATIONS, SHAPES, AND HER FAVORITE HOLIDAY: HALLOWEEN!

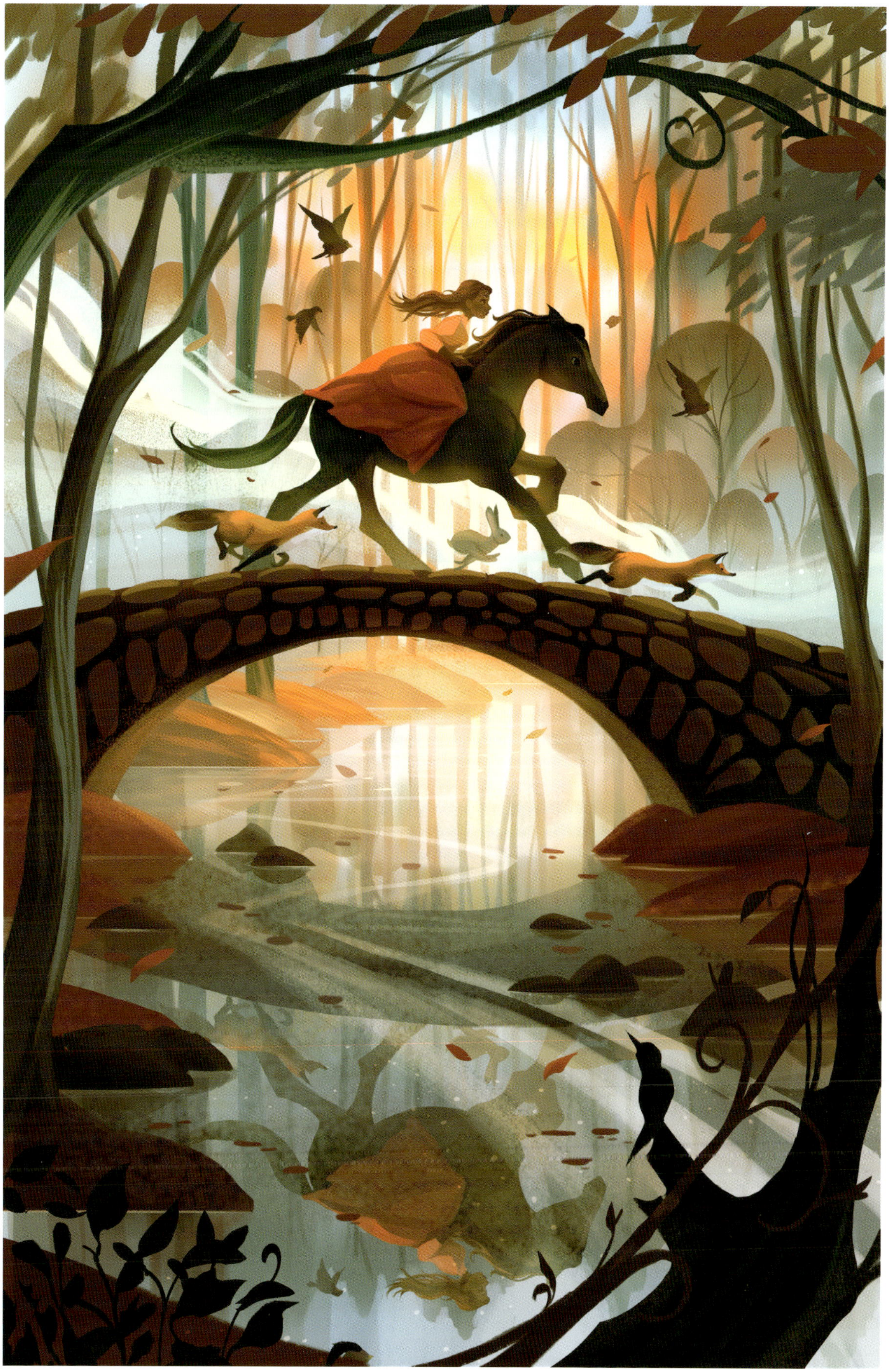

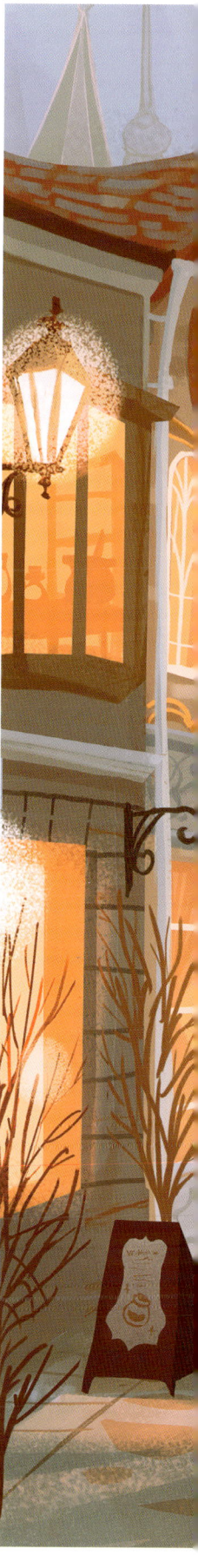

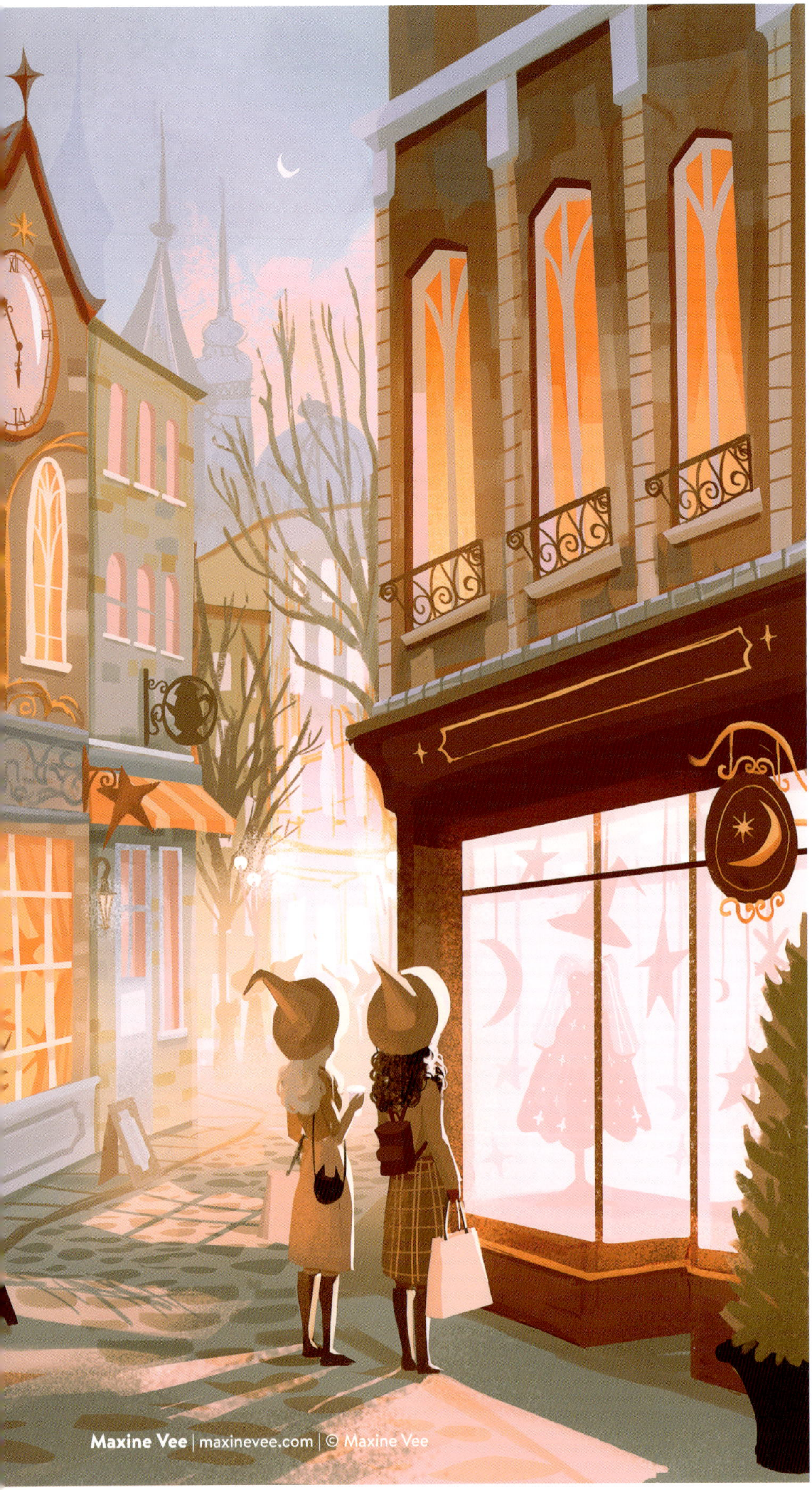

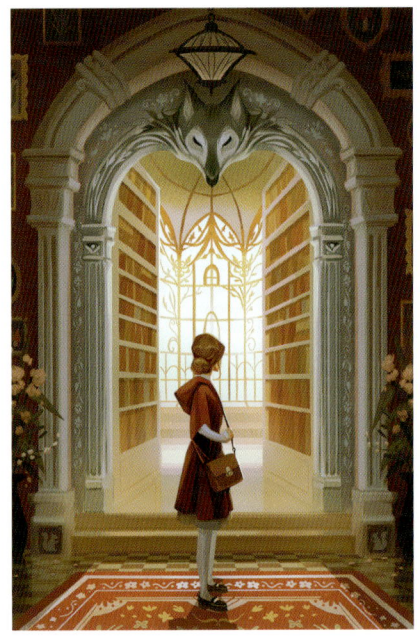

MAXINE VEE IS
A FREELANCE
ILLUSTRATOR AND
ARTIST BASED
IN THE GREATER
TORONTO AREA.
SHE LOVES CREATING
COLORFUL WHIMSICAL
ILLUSTRATIONS,
DREAMY MOMENTS,
AND MAGICAL SCENES.
SHE HAS WORKED IN
THE GAMING AND
ANIMATION INDUSTRY
AND HAS ILLUSTRATED
BOOK COVERS
FOR SCHOLASTIC,
HARPERCOLLINS,
PENGUIN RANDOM
HOUSE, BLOOMSBURY
PUBLISHING,
AND MORE.

Maxine Vee | maxinevee.com | © Maxine Vee

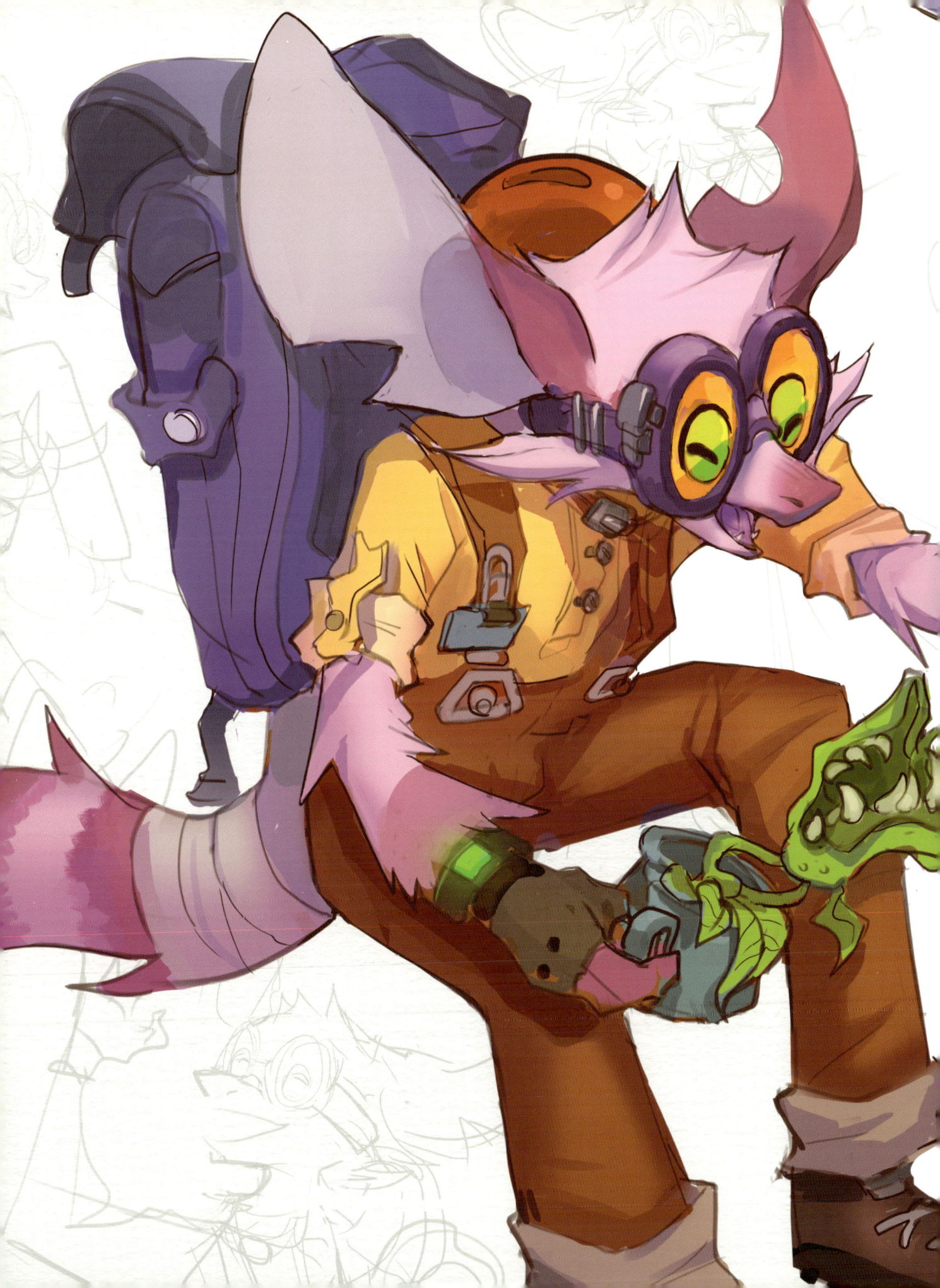

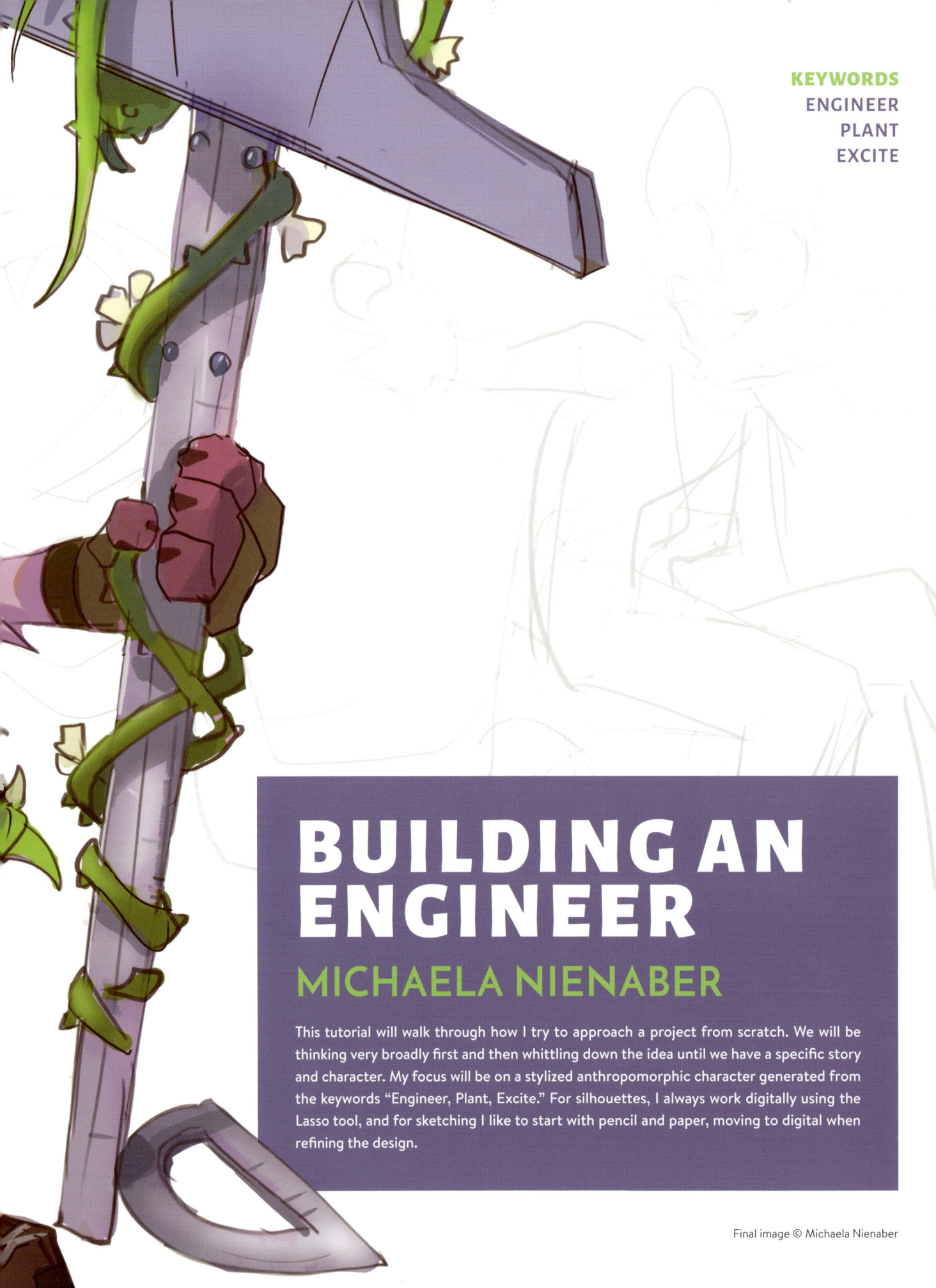

KEYWORDS
ENGINEER
PLANT
EXCITE

BUILDING AN ENGINEER

MICHAELA NIENABER

This tutorial will walk through how I try to approach a project from scratch. We will be thinking very broadly first and then whittling down the idea until we have a specific story and character. My focus will be on a stylized anthropomorphic character generated from the keywords "Engineer, Plant, Excite." For silhouettes, I always work digitally using the Lasso tool, and for sketching I like to start with pencil and paper, moving to digital when refining the design.

Final image © Michaela Nienaber

STARTING WITH SILHOUETTES

Creating silhouettes is a fun way to loosen up and not have to worry about detail. Whether you start with the Lasso tool or by drawing the shape and hitting the Fill button, focus less on line work, and instead try for readable shapes that feel interesting. Thinking about your big, medium, and small elements is also very helpful. What are going to be the interesting points of your possible designs? Spitball now so that you have a point of reference for the following stages.

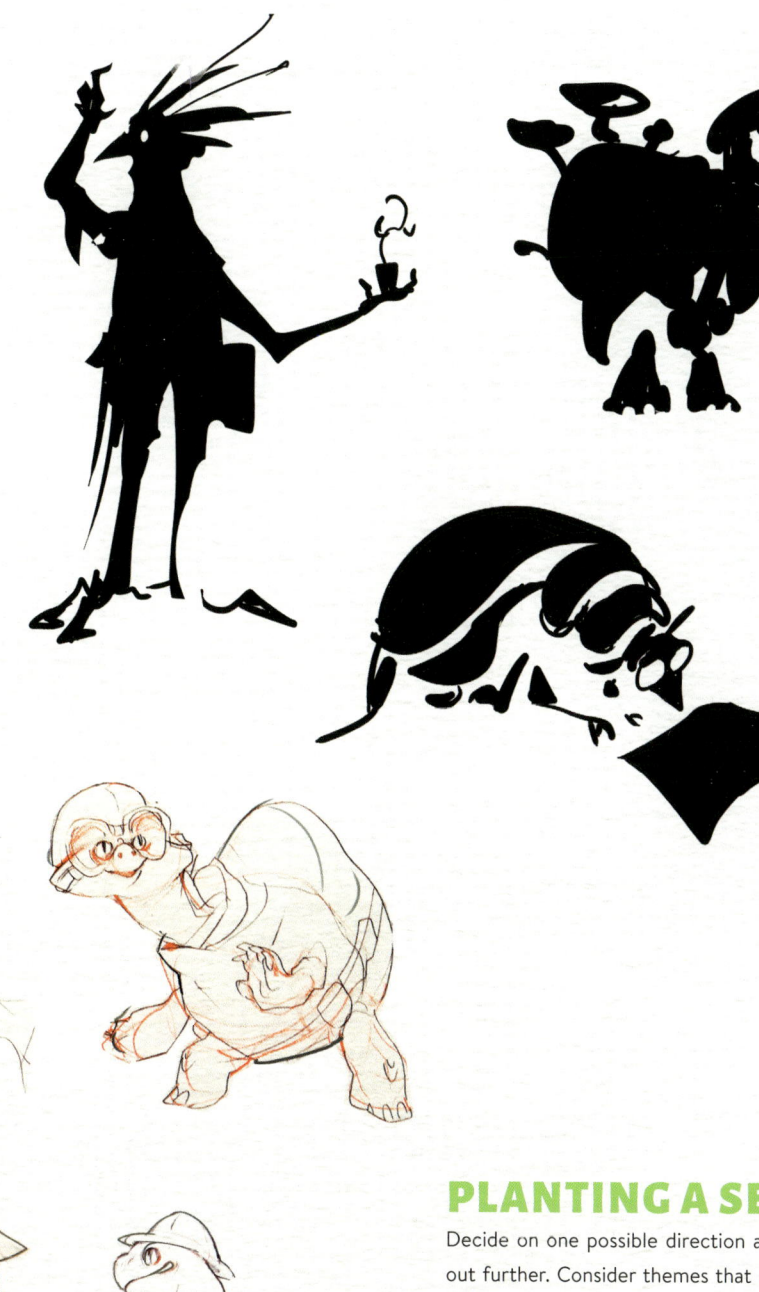

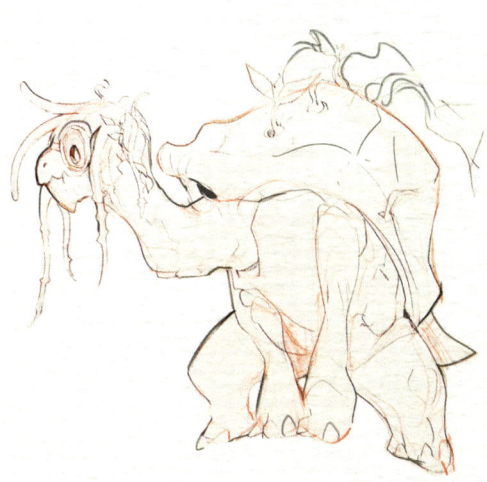

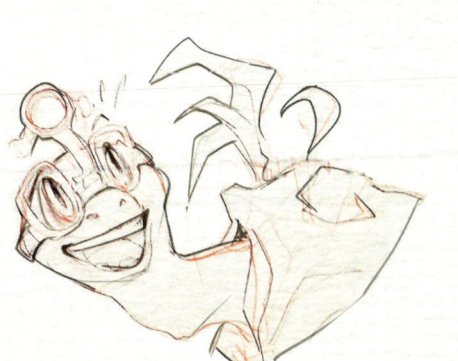

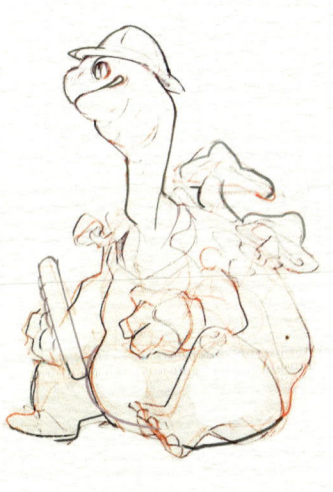

PLANTING A SEED

Decide on one possible direction and flesh it out further. Consider themes that might help give an extra hook to your character as you work; will your character be a mad scientist, or maybe a curious innovator? What sort of energy do you want them to have? Since my design is going to be an animal character, I start by exploring which species I want to draw – this is a huge part of choosing a direction for my design. First, I focus on tortoises with different props fulfilling the "plant" element of the brief. For example, I draw mushroom growths on the shell from his experiments, and a wig of plants draping from his head. Think of some of your own fun "hooks" and see where your imagination takes you!

"THESE EARLY STAGES ARE THE BEST TIME TO CHANNEL YOUR CREATIVE ENERGY INTO CASTING A WIDE NET FOR IDEAS"

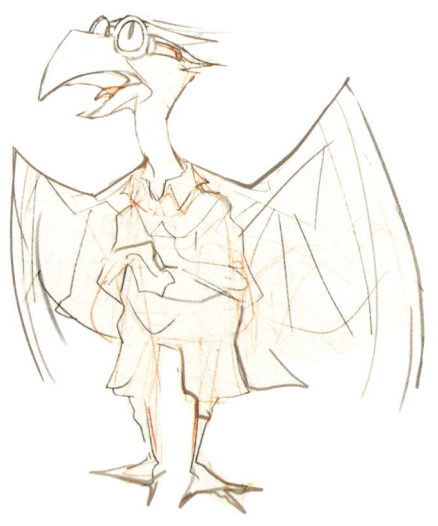

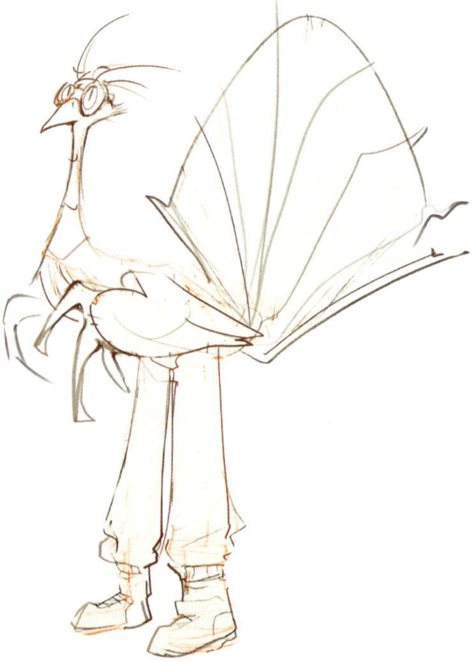

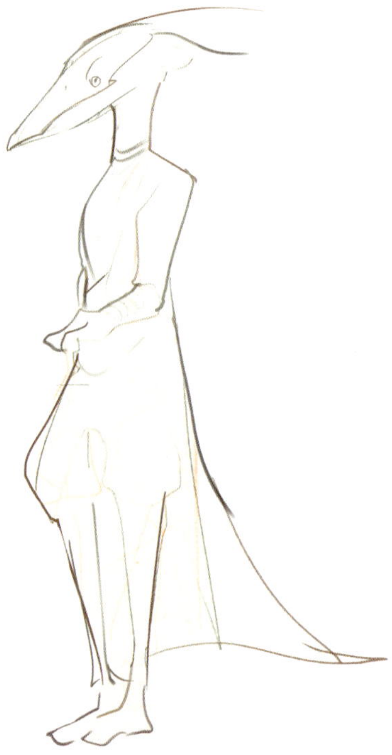

ANIMAL OPTIONS

Keep exploring further – juggle finding fun shapes that appeal to you with working out what the character's vibe will be. In this pass, I focus on birds as a species – could my character be an anxious peacock engineer using a cocktail of plants to grow their tail? How about a serious and more sinister type of character, like a cackling goose? These early stages are the best time to channel your creative energy into casting a wide net for ideas. Search for what will grab you, and your audience or client.

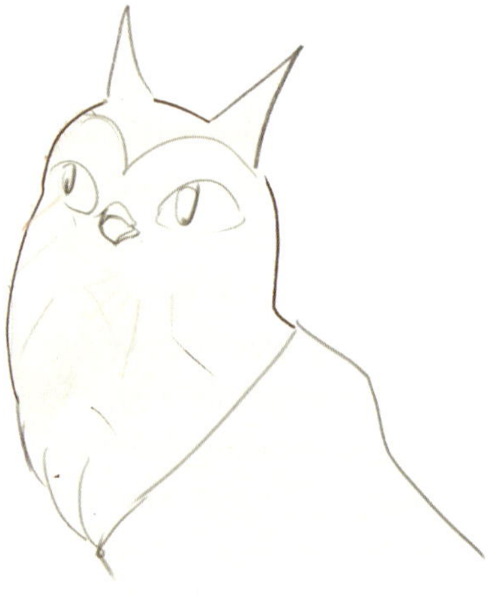

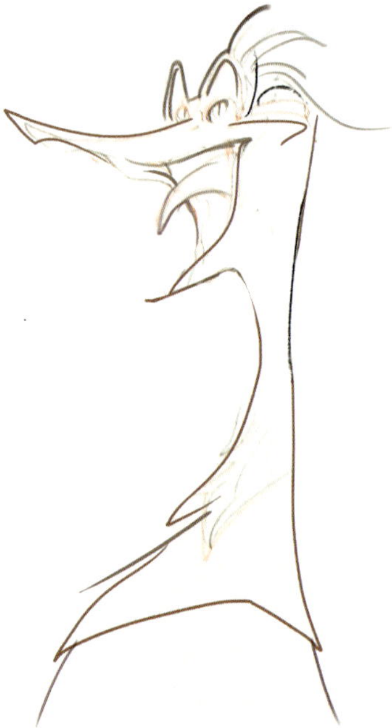

Opposite page (top): Opaque shapes will help you ideate quickly

Opposite page (bottom): Find an idea and explore its possibilities

This page: Explore design possibilities for your character

FINALIZING THE SKETCH

Consider what was missing previously to help dictate your choices in this last round of sketches. The earlier drawings I made don't quite hit the mark for me, so focus on thinking about specifics. I want something more cute and playful – maybe a character with big goofy glasses or goggles, and a hard hat to fulfill the "engineer" part of the brief. Maybe a better species fit could be a lemur or a fuzzy armadillo? Assess your sketches and ideas, and consider what else you can try. Ask yourself what you want a viewer to take from the first impression of your character.

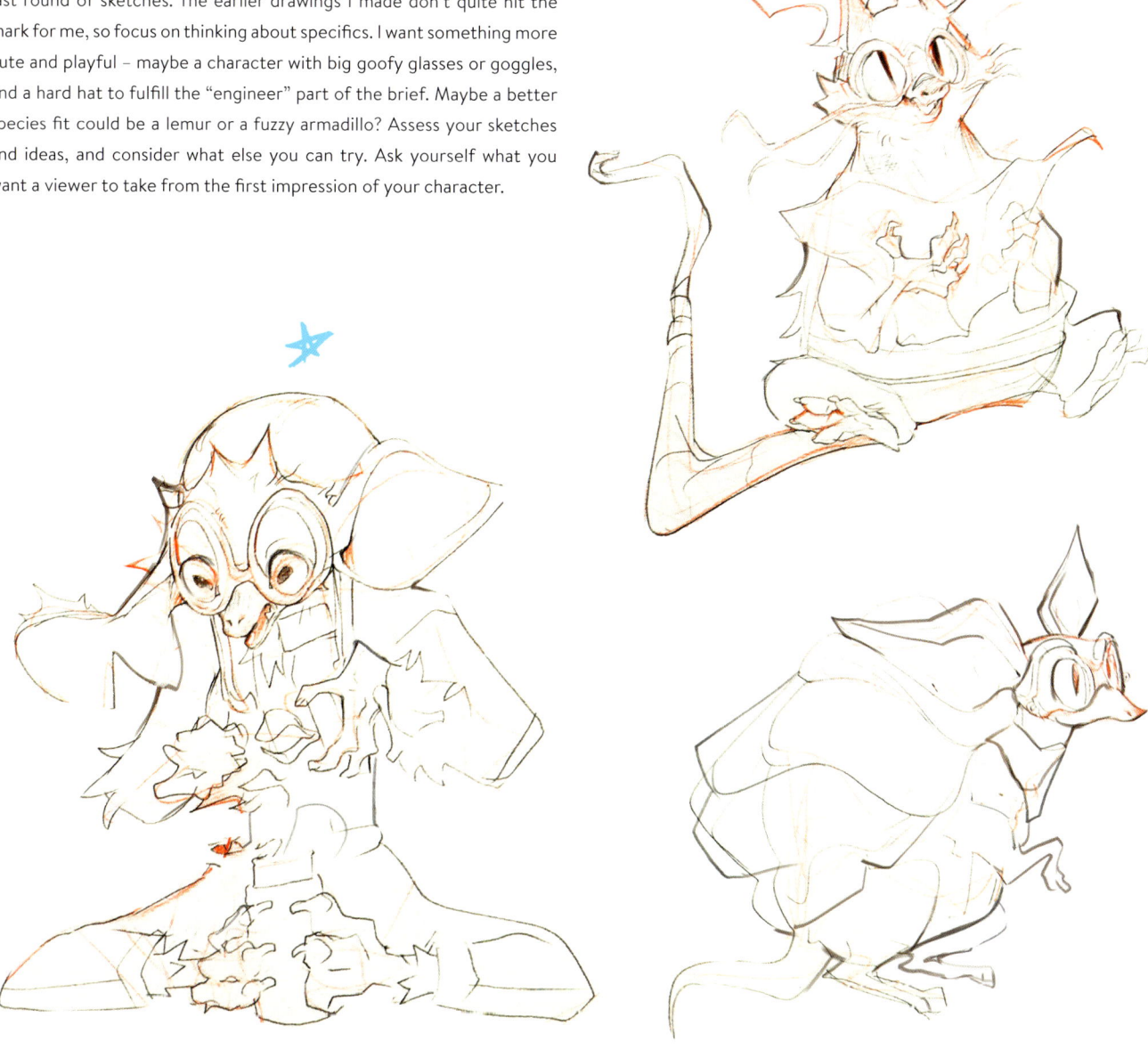

FRIENDLY FEEDBACK

Pitch your work to someone else and explain the direction so far – they can help you veto weaker ideas. Talk your ideas through with them and then jam on the suggestions that seem worth exploring. They may have a cool suggestion you hadn't thought of, or point out something that feels off. An extra pair of eyes can also help find inconsistencies you hadn't considered. Be open to feedback – two or more minds are always better than one. It's easy to get stuck at the concept stage – it's time to be decisive!

STORY SPECIFICITY

Think hard about what you want your character's story to be – who are they? What are they about? Are they sweet and cutesy, or tough and unruffled? Are they popular or a loner who avoids standing out? Jot down a 2–3 sentence biography for them that will help you choose any specific or relevant props or accessories you might want to add, then pull more specific keywords from there. This could take a few passes, but sometimes conceptual problems can be solved more easily with writing than through drawing. Figuring out their story will give you the context for what they should look like.

DESIGNING THE DETAILS

At this point, you have consulted others for their opinion and also decided on your own preference for the character's direction. Now it's time to get the final drawing down and to move on to the next stages of design. Did you need any style adjustments or proportions changed? Avoid adding too many last minute unnecessary details, but also be sure that the design fits the story outline you generated for yourself in the previous step. I add a protractor, nametag, and backpack to my character's overalls to touch on the "dorky student" vibe I'm going for.

ENGINEER, PLANT, EXCITE

story?

"A young student; dorky. maybe they carry hand-me-down tools. Peppy and growing a little baby flytrap.

- Button up shirt?   - Hard hat?
- Overalls
- Oversize boots?

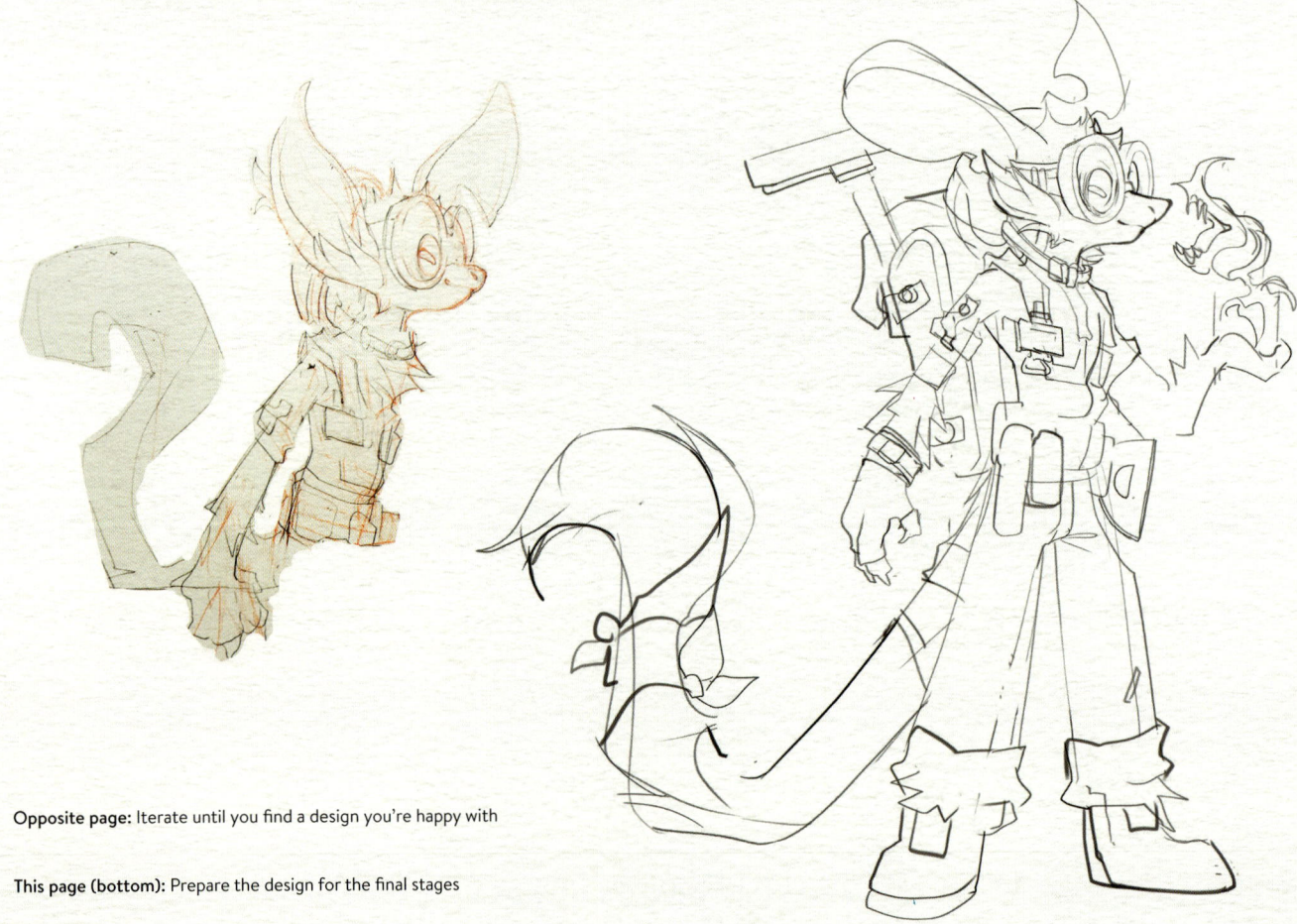

Opposite page: Iterate until you find a design you're happy with

This page (bottom): Prepare the design for the final stages

FIGURING IT OUT

When creating humanoid figures, it can help to draw straight lines across the page to use as a rough guide for checking your proportion variety. Think of it like dropping plumb lines in figure drawings, except even easier! It also pays to do this when studying faces – how far apart can eyes be? How close together? Don't be afraid of stylizing more than real life, it can add to the interest of the drawing if you're not aiming for realism. For body types, drawing simple primitive shapes for the torso will also help you check for variety. People come in many shapes and sizes, more than just large or thin.

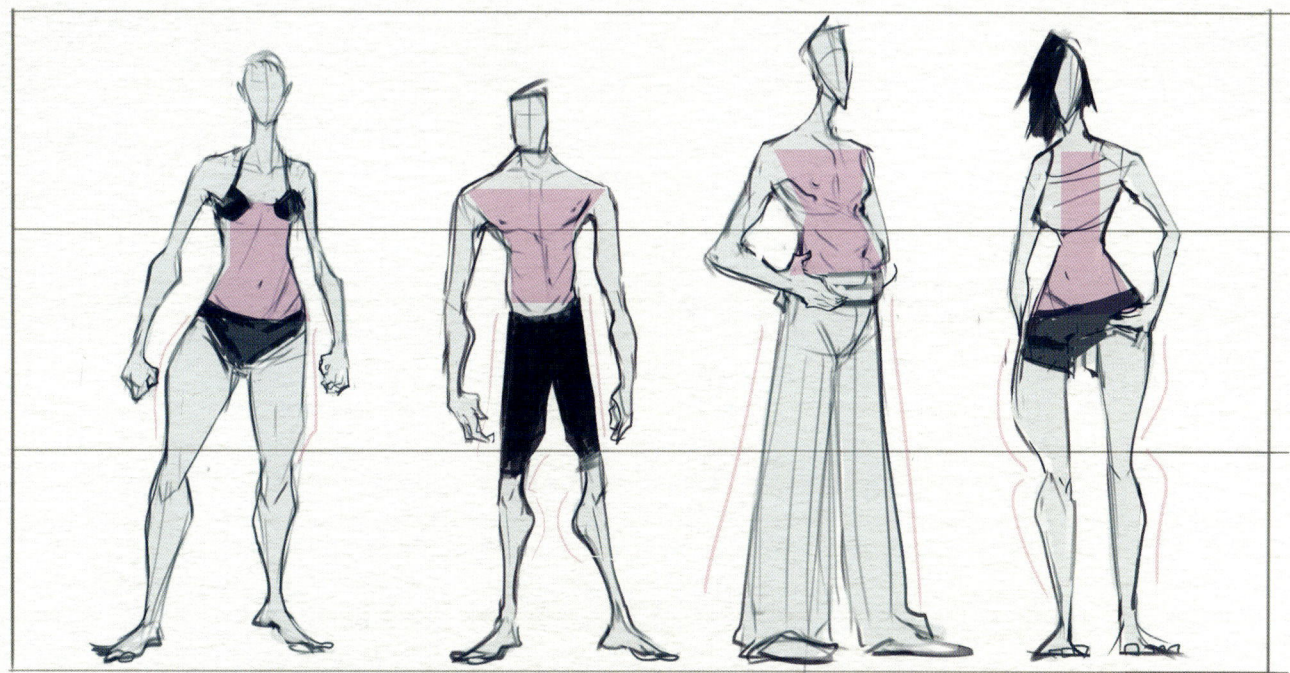

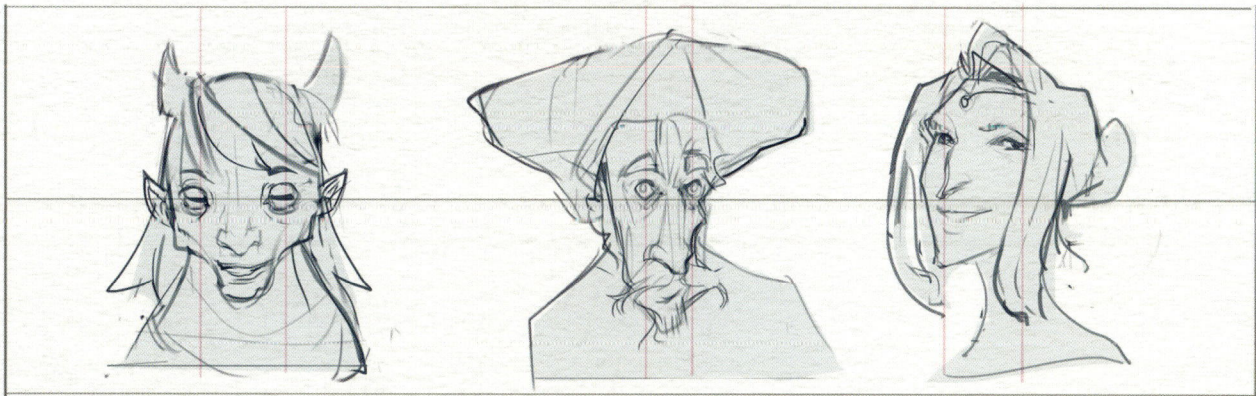

This page: Straight lines serve as a guide for working out character proportions

"IT'S IMPORTANT TO FIGURE OUT YOUR BASIC VALUE STRUCTURE BEFORE MOVING ON TO THE DETAILS"

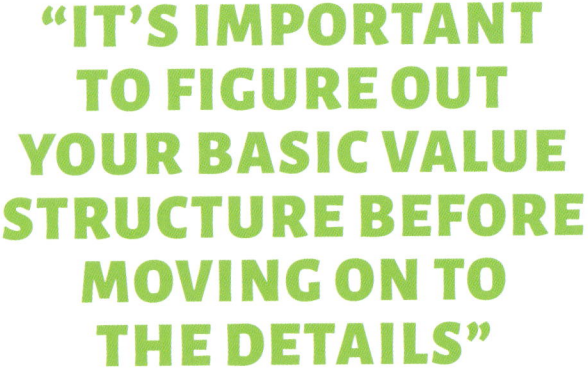

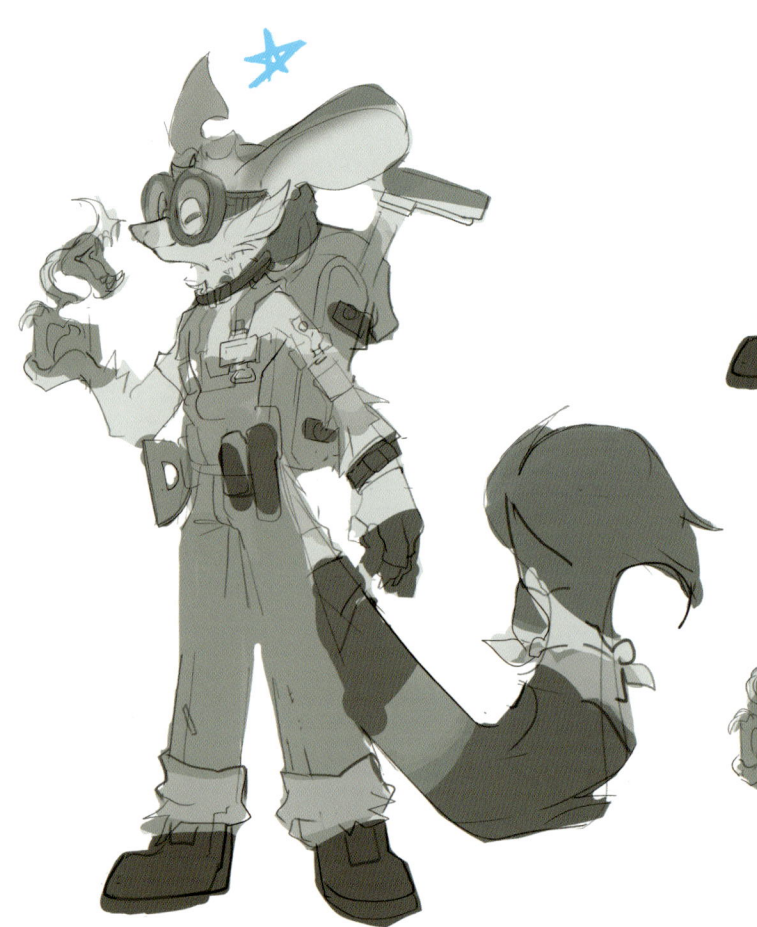

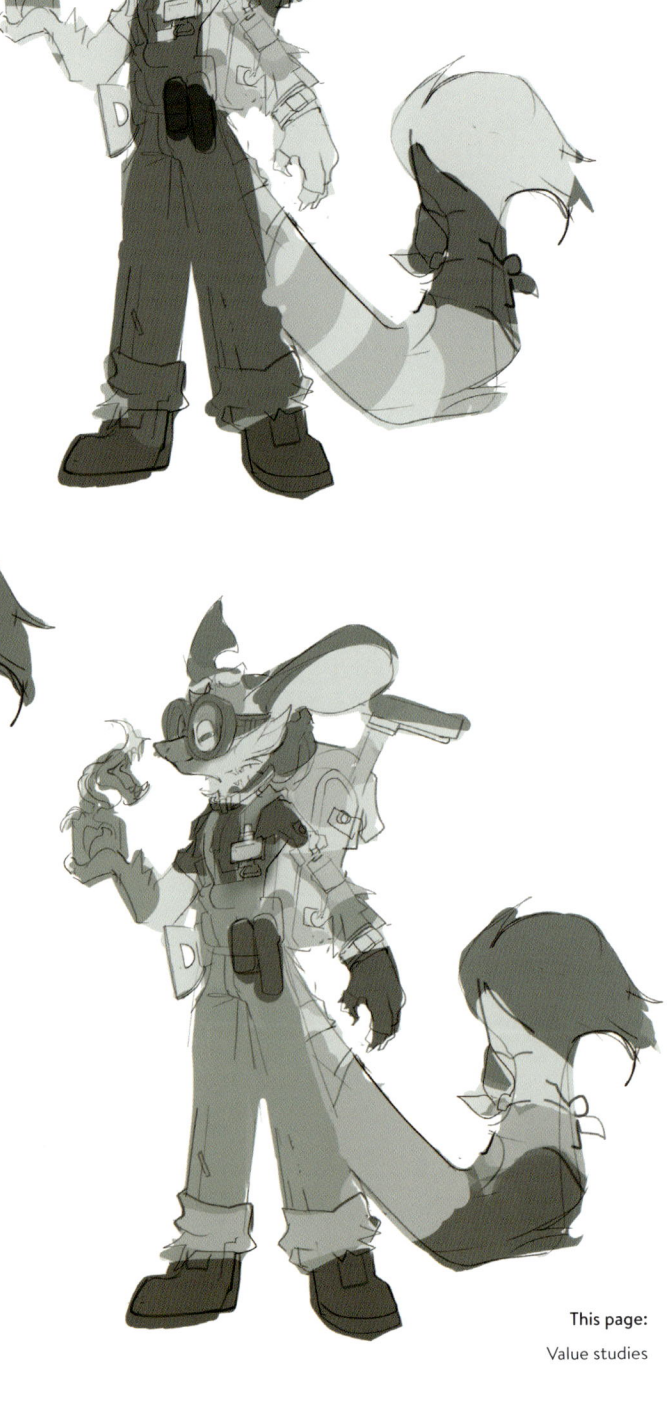

VERIFYING VALUES

Checking values is great for exploring things that are a pain to draw or sketch, like patterns in clothing, or markings on the face or body. It's important to figure out your basic value structure before moving on to the details. I'm pretty set on having darker clothing and a lighter character, with the eyes being a focal point, especially since "excite" was part of my prompt.

This page:

Value studies

"COLOR IS WHERE WE CAN START TO TRULY BRING THIS CHARACTER TO LIFE"

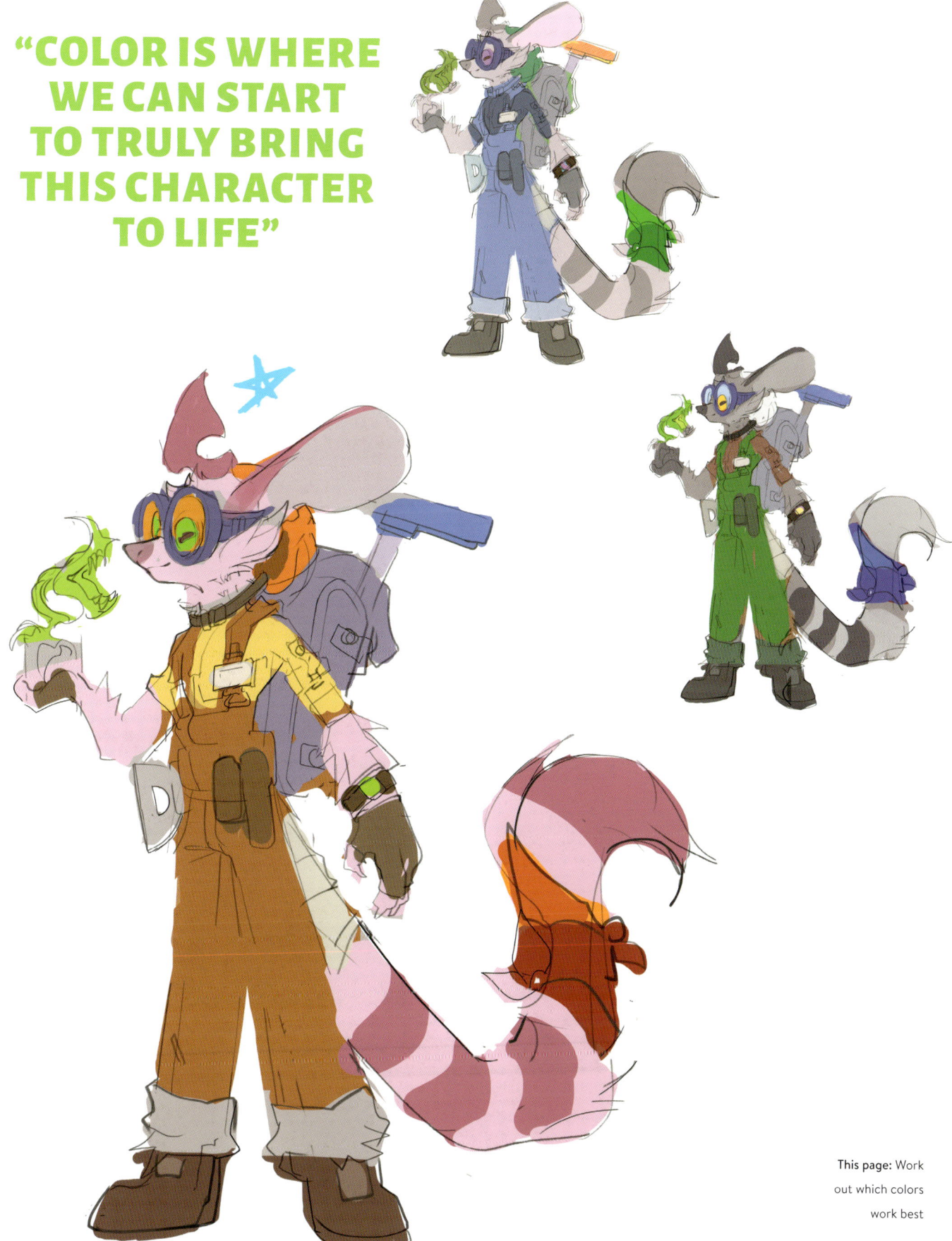

This page: Work out which colors work best

INTRODUCING COLOR

The hardest work is behind us now that we've pinned down the design – color is where we can start to truly bring this character to life. Using your value studies as a reference, and maintaining the value structure or patterns you liked most, now move into coloring. The best way to do this is to have your values visible as you work and just toggle your colors and values back and forth using the CTRL+Y trick I outline below. You can be as polished as you want, but remember we don't need to make a beautiful final work of art just yet – adding color is one step further along the design pipeline.

PLANNING THE POSE

Take a moment to jot down ideas you might want for posing in the final presentation. Given that "excite" was a keyword in the brief, I want to be sure that emotion comes across. Maybe the character will be jumping in midair, or simply standing with a hand on their hip to keep it neutral? There are times it's best to show off a character with a static pose, and others (especially in an early pitch phase) when injecting as much personality as possible is useful to convince others to get behind your idea.

Pose Planning

- Excited?
- Seated
- Standing?
- Holding plant?
- Laughing?

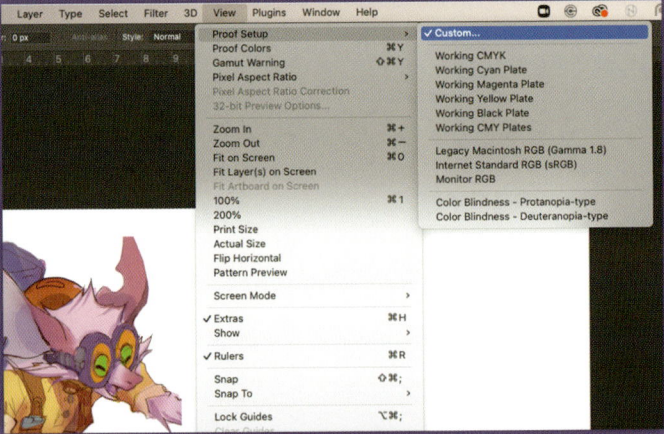

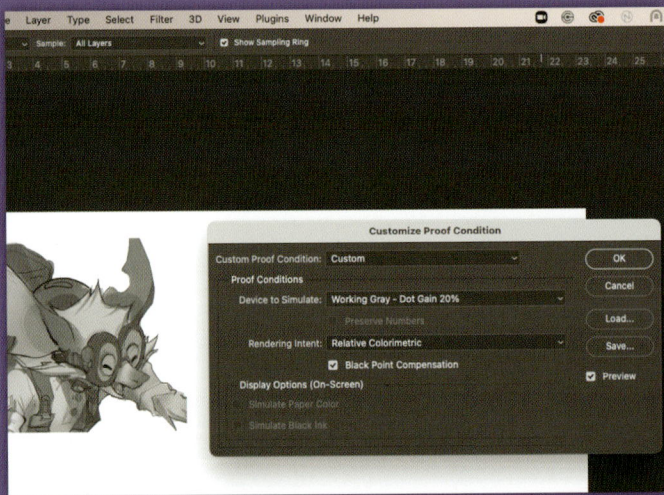

Photoshop screenshots showing the CTRL+Y tip

A VALUABLE TIP

In Photoshop, go to View > Proof Setup > Custom and set it to Working Gray – Dot Gain 20%. You can now hit CTRL+Y (or Command+Y on Mac) and see your painting in grayscale. This will make it super easy to check values while still working in color. Your Eyedropper tool will still choose true color as well.

"YOUR SKETCHES SHOULD BE FAST AND GESTURAL"

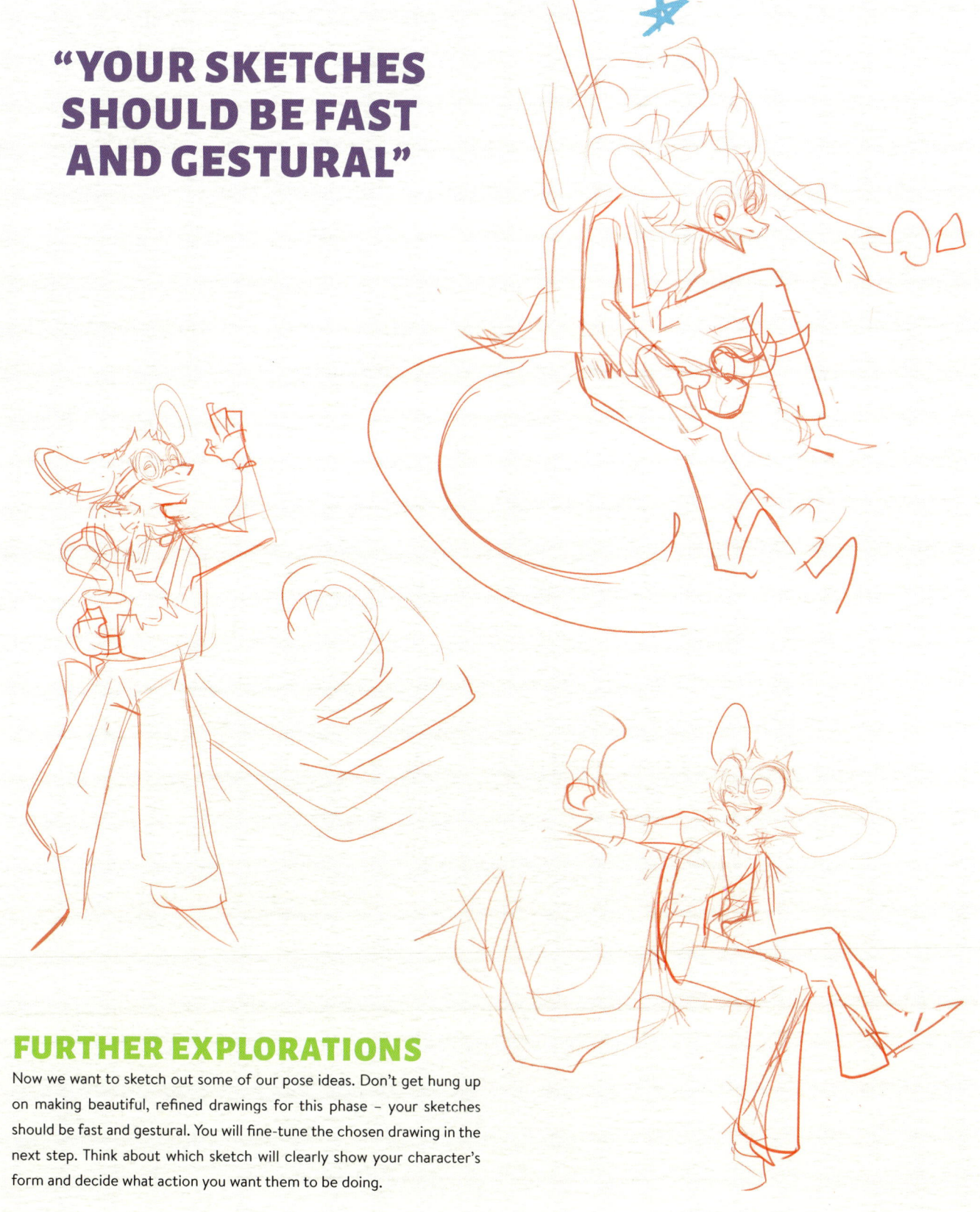

FURTHER EXPLORATIONS

Now we want to sketch out some of our pose ideas. Don't get hung up on making beautiful, refined drawings for this phase – your sketches should be fast and gestural. You will fine-tune the chosen drawing in the next step. Think about which sketch will clearly show your character's form and decide what action you want them to be doing.

PICKING THE POSE

Take your chosen rough sketch and flesh it out. It helps to do this in passes, building on a gestural sketch, working out any problems before drawing the final lines. Flip your image frequently so that your brain registers things that feel off. At this stage, it's important to focus on the style and proportions too, since sometimes we might leave placeholder scribbles in the sketch. I want to get the right shape for the backpack so that it feels chunky and stylized.

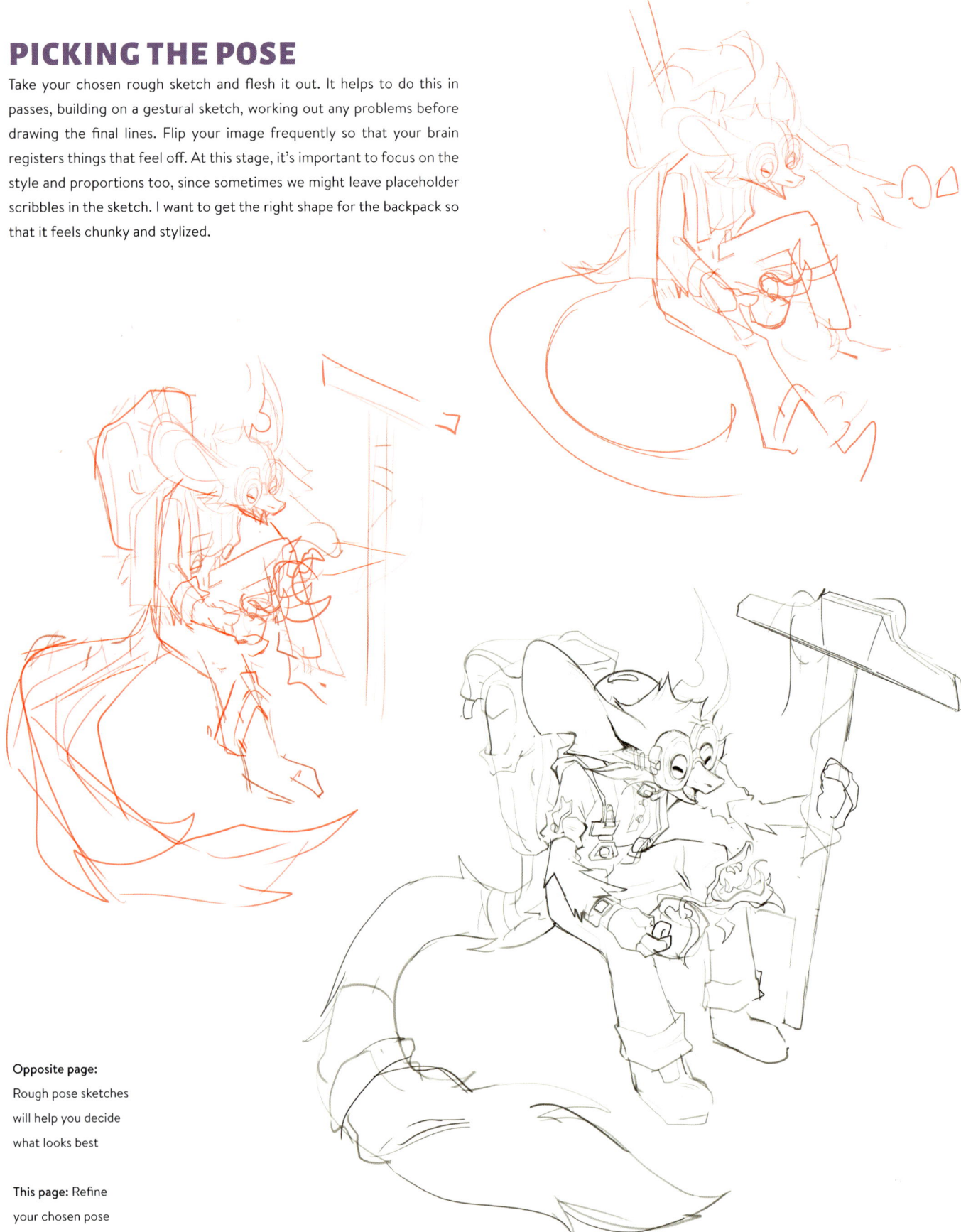

Opposite page:
Rough pose sketches will help you decide what looks best

This page: Refine your chosen pose

BLOCK IN COLOR

Referencing your chosen color design from earlier, start blocking in the character's colors. I make a big shape beneath the line-art layer, then add a Clipping Mask for the working layer. This will keep you locked to the silhouette shape and is a cleaner way to work. To do this, you can just right-click and scroll down to Create Clipping Mask, but be sure the layer sits above the block-in layer.

ADDING SHADOWS

I start suggesting shadows with a Multiply layer on top of the flat colors. Instead of using a basic gray, choose a color that is either warm or cool so that things don't become dull – I often key it purple, red, or blue. Use the Value tip from earlier to make sure your forms are reading well – this is crucial since this is the basis for your final painting. Think about where your darkest darks will be and avoid any shadows getting darker than that. Always keep the color temperature in mind as you're working on each section of your character.

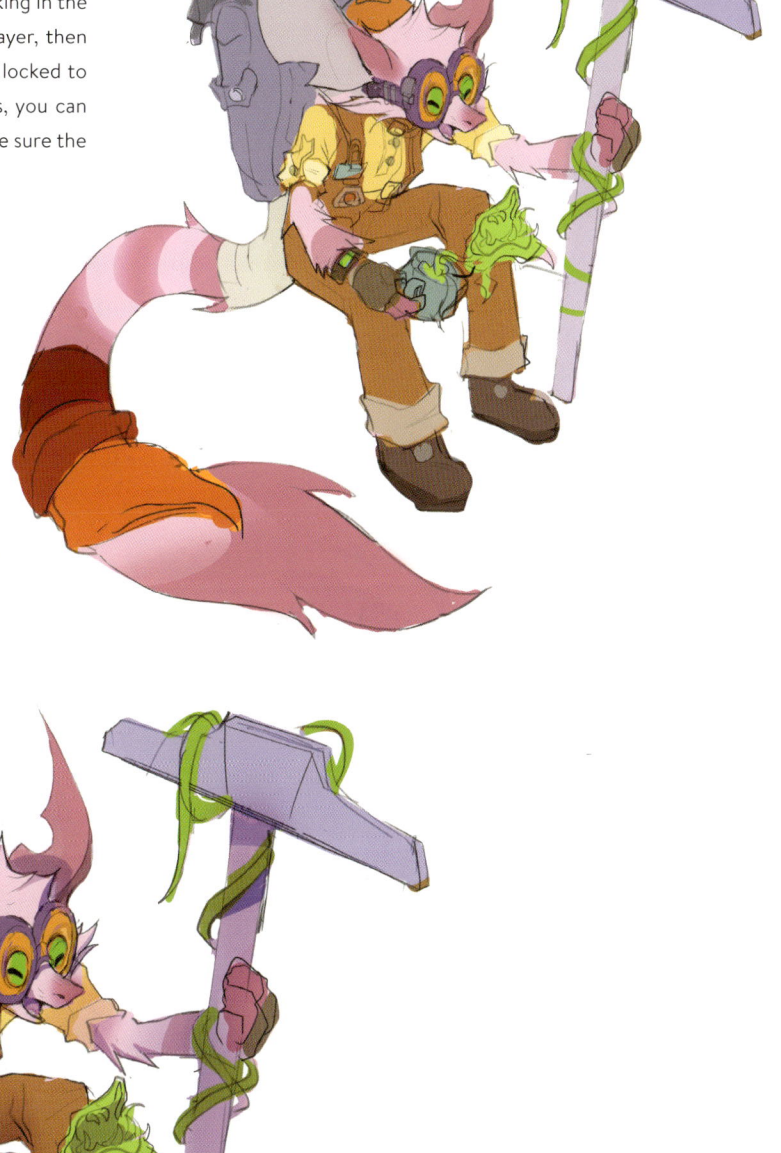

This page (top): Add your chosen colors to your line drawing

This page (bottom): Adding shadow and showing form

Opposite page: Our engineer is alive!

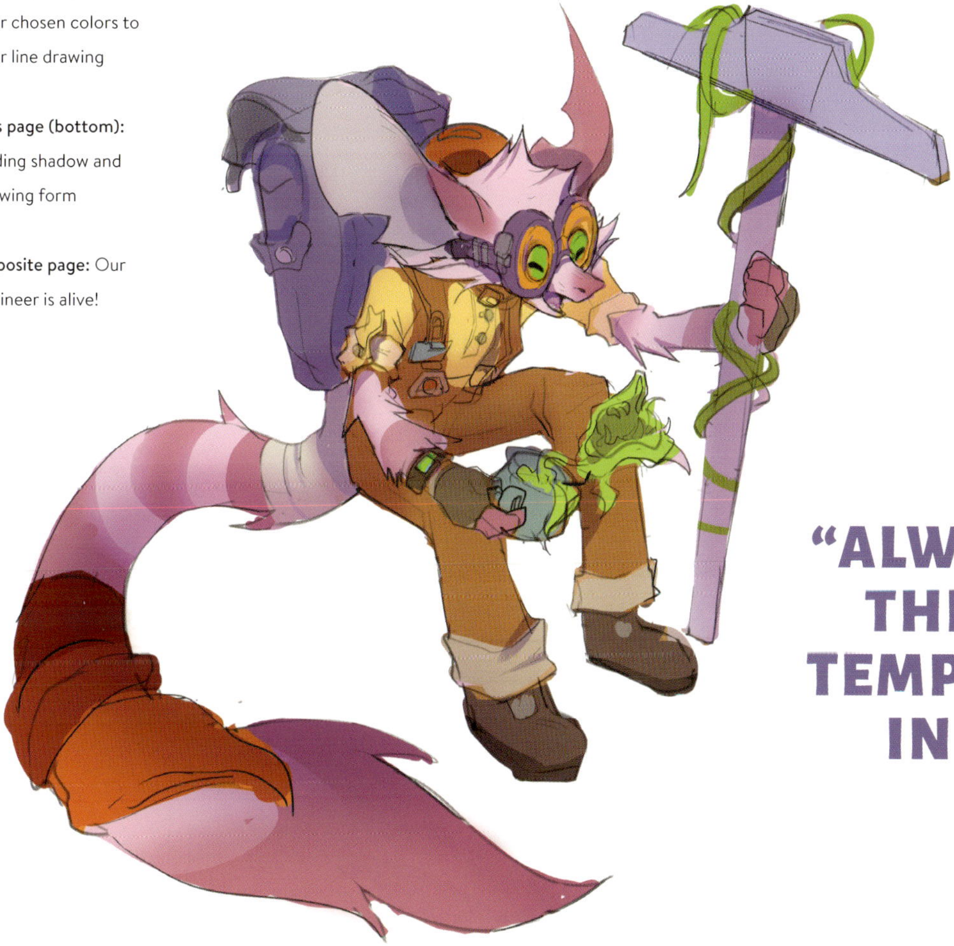

"ALWAYS KEEP THE COLOR TEMPERATURE IN MIND"

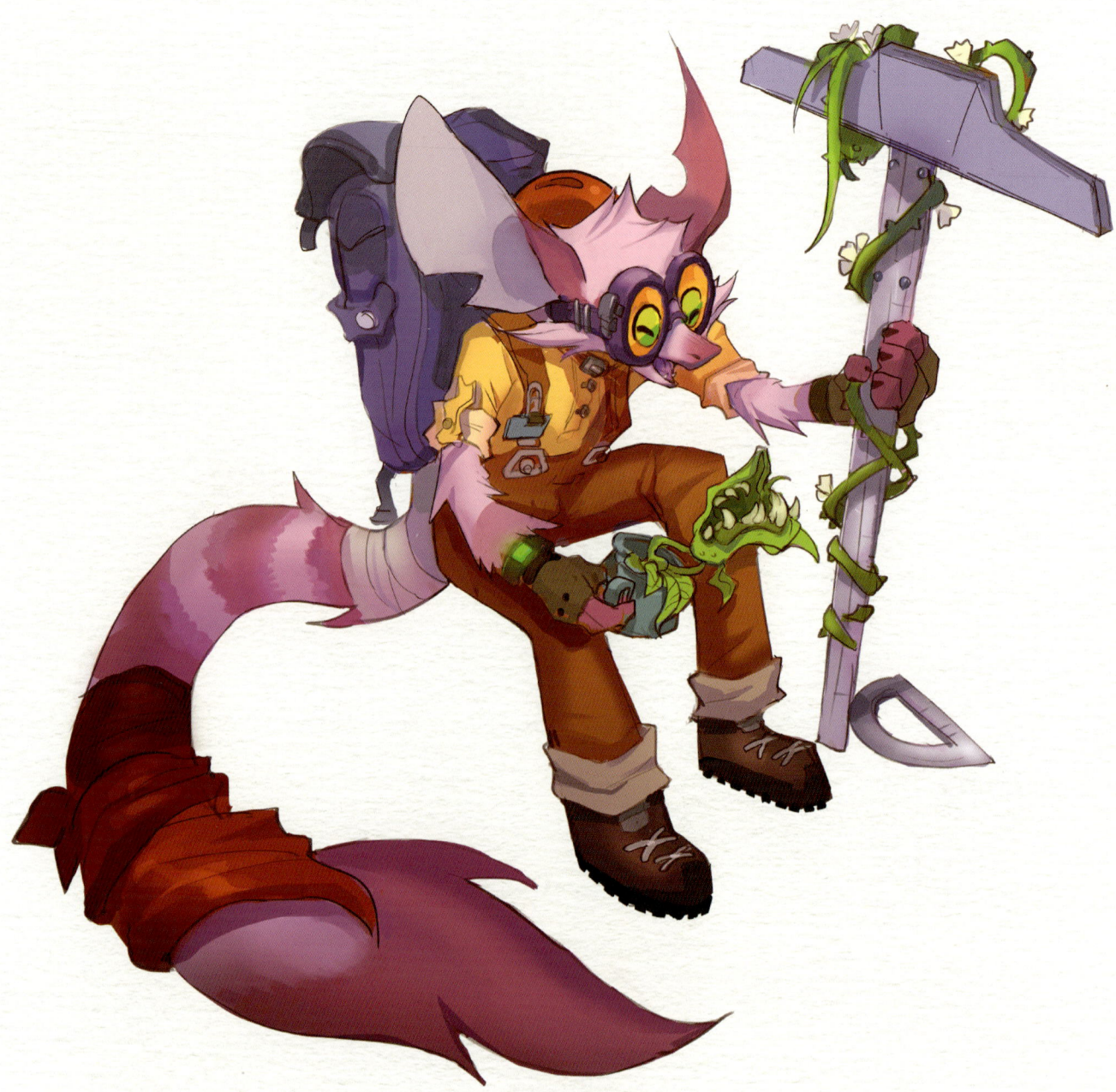

THE ENGINEER LIVES

You made it – your character lives and breathes! You hopefully should feel you have made something you are confident to present to others. Make sure any specific materials are reading well – do you have specular reflections on your metal? Did you indicate where an element is transparent or has emissive light? Does fur read as soft? Zoom out and make sure there is enough contrast in your final image, so that the character pops off the page whether viewed up close or from afar. A simple neutral background can also help to ground them.

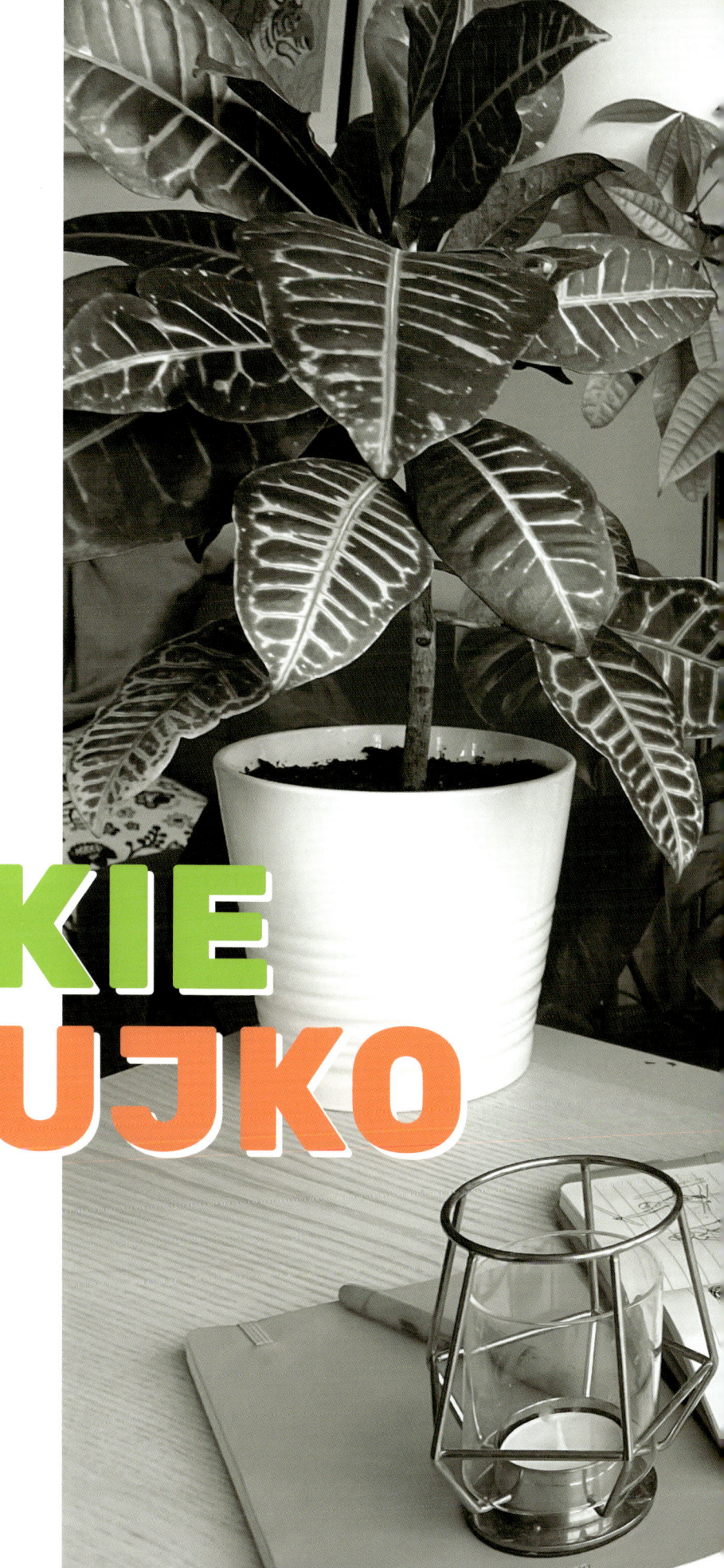

MEET THE ARTIST:
JACKIE
DROUJKO

Jackie Droujko is a character designer working professionally in the animation industry. Her bold, colorful designs have earned her a healthy following on Instagram, Patreon, TikTok, and YouTube. She has also previously created a tutorial for *CDQ*. We caught up with Jackie to chat about how she manages her busy schedule, the inspiration behind her art style, and much more.

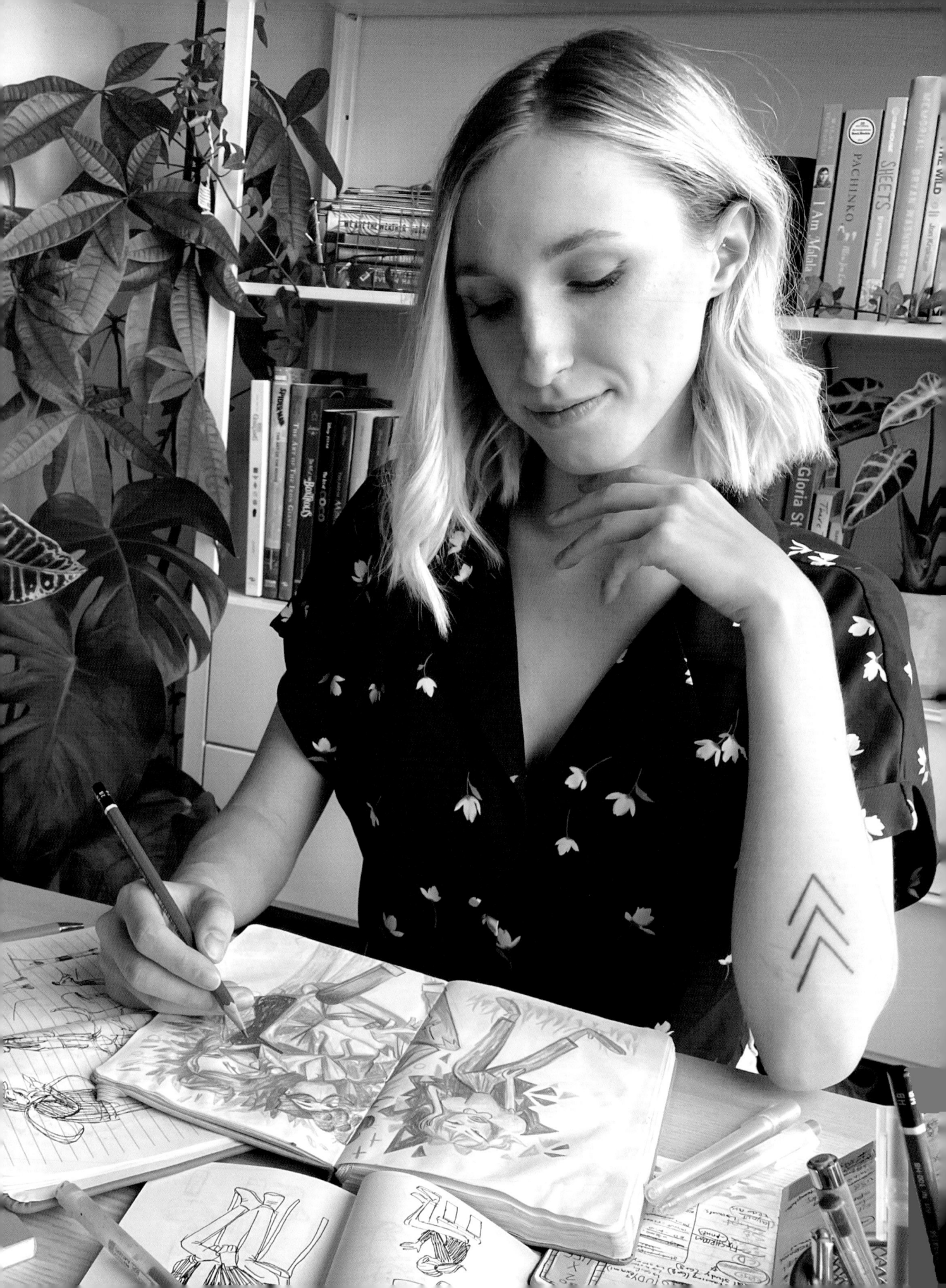

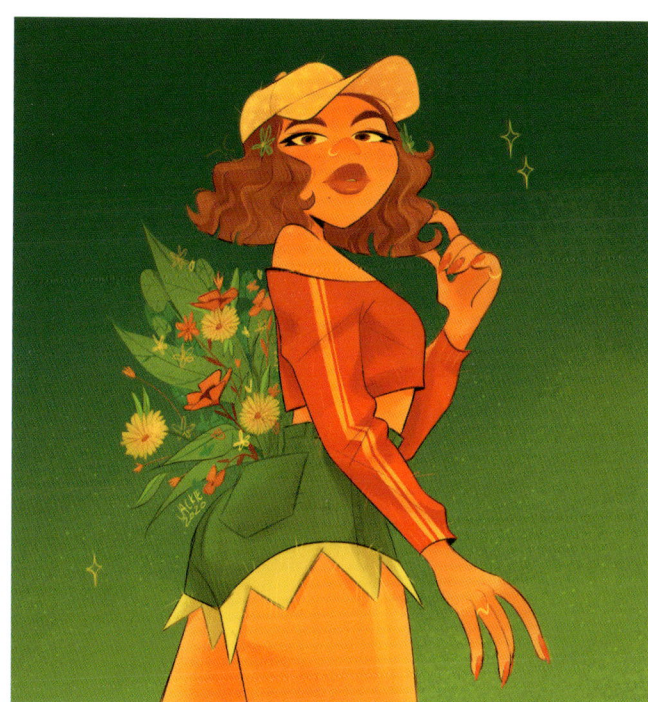

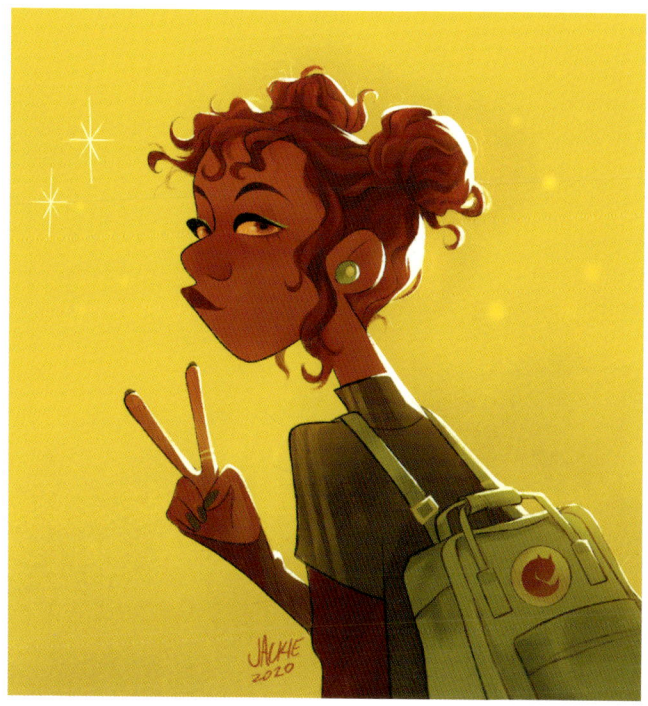

Hi Jackie. Can you tell us a little about your career so far, and how you got started in the industry?

Sure thing. I've been in the industry for around four years now, since I graduated from Sheridan College's Bachelor of Animation program in Ontario. I was offered a character-design assistant position on Dreamworks' *Cleopatra in Space* halfway through my fourth year of college, so after school I moved across the country to Vancouver to start at Titmouse. I stayed there for a year or two, working briefly on shows like *Archibald*, *Star Wars: Galaxy of Adventures*, *Deathstroke*, and some unannounced projects. I then worked as a character-design assistant on Netflix's *Arlo the Alligator Boy* movie. In early 2020, Netflix reached out to me about working on *Charlie and the Chocolate Factory* because their lead artist loved my work on Instagram – the power of social media! This was huge for me. I was so excited to move to LA and start my first real character-design job with the big boys (finally graduating from assistant work). But then we all know what happened in 2020. I couldn't move because of COVID. I worked with Netflix for about two years on my third feature project before the mass layoffs there. I've also had the opportunity to do freelance work for an unannounced Warner Bros series and create primary character designs for Nickelodeon's *Monster High*.

With all the various projects you have on the go, it seems like you keep very busy. Do you have any tips to help our readers maximize the use of their time?

Ha-ha, yes, I always give myself side projects for no other reason than I enjoy keeping busy. I keep up with my Patreon, my online shop, freelance, selling art at conventions, making films, hosting workshops, giving presentations at schools, and a boatload of other things. It's definitely tiring, and I'm also a huge advocate for taking breaks. We often feel guilty about not being productive or capitalizing on our hobbies, but I always make sure I give myself the space to turn down opportunities in the name of rest. I'm hesitant to advise how to maximize your time when, if I was a reader, I would definitely benefit from advice on how to minimize my time on the grind. For example, when I was in college, I would often pull all-nighters to get as much work done as possible, and it was so normalized because so many other students were doing it too. So, I'm going to flip this question on its head – how do I not feel guilty about resting? It's like any habit, if you start giving yourself a set time when you're not allowed to create, it'll get easier to rest. I made it a habit never to create on weekends because that's when I recharge, so I don't burn out during the week. I also surround myself with people who value rest – it's easy to get caught up in the 24/7 grind when everyone around you is doing it too. Your value is not your artwork. It took me a long time to discover that.

This page (top left): I went through a floral phase

This page (top right): I drew this for an advert, but I ended up loving it

Opposite page: I drew this for an exclusive Patreon print; it's always been one of my favorite pieces

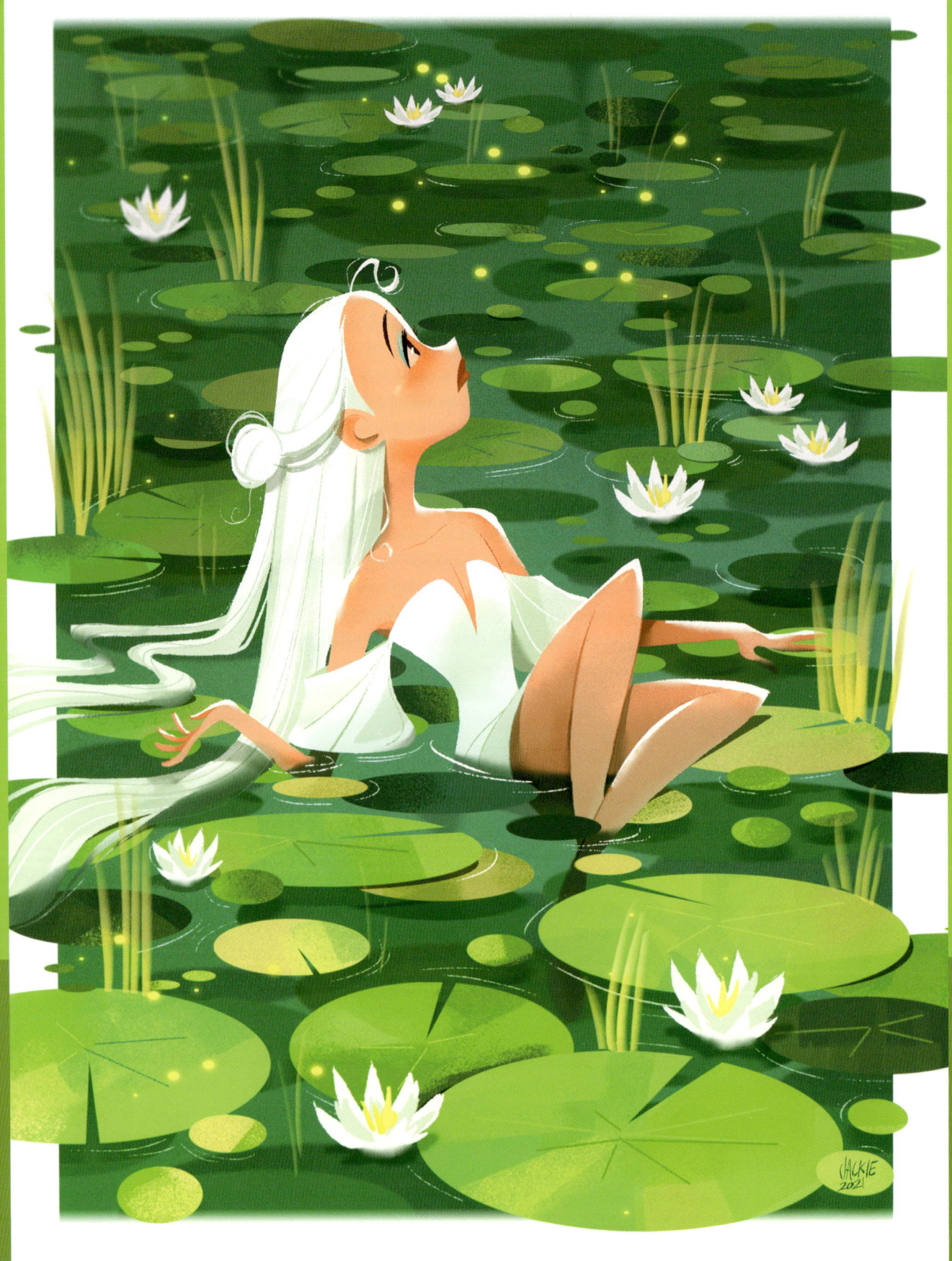

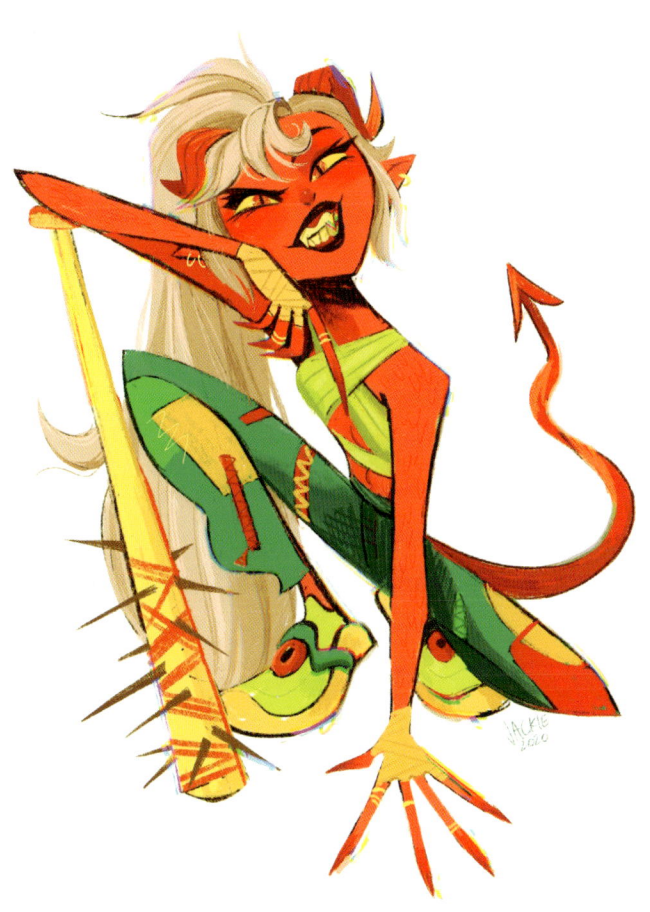

This page: I love playing with sharp shapes to depict a character

Opposite page: Starting and completing a piece on one layer is really freeing – you embrace your mistakes

The first thing that stood out to us in your amazing designs is your bold use of color. How important is color to you when designing a character?

Thank you. Color is such an important part of design to me – I love experimenting with palettes to invoke an emotion. I love playing with "ugly" color schemes (like yellow and green) and attaching them to beautiful designs, and to create something new and exciting that maybe hasn't really been seen much before. Bold and bright colors are often associated with "young animation," which some people might even call unsophisticated. I like playing with slightly more mature themes like fashion, sex appeal, and violence, juxtaposed with bold and bright color palettes to create interesting ideas. Lately, I've been focusing on lighting and environments, and as I learn more about light, I start to apply my new findings to my characters, which is really cool to see.

What are the key influences behind your style of character design?

Definitely fashion and modeling – I treat my designs like they're in an editorial magazine. I love playing with intense gazes, fun clothes, and model poses. I also take a lot of inspiration from artists I admire. Whether it's Sophie Li's energy, Jason McLean's shape language, or James Woods' strong line, there's always artists inspiring my color palette and designs. Sometimes seeing the flow of a houseplant will inspire me to draw a certain shape, or seeing a certain color combination out in public will spark inspiration. If you look at everything through the lens of design, anything can become inspiration.

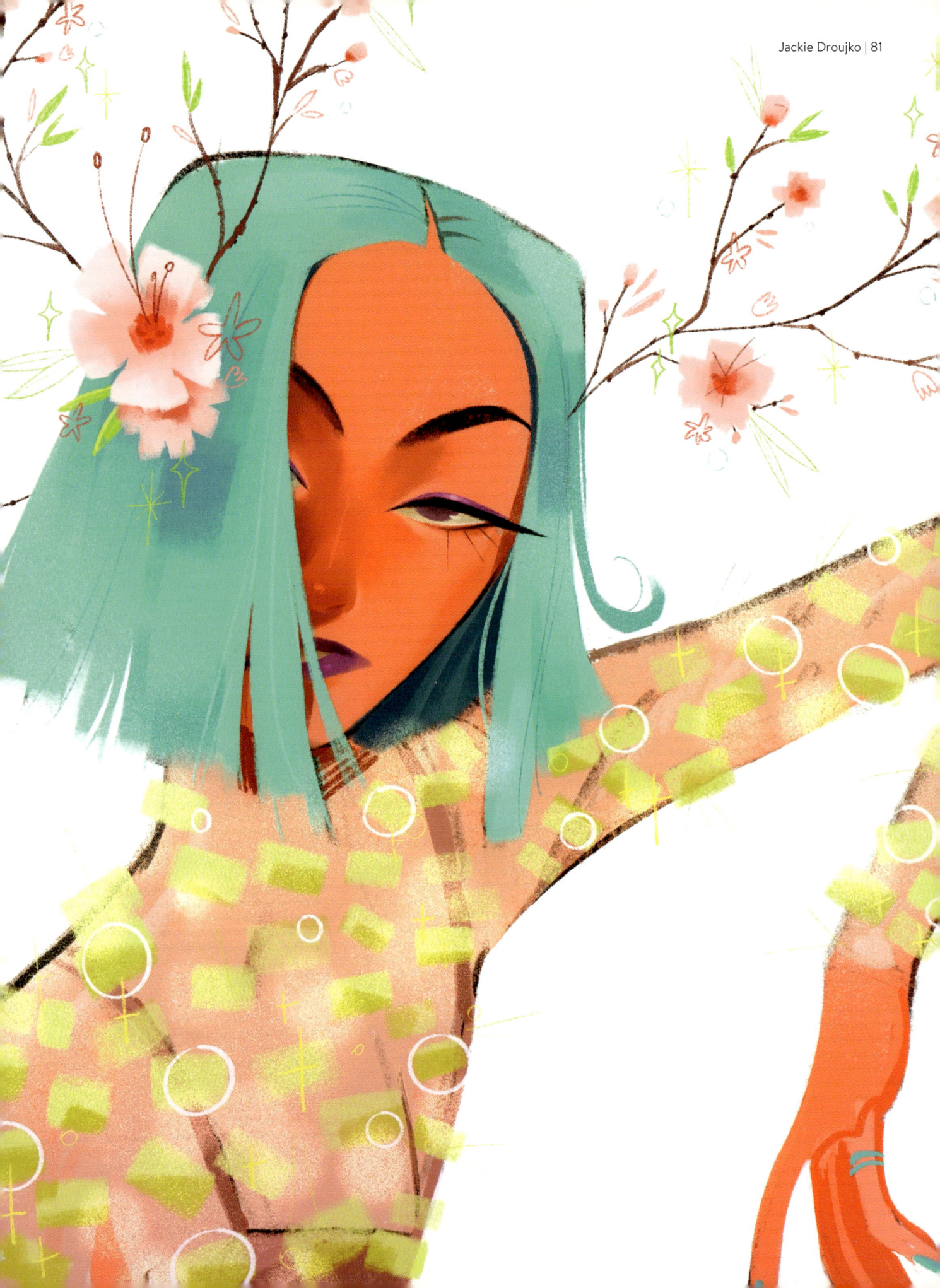

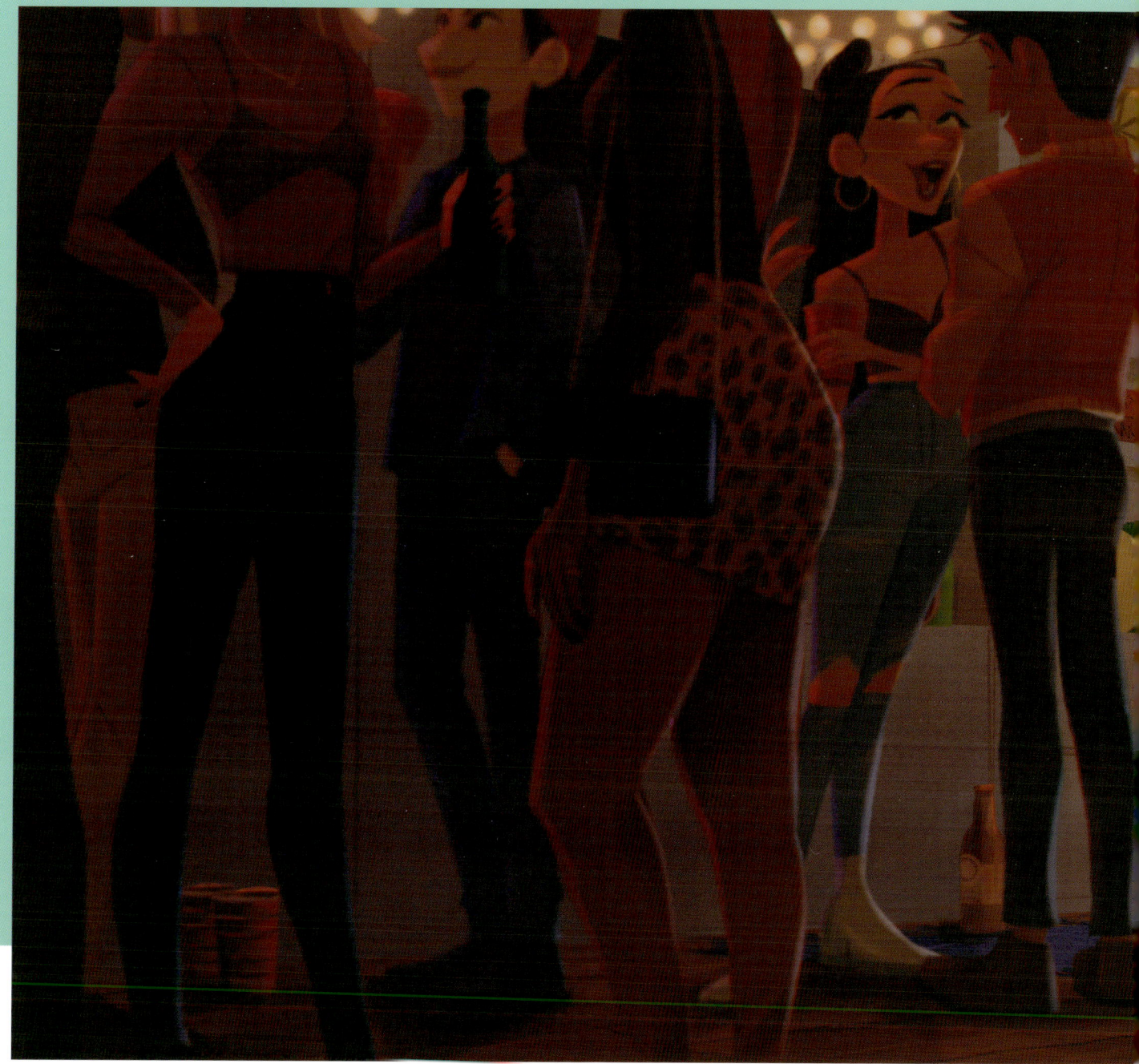

I believe you created a short film almost entirely single-handed, is that right? Is making your own animation projects something you want to continue to do?

That's absolutely right. In my fourth year of animation school, with the help of a 3D animator for props, sound artists, and a few color-fill helpers, I made a one-minute-long film called *Bang! Bang!* Filmmaking is something that really excites me; I try to make a short film every year with a small group of people. This year I've been working on a film entirely by myself (other than a musician for the score), which is my first solo film project since college. I felt pretty directionless after being stuck at home during COVID, and I was reminiscing on the excitement and passion I had while making my first short film. So, I put my last two brain cells together to come up with a simple story that I would be able to take from start to finish. Since I'm only able to work on it between my full-time job and other side projects, it's definitely taking longer than expected, but I hope to finish within the next few months.

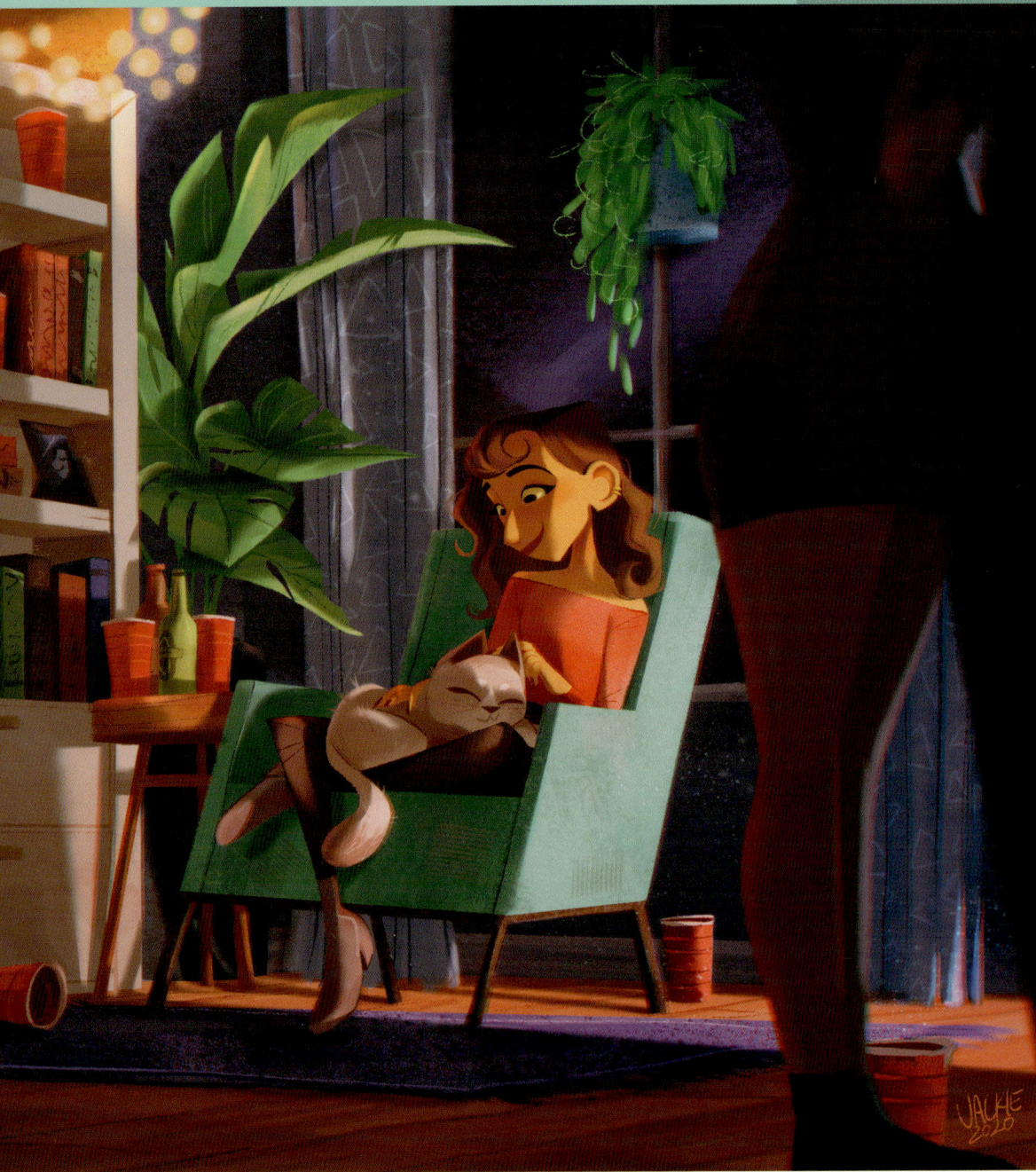

These pages:
I don't do many full
scenes so this piece
is very dear to me

You've worked on lots of big properties for Netflix, Lucasfilm, and others. What challenges come from working with pre-existing characters?

Good question. As a character-design assistant, you don't get to work in your own style or really create your own characters, apart from background characters. The difficulty, especially in 2D animation, is matching the style of the lead character designer, or the style of the existing property. In 2D, these characters are going to appear on screen as they are drawn – you have to match the exact hand of the lead, or it will look jarring. You need to be a chameleon. When I worked on *Charlie and the Chocolate Factory*, the challenge was taking beloved existing characters and finding a way to modernize them, so new audiences would warm to them as much as we did growing up. Since working on my last project at Netflix, I've been lucky enough to create many exciting characters from scratch – I'm only limited by my imagination (and what the director thinks!).

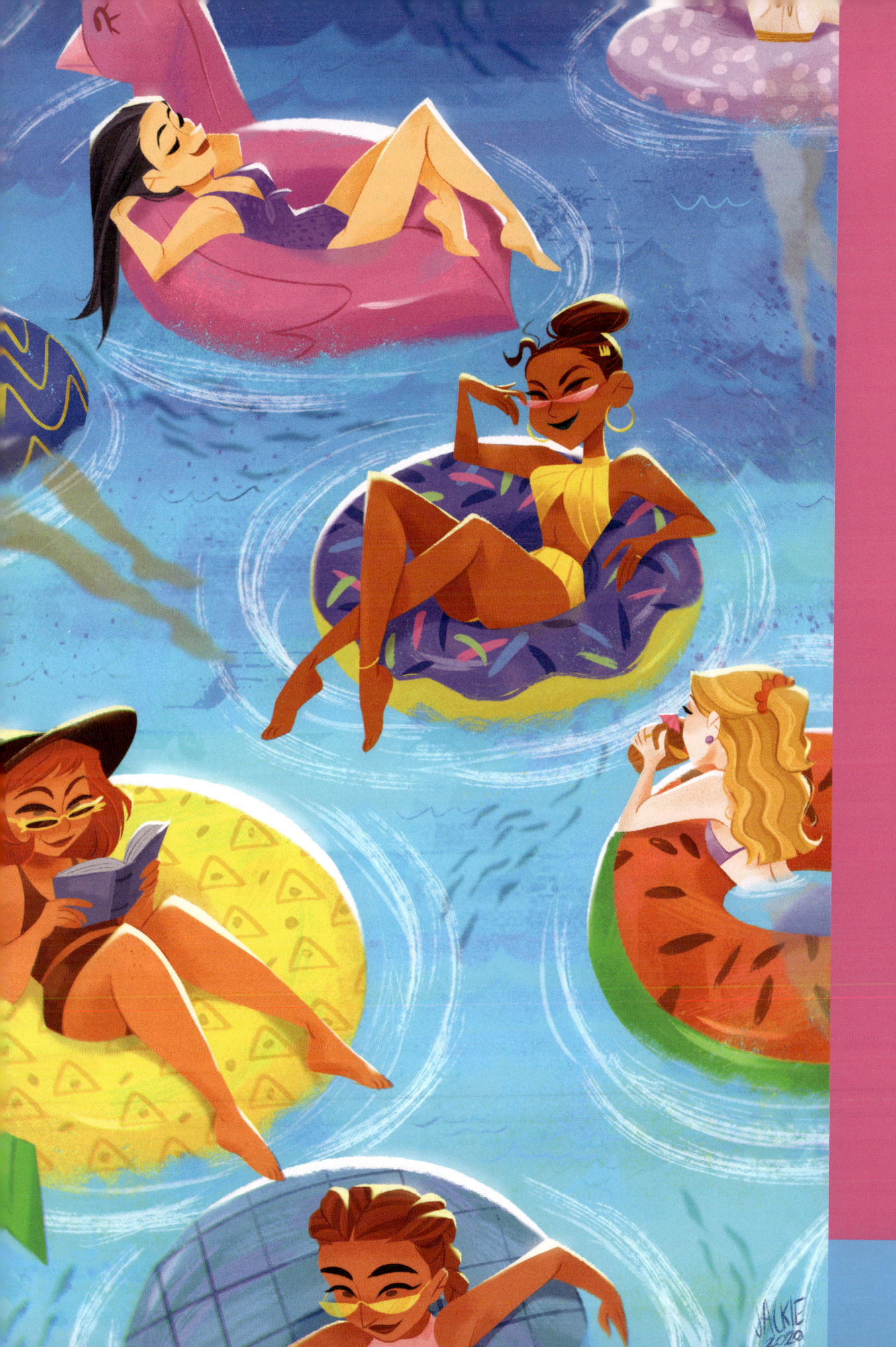

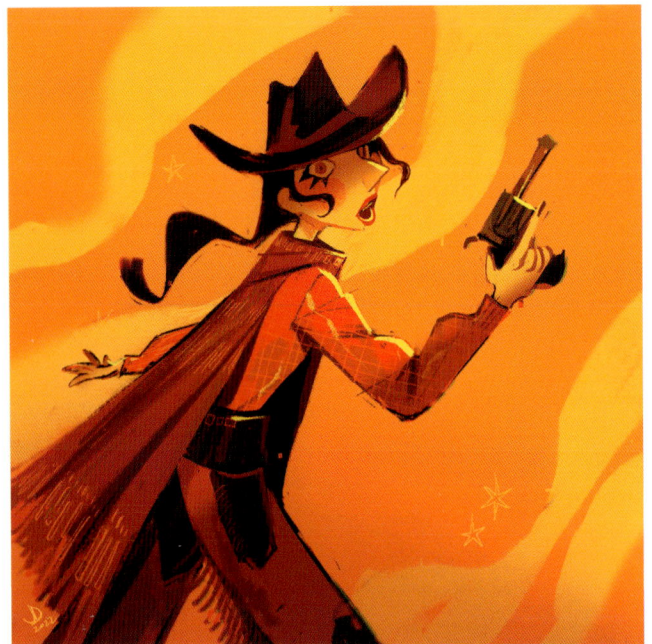

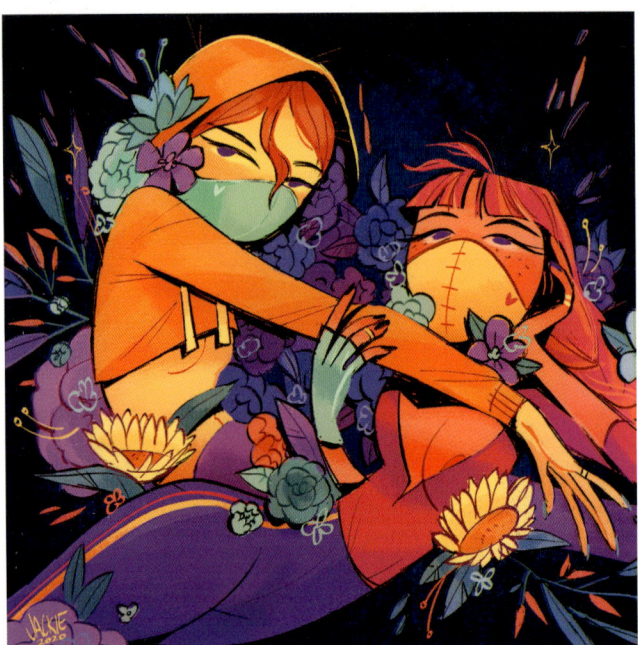

Opposite page: I love the contrast in colors in this piece – I wish I was there

This page (top): I love using a monochromatic color palette to emphasize a feeling; in this case, I'm accentuating the sepia Western vibe with desert orange colors

This page (bottom): Trying to make masks cool in 2020

You mentioned social media got your foot in the door at Netflix – do you have any advice for our readers about getting noticed in a similar way?

Social media has literally gotten me every job I've worked on – it's the foundation of my career. When you don't live in the LA hub, it's nearly impossible to network, but with the power of the internet, you can get eyes on your work from all around the world. I grew my presence on Instagram in college by posting every day. It wasn't a challenge because I was passionate about drawing, and receiving positive online feedback was really motivating. When I posted fanart, participated in internet challenges, and hosted giveaways, I also noticed a higher engagement. I connected with others in my field and benefited from a community of passionate artists. My greatest advice is to post what you like to draw. If you post what you think your audience wants to see, then you'll be stuck in the loop of drawing for others, rather than yourself. It's better to have an audience that wants to see your personal growth, rather than one you have to cater to.

Do you think the disruption caused by the pandemic is here to stay? Would working from home permanently have its advantages, or would you rather be physically at a studio?

I think about this a lot. I'd like to live in LA for a few years, but when I hear my colleagues complain about the traffic, I'm less inclined. I think many studios will move to a hybrid studio-and-home work style, as they've been benefiting from working with remote artists from all over the world. Working from home definitely has its advantages – I can choose my own hours, I can go for long walks, and I don't have to commute. But I do miss physically hanging out with co-workers, it definitely can get lonely being so isolated. I'd like to work in-house in LA if I get a great position on a really cool project, like a lead on a film. Until then, I'm happy reaping the benefits of staying in Canada and working for an American studio – although I would love more free lunches.

Thanks for chatting to us, Jackie. Finally, do you have any projects coming up that we should look out for?

Sure! My short film *Mismatched* will come out this year, and keep your eye out for a character design course from me. I expect a lot of projects I've been working on will finally be announced, too. It's hard to keep quiet about all these exciting things I've been a part of, especially when they go public years after I got my hands on them.

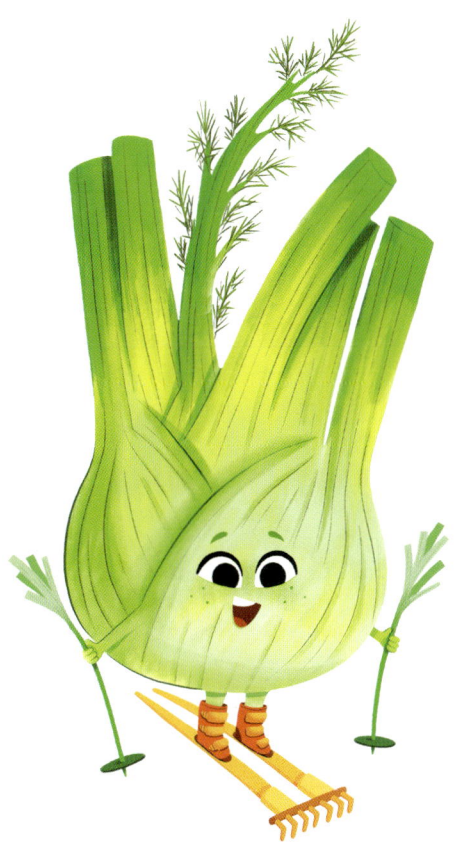

TELLING VEGGIE-TALES

ELÉONORE PELLUAU

In this article we will explore the main points to consider when creating a character for a young audience. We will see that it's important to respect some basic principles: shape, proportions, facial structure, and colors. I'll also remind you of the importance of drawing in your own style. It can be tempting to search online for existing artwork when you want to create a character, but it's good practice to try basing your drawings on reality or your own imagination – and to design them your own way.

"TAKE A STEP BACK AND CHOOSE ONE OF THE ELEMENTS THAT SPEAKS TO YOU THE MOST"

CHOOSE YOUR CHARACTER

Take a few minutes to relax, listening to your favorite music or the birds singing. Grab a piece of paper and a pen, and draw. After filling your paper, take a step back and choose one of the elements that speaks to you the most. Now, on a fresh sheet of paper, explore this new idea.

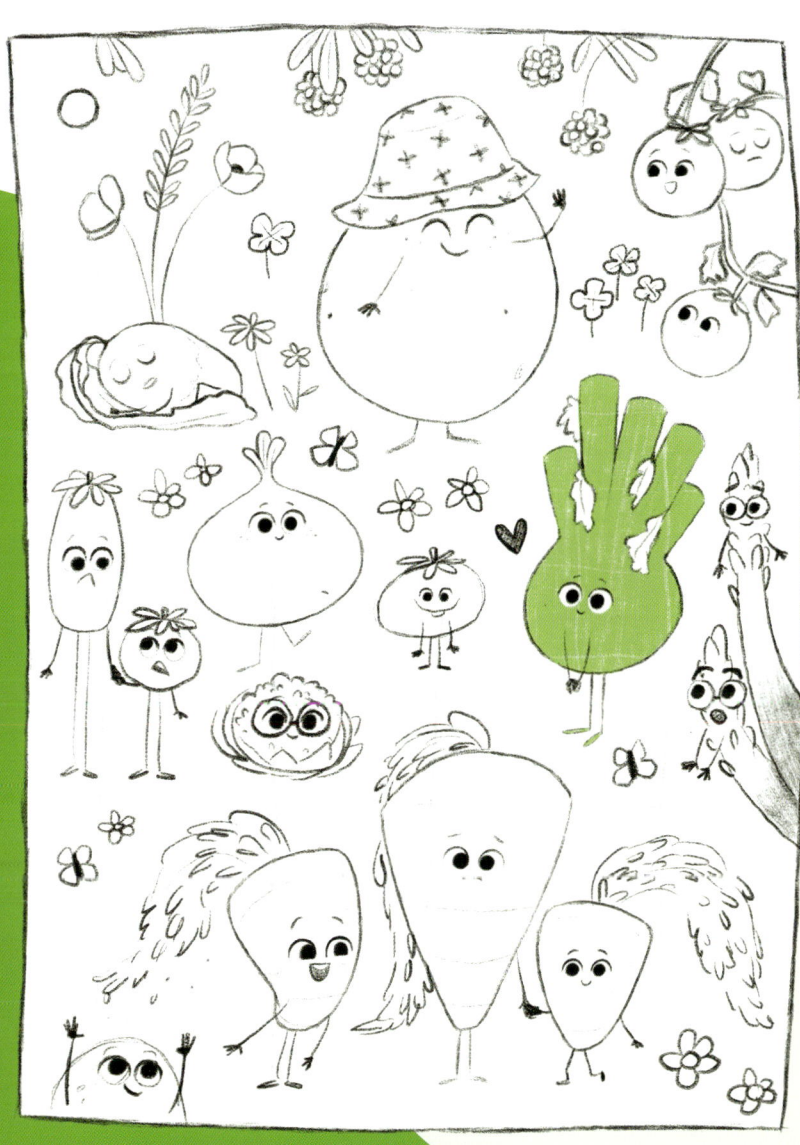

DRAWING FROM MEMORY

At the beginning of the process it's helpful to draw your subject, for example, a fennel, from memory. You don't have to look at references straight away. This exercise will allow you to use your memory and give you confidence as you draw.

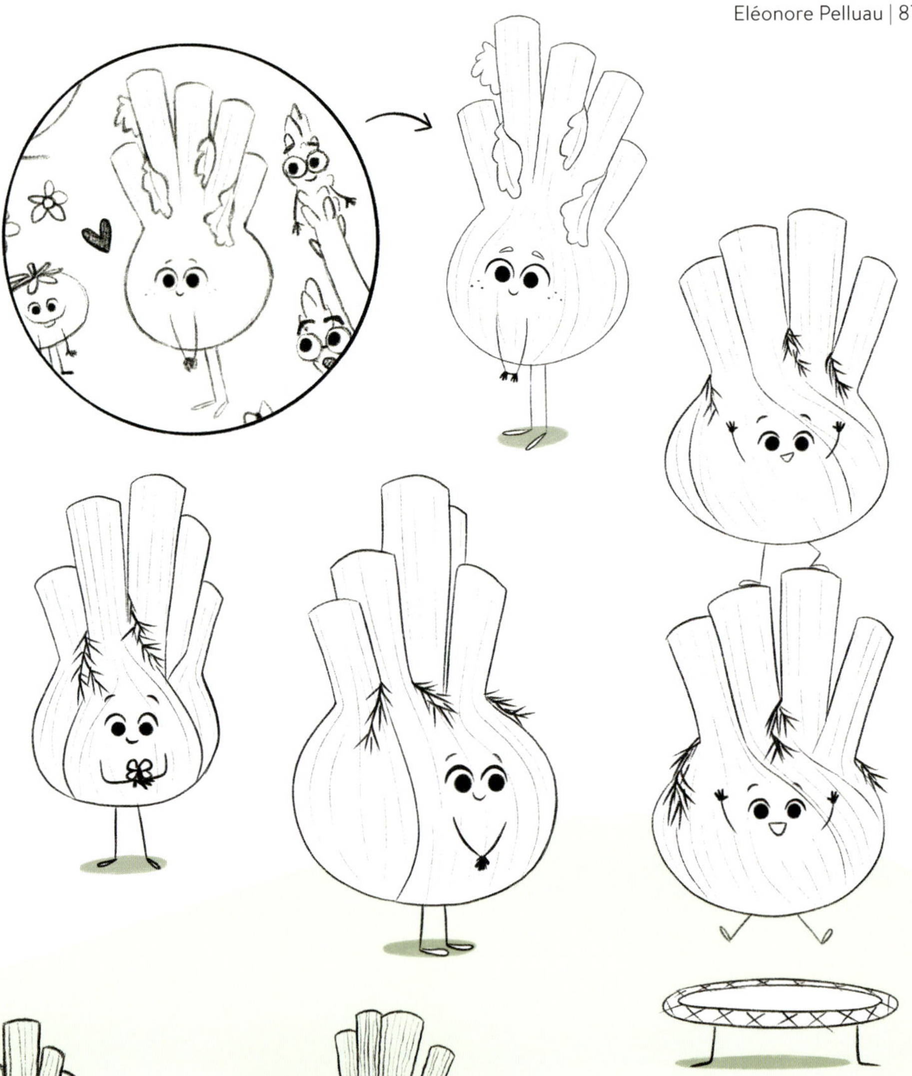

SELECTING A SHAPE

Next, we will define a simple geometric shape which will allow young children to understand the drawing immediately. Test each shape to see which one fits your character. Fill the silhouettes with a solid color to see if the shape works well.

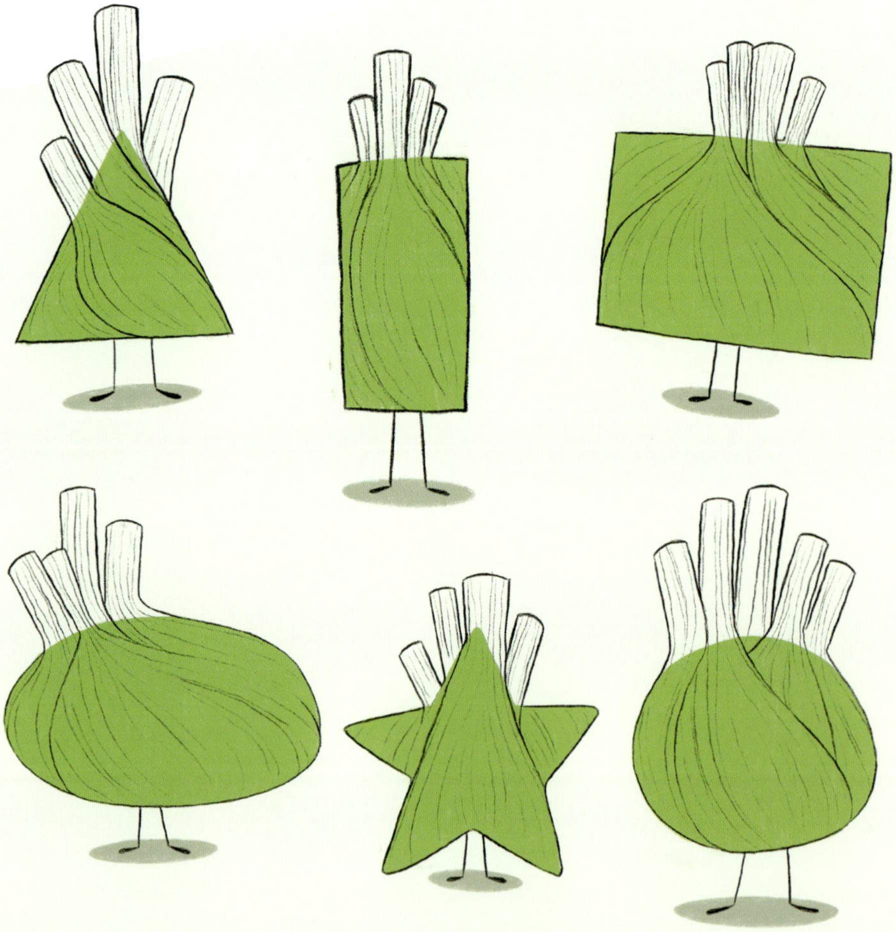

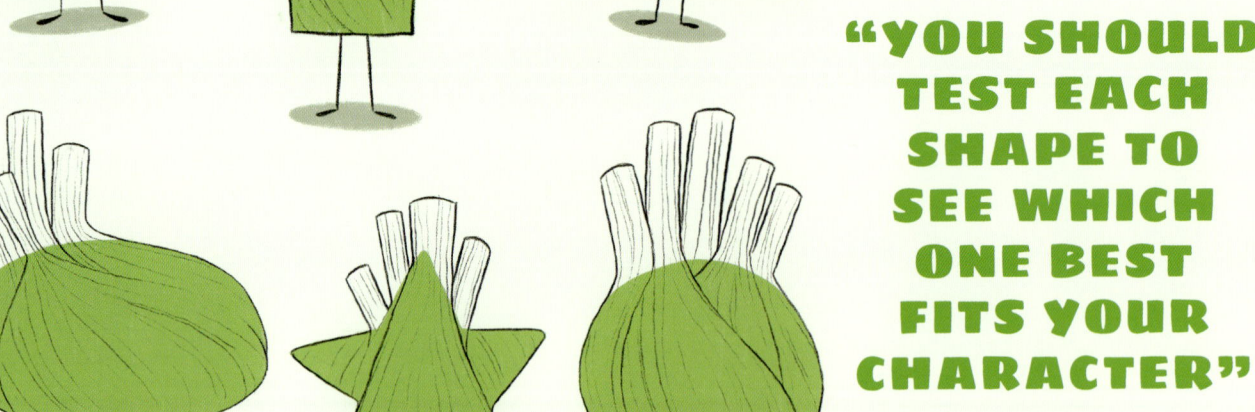

"YOU SHOULD TEST EACH SHAPE TO SEE WHICH ONE BEST FITS YOUR CHARACTER"

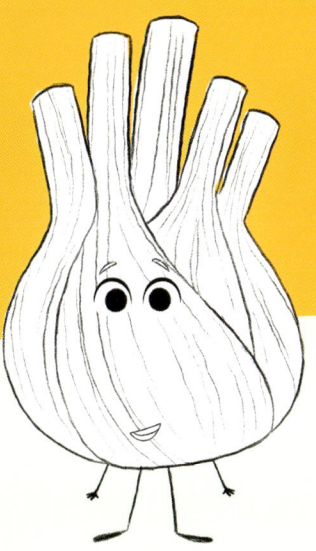
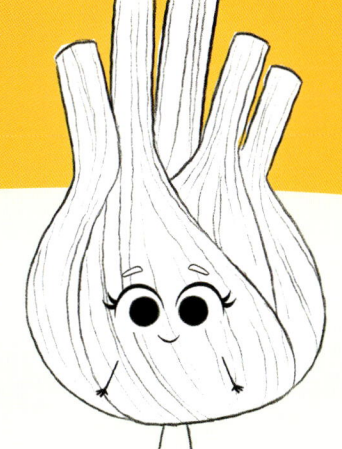
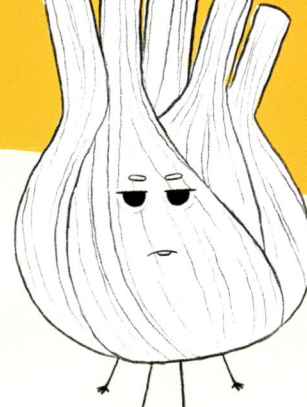

MAKING FACES

With the shape and the character defined, it's time to find a suitable face. Young readers must be able to quickly identify the character and intended mood. Try not to make the face too complicated. Aim for the simplest look that is still readable and don't forget that the closer the elements are together (eyes, nose, mouth) the cuter and more endearing your character will be.

OUT OF PROPORTION

The key design decision when creating characters for children is how to balance the proportions of the body. It's a good idea to favor big heads and small legs, or vice versa. Your character will ideally not be perfectly proportioned, but rather totally out of place – this will make them look much more endearing.

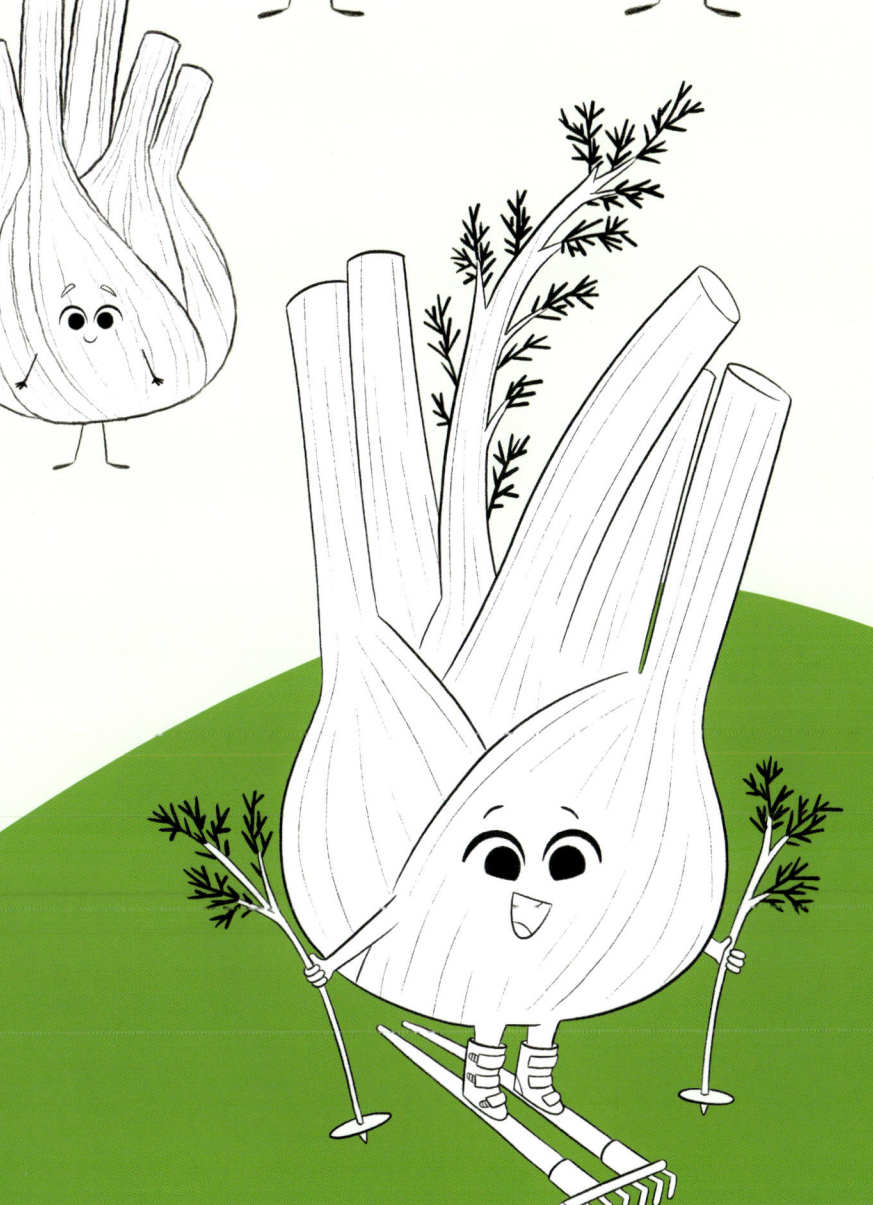

A COLORFUL CONCLUSION

Children are attracted to bright colors – a child will linger in front of a colorful design longer than they would a dull or black-and-white drawing. Choose complementary colors, but be careful not to use too many. Instead, start with one or two main colors, so a child can easily read the character. The final design is bright, friendly, and recognizable – perfect for young people to enjoy.

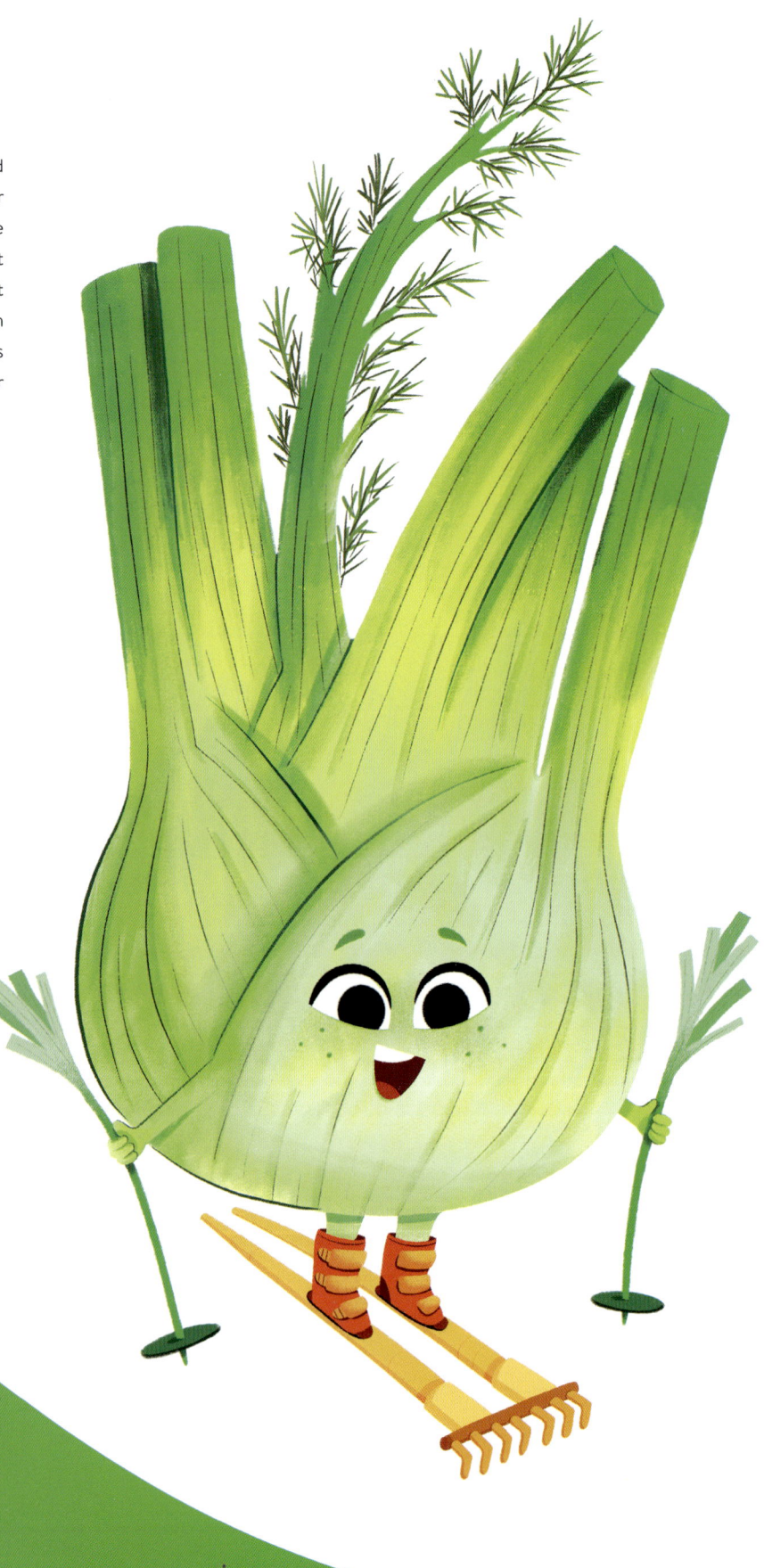

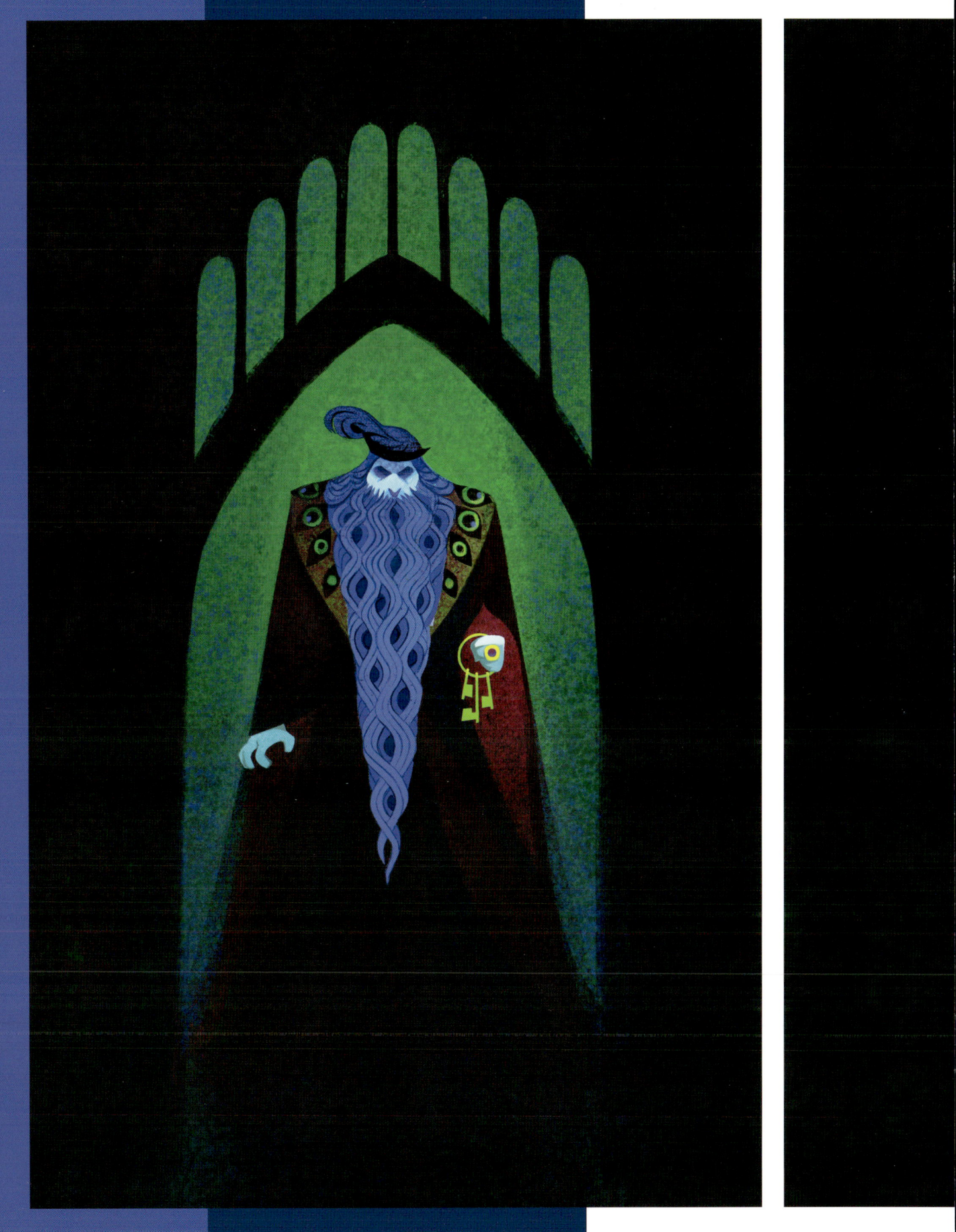

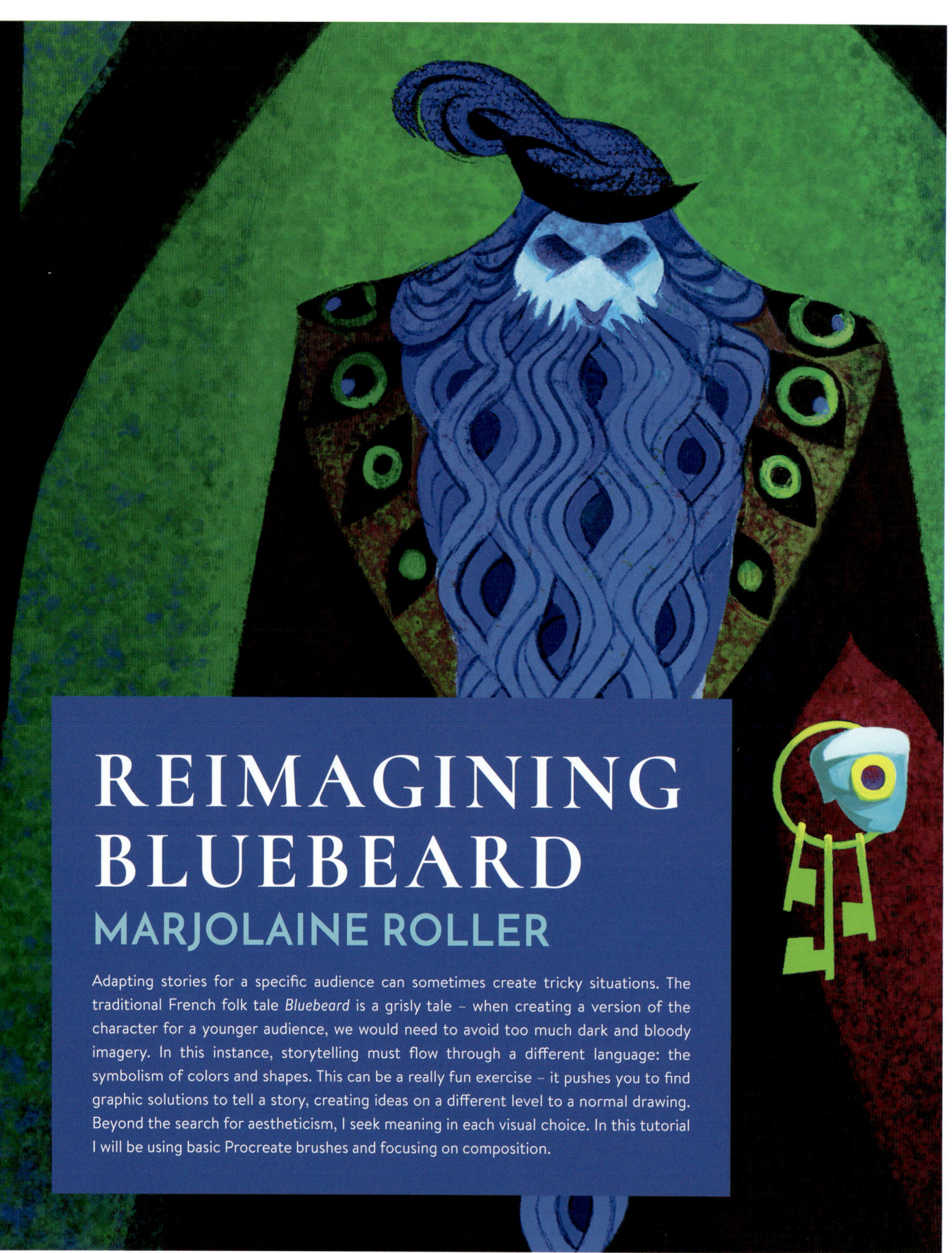

REIMAGINING BLUEBEARD
MARJOLAINE ROLLER

Adapting stories for a specific audience can sometimes create tricky situations. The traditional French folk tale *Bluebeard* is a grisly tale – when creating a version of the character for a younger audience, we would need to avoid too much dark and bloody imagery. In this instance, storytelling must flow through a different language: the symbolism of colors and shapes. This can be a really fun exercise – it pushes you to find graphic solutions to tell a story, creating ideas on a different level to a normal drawing. Beyond the search for aestheticism, I seek meaning in each visual choice. In this tutorial I will be using basic Procreate brushes and focusing on composition.

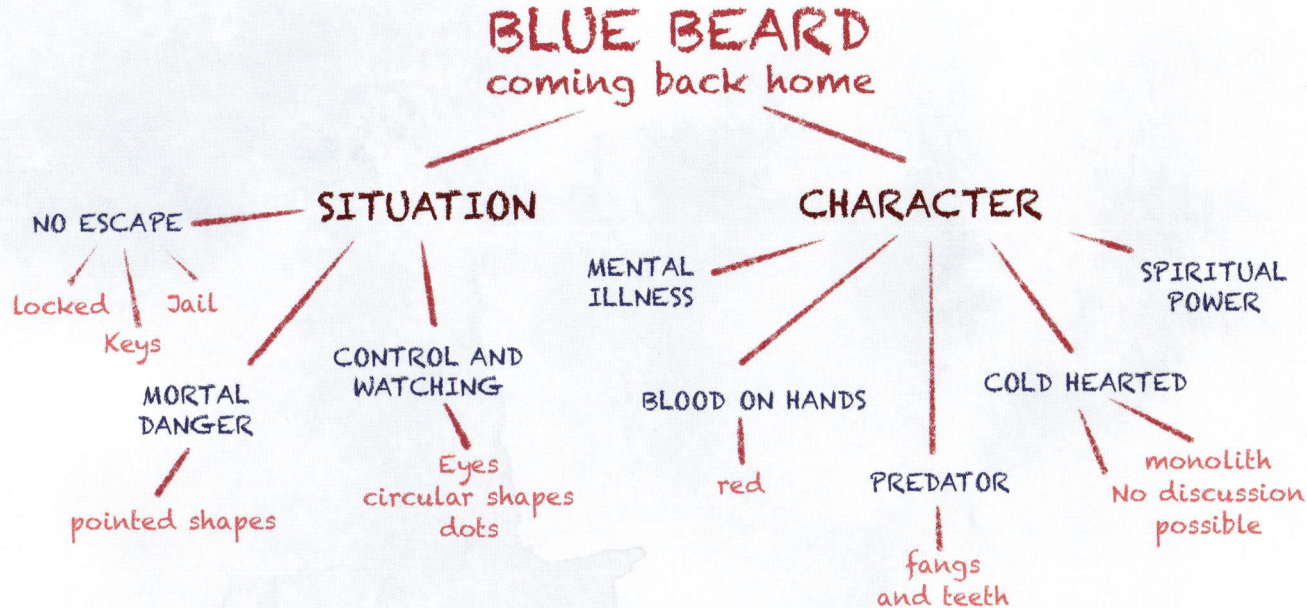

BLUE BEARD
coming back home

SITUATION

CHARACTER

NO ESCAPE

locked — Jail

Keys

MORTAL DANGER

pointed shapes

CONTROL AND WATCHING

Eyes
circular shapes
dots

MENTAL ILLNESS

BLOOD ON HANDS

red

PREDATOR

fangs
and teeth

COLD HEARTED

SPIRITUAL POWER

monolith
No discussion
possible

STEPPING INTO THE STORY

I see Bluebeard as the archetype of a psychopath – today we would describe him as a serial killer and a control freak. He pushes his wives to disobey him during his absence, thus having a good reason to kill them when he returns. Sometimes an idea just pops into your mind and you feel you can start to draw at once. However, taking time to focus on keywords is always a good idea. It will be like a chart to guide you through the process, and it may even lead to early graphical solutions.

MAKING NARRATIVE CHOICES

Even when working from a detailed brief, there is always room for interpretation and there are visual choices to be made. This step is so important – your final work will be more meaningful if you make sharp narrative decisions. The first thing to ask yourself is: What story do I want to tell? I imagine Bluebeard is returning home after a long journey. I need to decide which characters to focus on, and what attitude and body language they will have. I think the best choice here is to show Bluebeard, but to hold back his anger and impatience. We know he's mad, but he's not reacting yet, so we expect the worst, creating suspense. Sometimes, less is more.

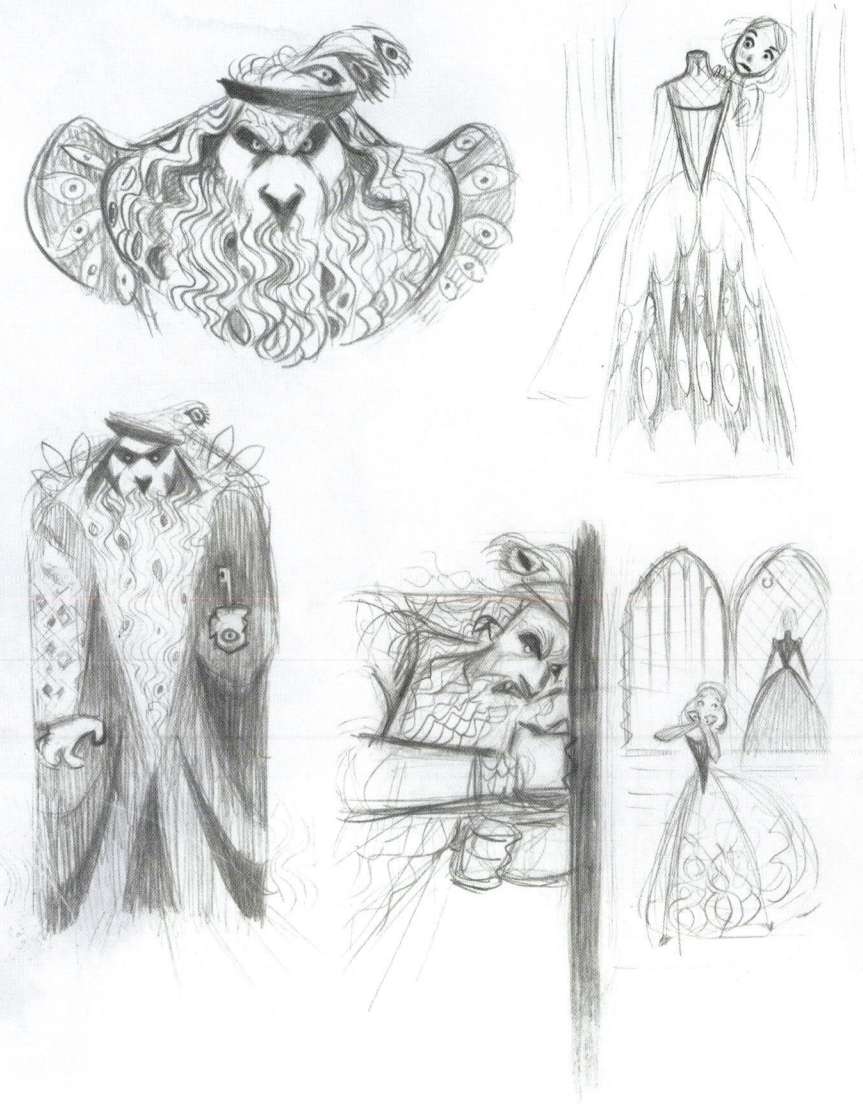

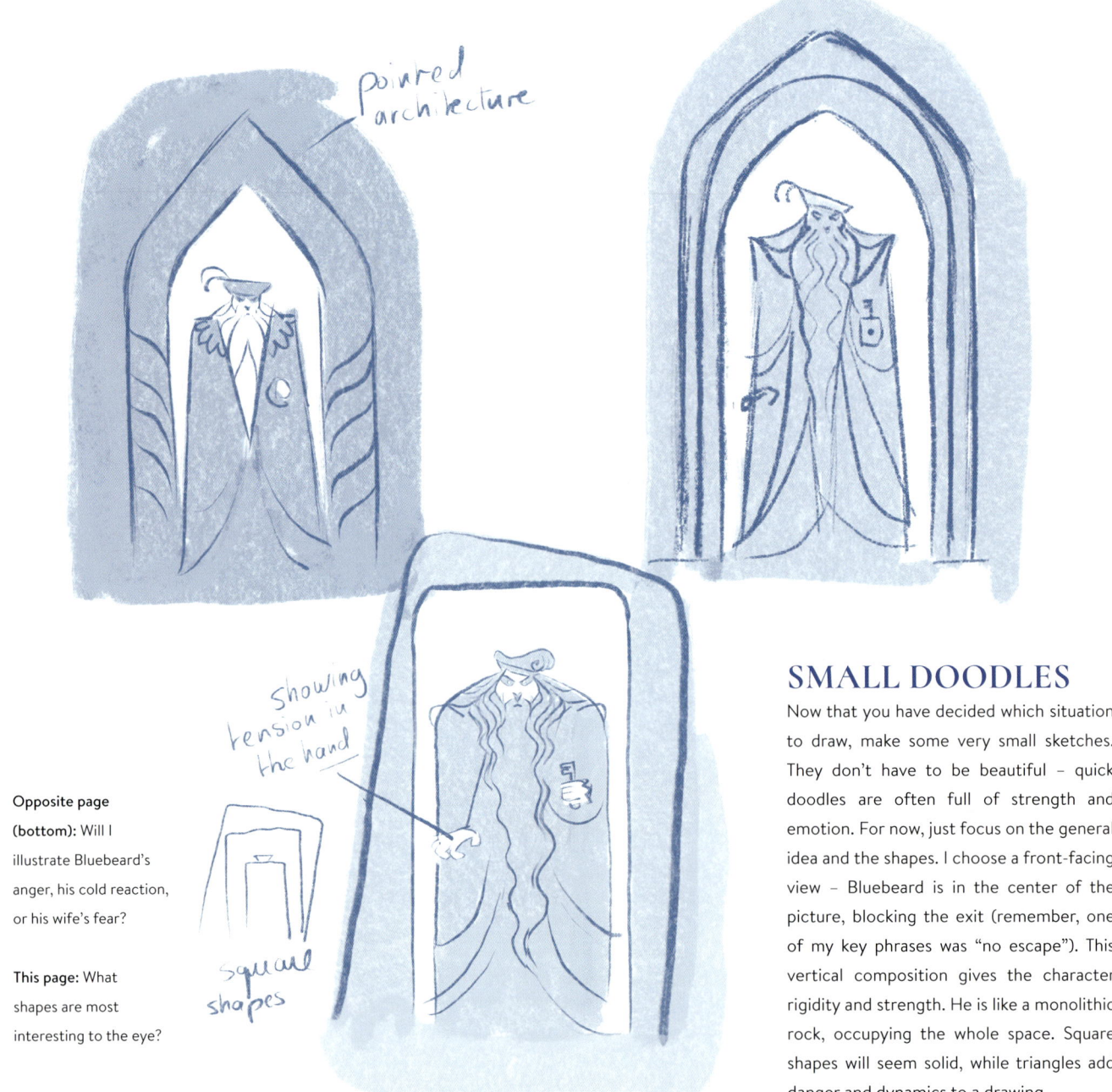

pointed architecture

showing tension in the hand

square shapes

Opposite page (bottom): Will I illustrate Bluebeard's anger, his cold reaction, or his wife's fear?

This page: What shapes are most interesting to the eye?

SMALL DOODLES

Now that you have decided which situation to draw, make some very small sketches. They don't have to be beautiful – quick doodles are often full of strength and emotion. For now, just focus on the general idea and the shapes. I choose a front-facing view – Bluebeard is in the center of the picture, blocking the exit (remember, one of my key phrases was "no escape"). This vertical composition gives the character rigidity and strength. He is like a monolithic rock, occupying the whole space. Square shapes will seem solid, while triangles add danger and dynamics to a drawing.

USING LINES IN COMPOSITION

Horizontal, vertical, and diagonal lines subconsciously evoke different feelings for the viewer. Use them to compose your image and reinforce your storytelling. Horizontal lines are associated with a sense of balance, harmony, tranquility, and peace. Vertical lines induce a sense of power, strength, and sometimes even drama, depending on what is being represented. Diagonal lines convey the idea of movement, dynamics, or tension.

THE RELATIONSHIP BETWEEN THE SET AND ITS CHARACTER

The background needs to make sense. Bluebeard is a manipulative man who mind-controls his wives – he has a kind of spiritual power. I decide to use gothic architecture for the background, to evoke a church and the spiritual authority such places have embodied for centuries. It can be interesting to use symbols and archetypes out of their traditional context. Gothic motifs also continue the vertical design of the drawing and accentuate the drama through their pointed shapes. When you design your set, start with simple shapes before moving on to details, like furniture and patterns.

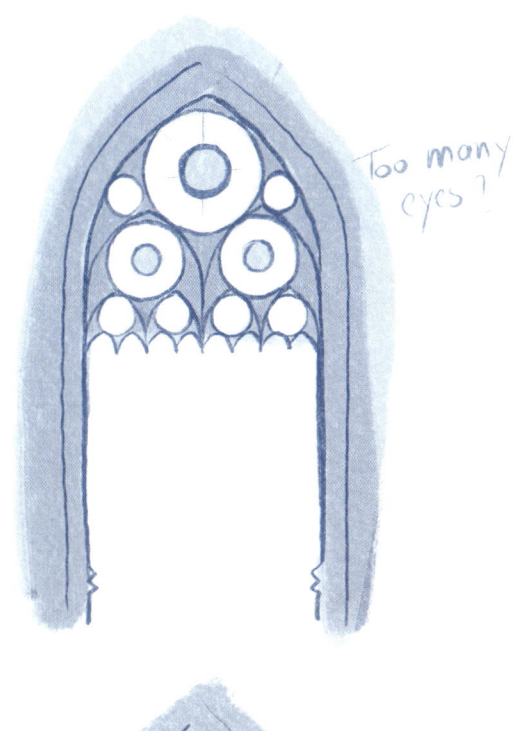

Too many eyes?

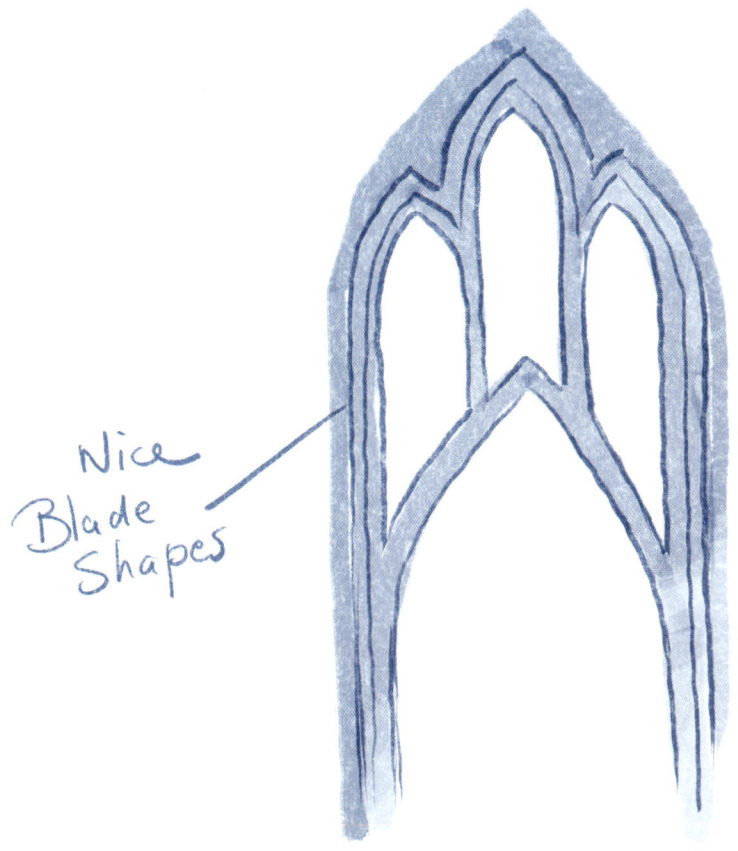

Nice Blade Shapes

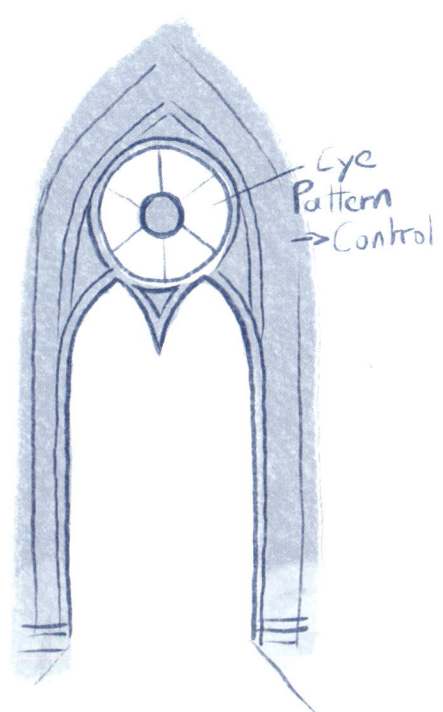

Eye Pattern → Control

THE MEANING OF SHAPES

Shapes, like lines, can affect people's feelings. Squares suggest stability, order, solidity, honesty, reliability, and security. However, squares can also be a boring form and look a little monotonous! Circles represent completion, fullness, harmony, unity, and protection. Their lack of angles gives them a softer, more comforting feel. Upward pointing triangles represent strength, power, and stability – it's an energetic and dynamic shape that can also represent movement and direction. Downward pointing triangles suggest instability and conflict. They suggest action, tension, and sometimes aggressiveness.

TIME FOR TRIANGLES

Try to balance your composition by using different shapes: triangles, circles, squares, and other organic shapes, using both straight and curved lines. Varying shape design adds visual interest and subtlety to your image. For this piece, I decide to deviate from this rule and base my entire composition on the triangle. Sometimes, rules can be broken – especially when dealing with a psychopath! I choose to keep him immobile and relatively expressionless, so I have to convey all the danger, instability, and aggressiveness of the situation in other ways. The inverted triangles, like repeated blades directed toward us, will convey this mood to the audience.

DEVIL IN THE DETAILS

As you start adding detail, go back to your keywords and try to translate them into visual shapes. Here, I use the word "predator," which I associate with teeth and try to find a way to introduce this pattern into my drawing. Experiment with different ideas but remember that not everything will work. Be open to twisting and simplifying shapes to match the rest of the sketch – the main composition must remain legible. Details must bring something to the story you're trying to tell – be selective about what you add. Sometimes, it's better to draw less and stay clear and punchy.

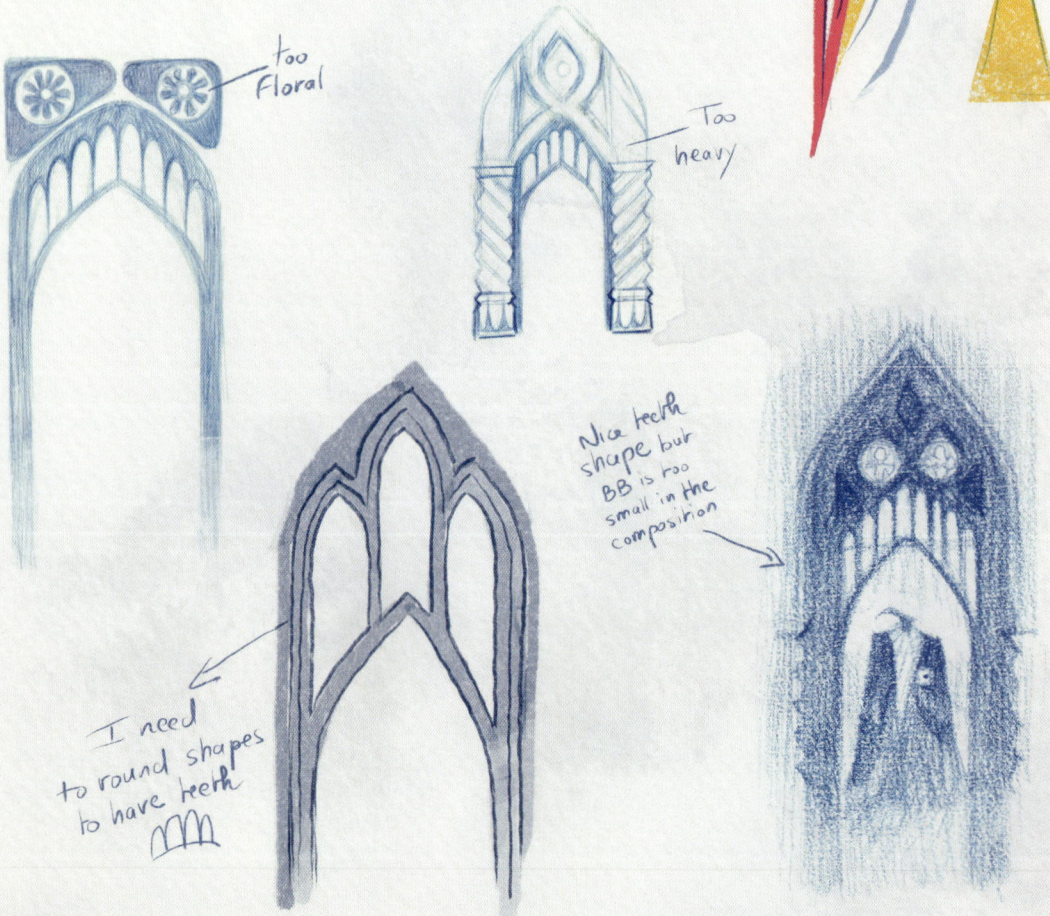

too floral

Too heavy

Nice teeth shape but BB is too small in the composition

I need to round shapes to have teeth

Opposite page: Mixing gothic architecture with eye patterns and blade shapes

This page (top): The triangle is the recurring shape of my composition

This page (bottom): Referencing gothic architecture to suggest teeth

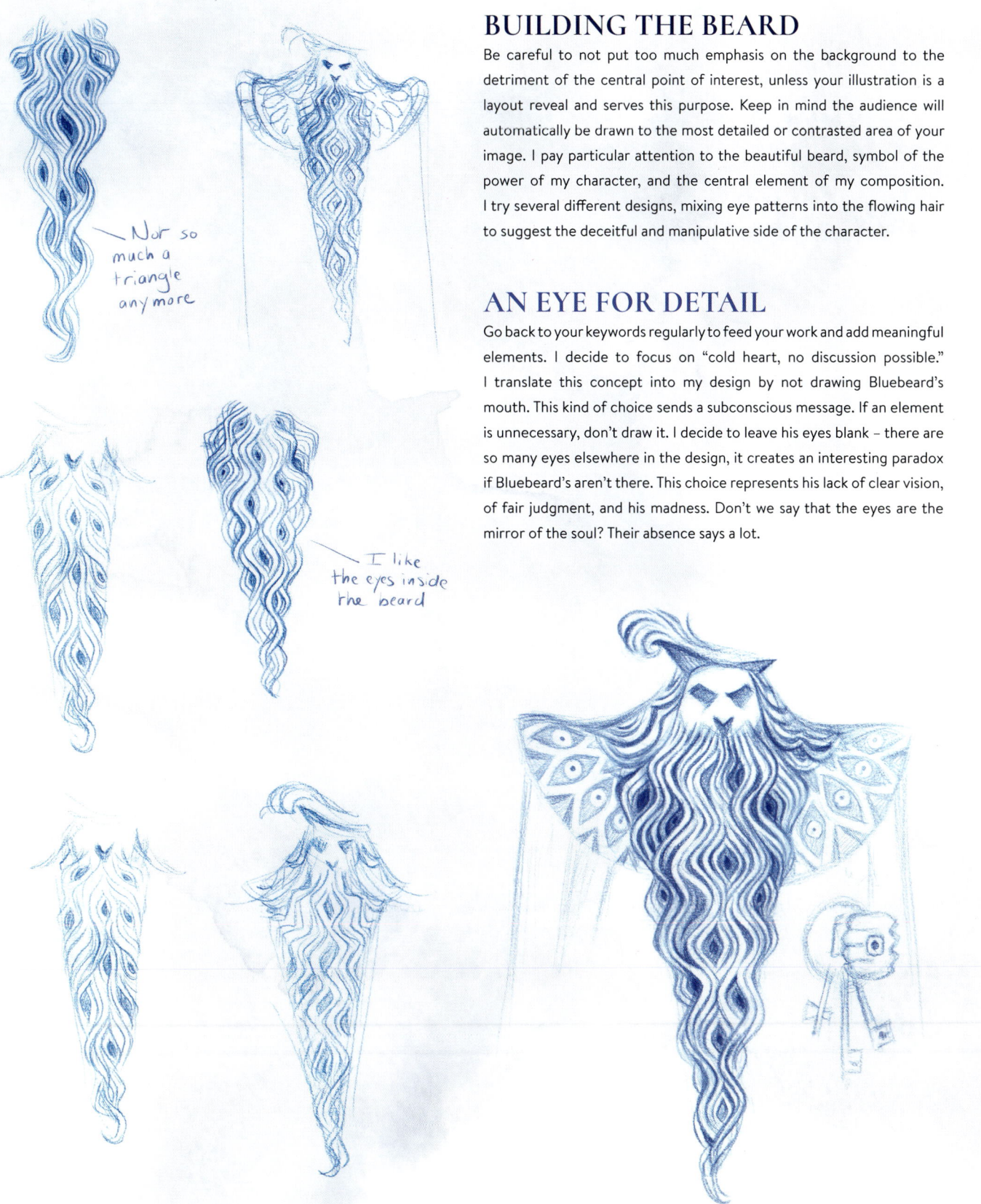

Nor so much a triangle anymore

I like the eyes inside the beard

BUILDING THE BEARD

Be careful to not put too much emphasis on the background to the detriment of the central point of interest, unless your illustration is a layout reveal and serves this purpose. Keep in mind the audience will automatically be drawn to the most detailed or contrasted area of your image. I pay particular attention to the beautiful beard, symbol of the power of my character, and the central element of my composition. I try several different designs, mixing eye patterns into the flowing hair to suggest the deceitful and manipulative side of the character.

AN EYE FOR DETAIL

Go back to your keywords regularly to feed your work and add meaningful elements. I decide to focus on "cold heart, no discussion possible." I translate this concept into my design by not drawing Bluebeard's mouth. This kind of choice sends a subconscious message. If an element is unnecessary, don't draw it. I decide to leave his eyes blank – there are so many eyes elsewhere in the design, it creates an interesting paradox if Bluebeard's aren't there. This choice represents his lack of clear vision, of fair judgment, and his madness. Don't we say that the eyes are the mirror of the soul? Their absence says a lot.

CONTRAST MANAGEMENT

Contrast management is a very useful tool for directing the viewer's eye to the right place. The higher the contrast, the better the readability. You have seven kinds of contrast: contrast of hue, light–dark contrast, cold–warm contrast, complementary color contrast, simultaneous contrast, contrast of saturation, and contrast of extension (relative areas of two or more patches – the contrast between great and small).

THE FINAL SKETCH

The research sketches are done – I can now put all this work together in one drawing. I add the hand that holds the key, with an eye-shaped ring. I keep the eye patterns in the beard and Bluebeard's clothes, but I remove the eye-shaped windows – they draw too much attention away from Bluebeard. The focus has to be on the character. I add two twisted columns, which take us away from the gothic style but add a phantasmagoric touch and bring to mind the shape of the beard. When possible, it is interesting to create a dialogue between the character and their background by using similar elements.

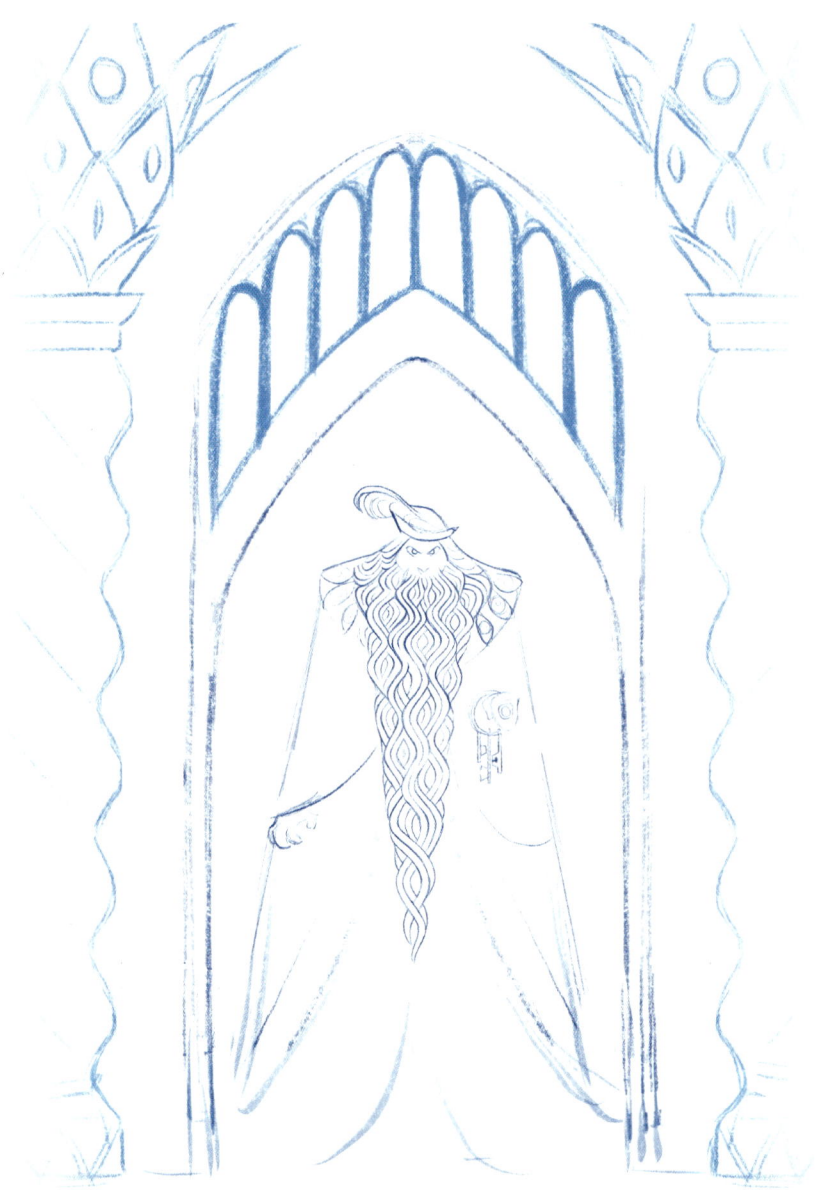

Opposite page (left):
Take extra care exploring possible patterns for the beard

Opposite page (right):
Deepening the psychology of the character by thinking about the details – each element (or its absence) delivers a message

This page: Making the final compositional adjustments

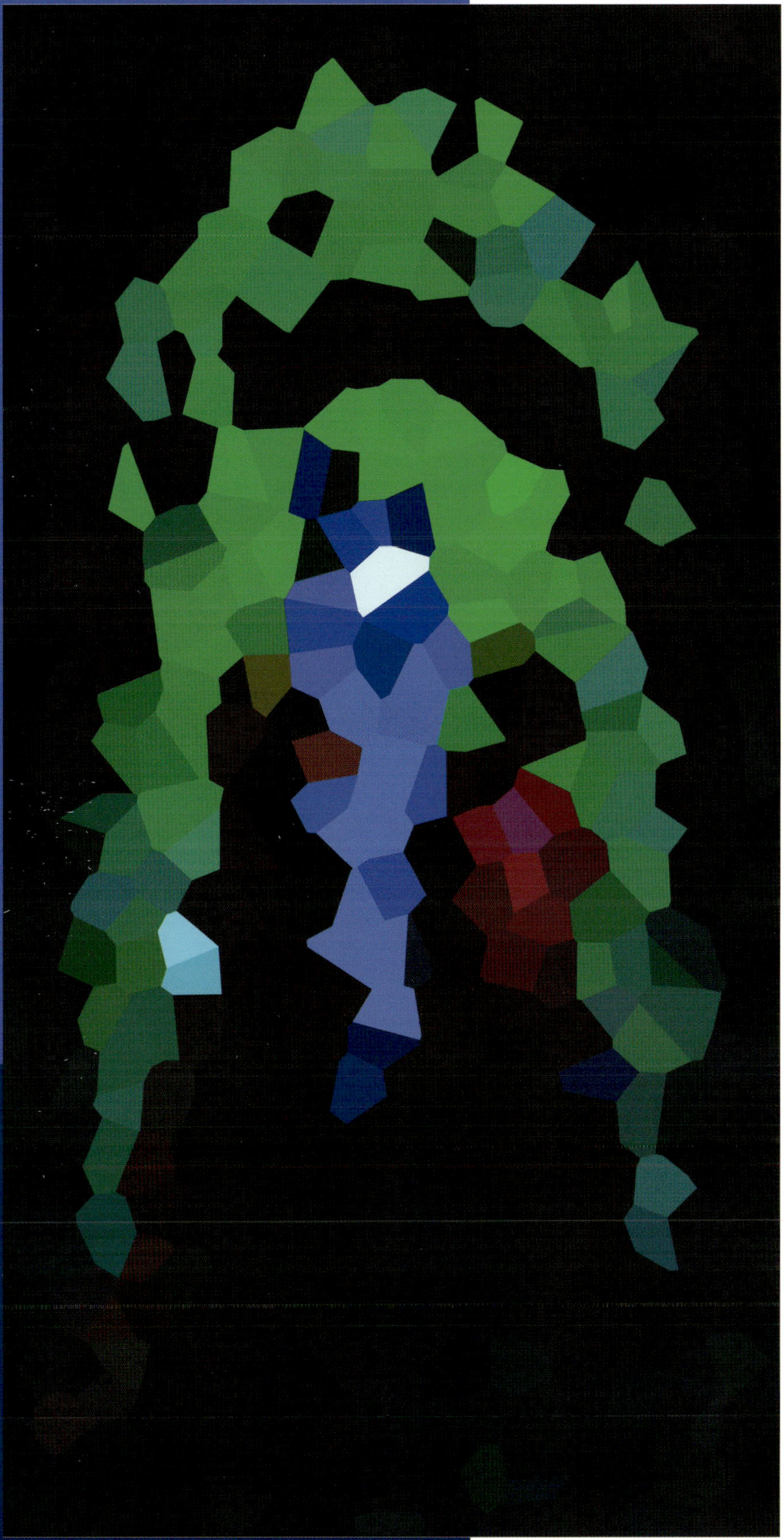

THE COLOR CHART

For this design, I need an intense and dramatic color choice. I choose a triadic color scheme, meaning three colors evenly spaced around the color wheel. This pattern can cause discomfort for the viewer if the hues are too intense, so I need to make value and saturation adjustments for them to coexist. For a calm and relaxing feeling, choose an analogous color palette: 3 adjacent colors on the chromatic circle that are easy and soft on the eye. Complementary colors will grab attention but require careful adjustment to maintain balance. A split complementary color scheme is a slight deviation that introduces more diversity.

TRIADIC COLOR SCHEME

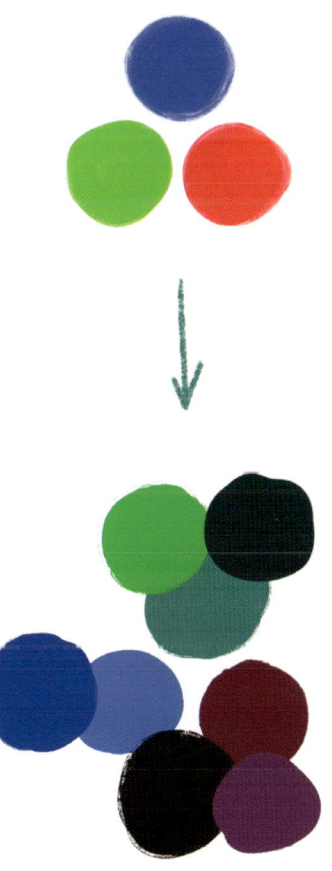

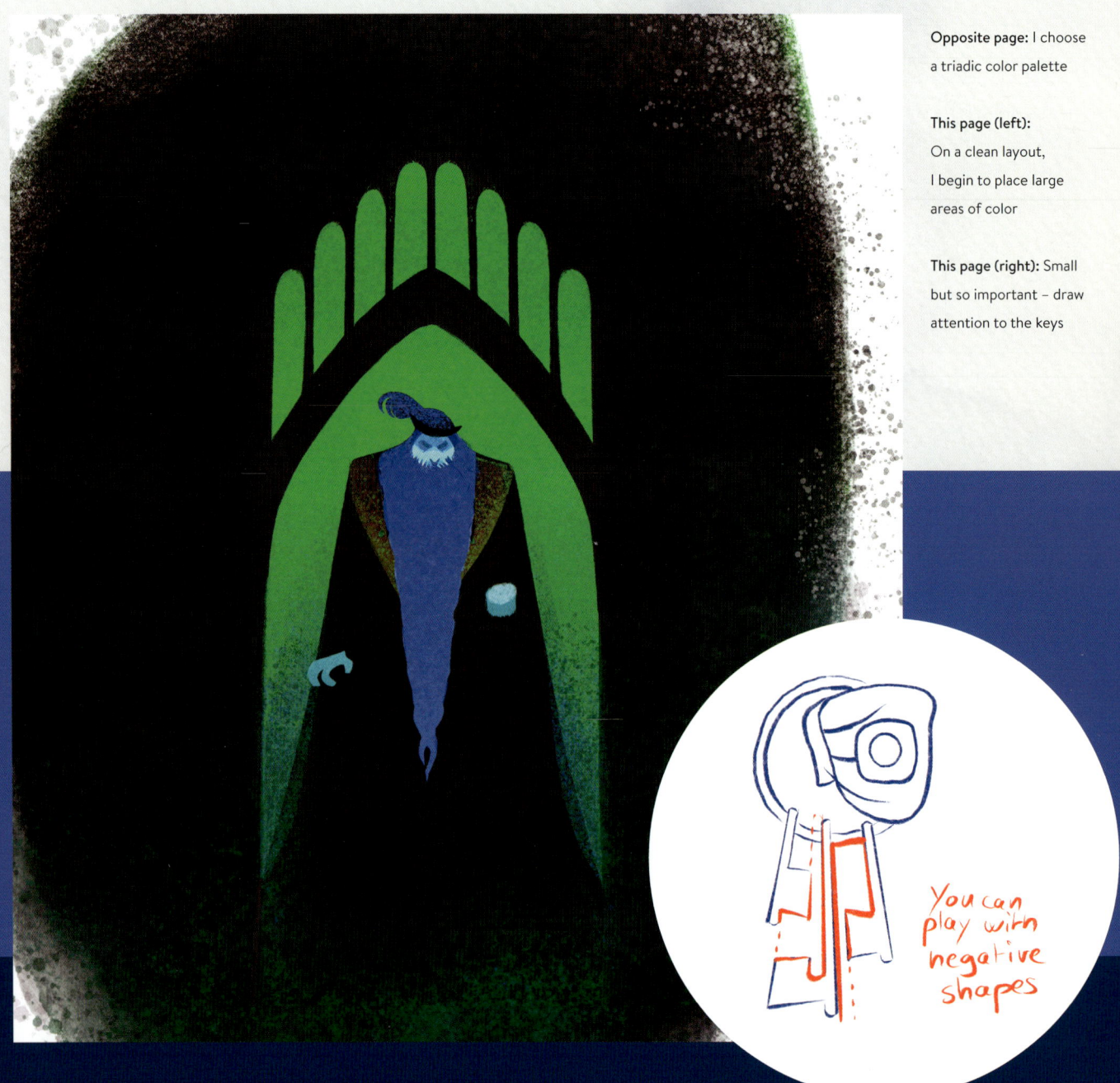

Opposite page: I choose a triadic color palette

This page (left): On a clean layout, I begin to place large areas of color

This page (right): Small but so important – draw attention to the keys

You can play with negative shapes

LAYERING COLOR

Start by thinking about the main areas of your drawing. If the colors don't fit together yet, I won't worry too much because I like to work by adding transparent layers on top of each other, refining the shades little by little. It's just like working with traditional techniques, such as colored pencils or ink. Juxtapose layers until you find the right hue, saturation, and value. Even if digital painting allows you to directly pick the right shade, I find that the result is much livelier and more natural if you obtain it by mixing colors.

THE KEYS ARE THE KEY

A crucial point of the composition are the keys and the eye-shaped ring that watches over them – the story hinges on the bloodstained keys that unveil Bluebeard's wife's disobedience. I focus on the keys, adjusting value, saturation, and pushing detail. They will be the brightest point of the whole piece. I pay attention to negative spaces too, so that the keys remain legible even if small.

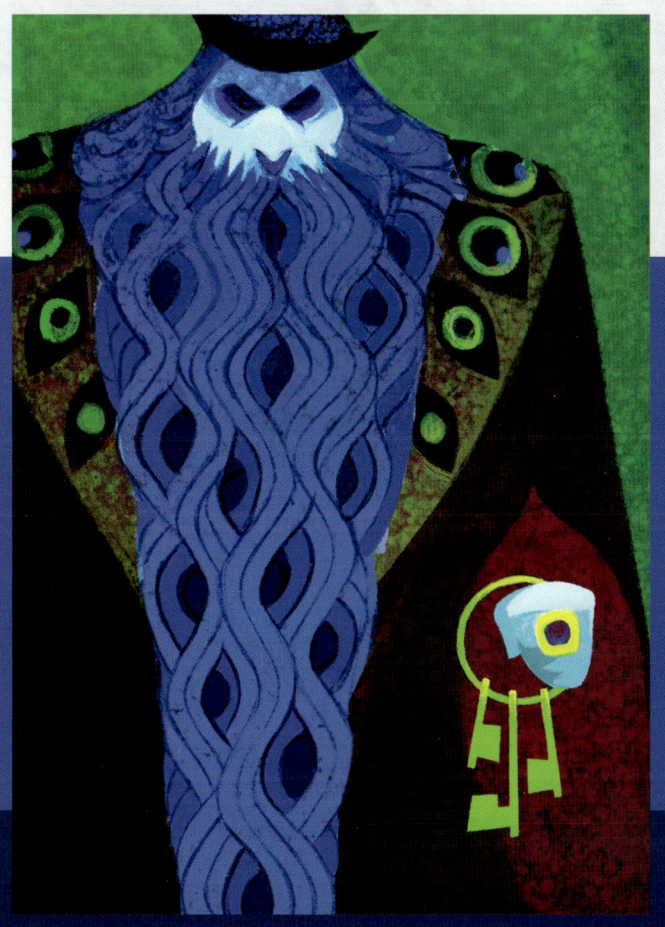
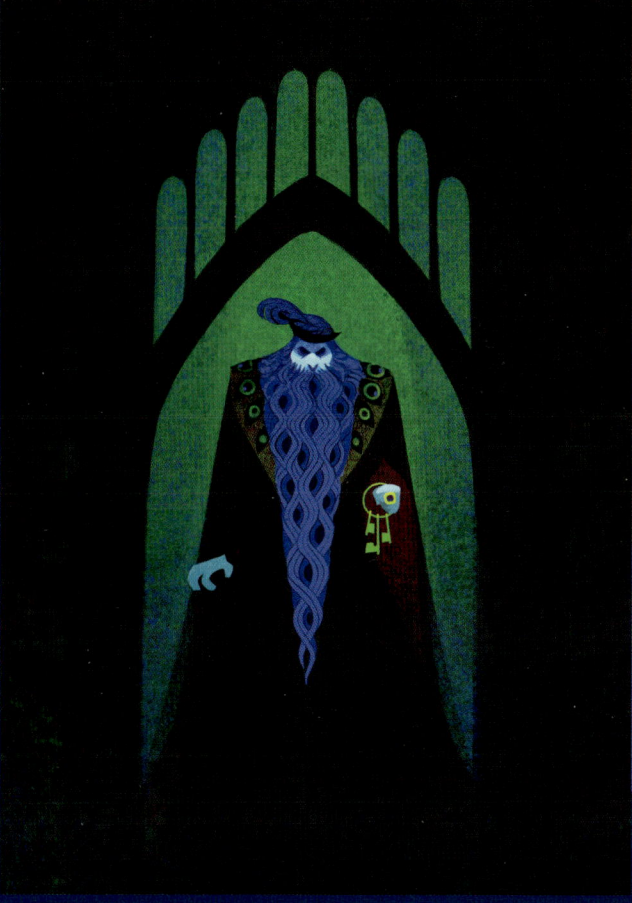

BLOOD SIMPLE

To suggest blood without showing it, I color the inside of Bluebeard's sleeve red, giving it a fluid shape. Design is always about using symbols and archetypes to tell the story. It's not necessarily easy to introduce a bright red in the middle of a predominantly blue and green composition, but a pop of color under the keys will help to draw attention to this area. It can become difficult to harmonize a drawing with a lot of different colors – sticking with two or three makes the job easier.

INTO THE BACKGROUND

Though my drawing is quite precise, I want to keep the background blurred – it must remain in the shadows. Even in a daylight setting, the background should still highlight the action or the characters, unless it's a set reveal. My color choice here recalls religious stained glass, as does the front-facing composition, the stiff poses, and the simple geometric shapes. These references can work really well when illustrating an ancient fable. Stained glass windows were meant to teach by impressing the spirits, using very bright colors. Here it reinforces Bluebeard's position of power, giving him an almost mystical aura.

FINAL ADJUSTMENTS

I decide that the column background adds nothing – it doesn't help to highlight Bluebeard. It's not always easy to remove something, especially if it's an element that has taken a lot of time and effort to produce, but sometimes the simplest solutions are the most effective. Giving the eye some empty space to rest lightens the composition, allowing us to focus on the essentials. Finally, I adjust the contrasts and the colors, refine the details, add some highlights, and try to take a step back to see if the whole work is harmonious or if something is missing. Now, away to your pencils, and have fun!

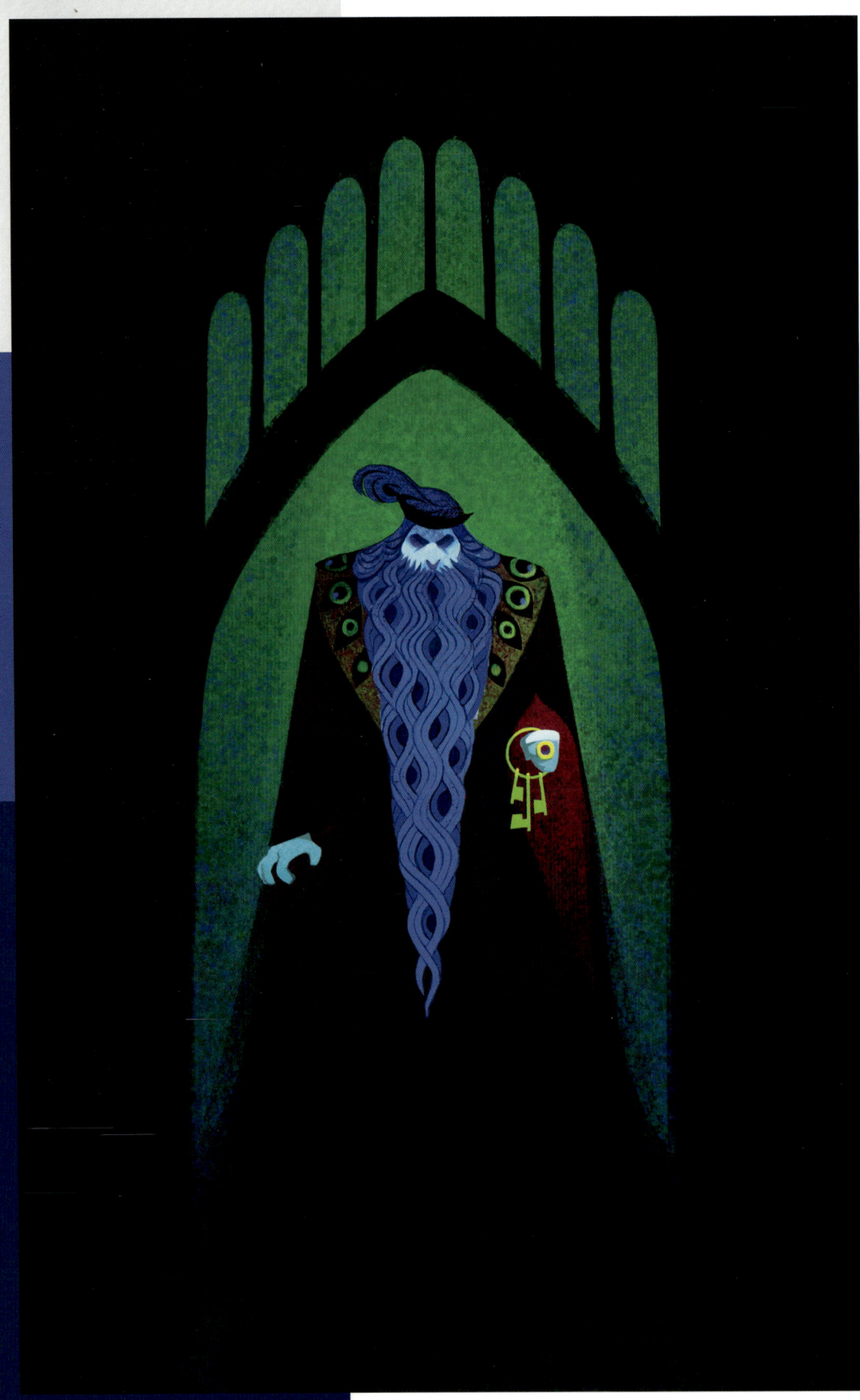

Final image © Marjolaine Roller

Opposite page (left):
Carefully introducing a
touch of bright red

Opposite page (right):
I try to suggest the
castle without going
into too much detail

This page: Last but not
least, the final touches

CONTRIBUTORS

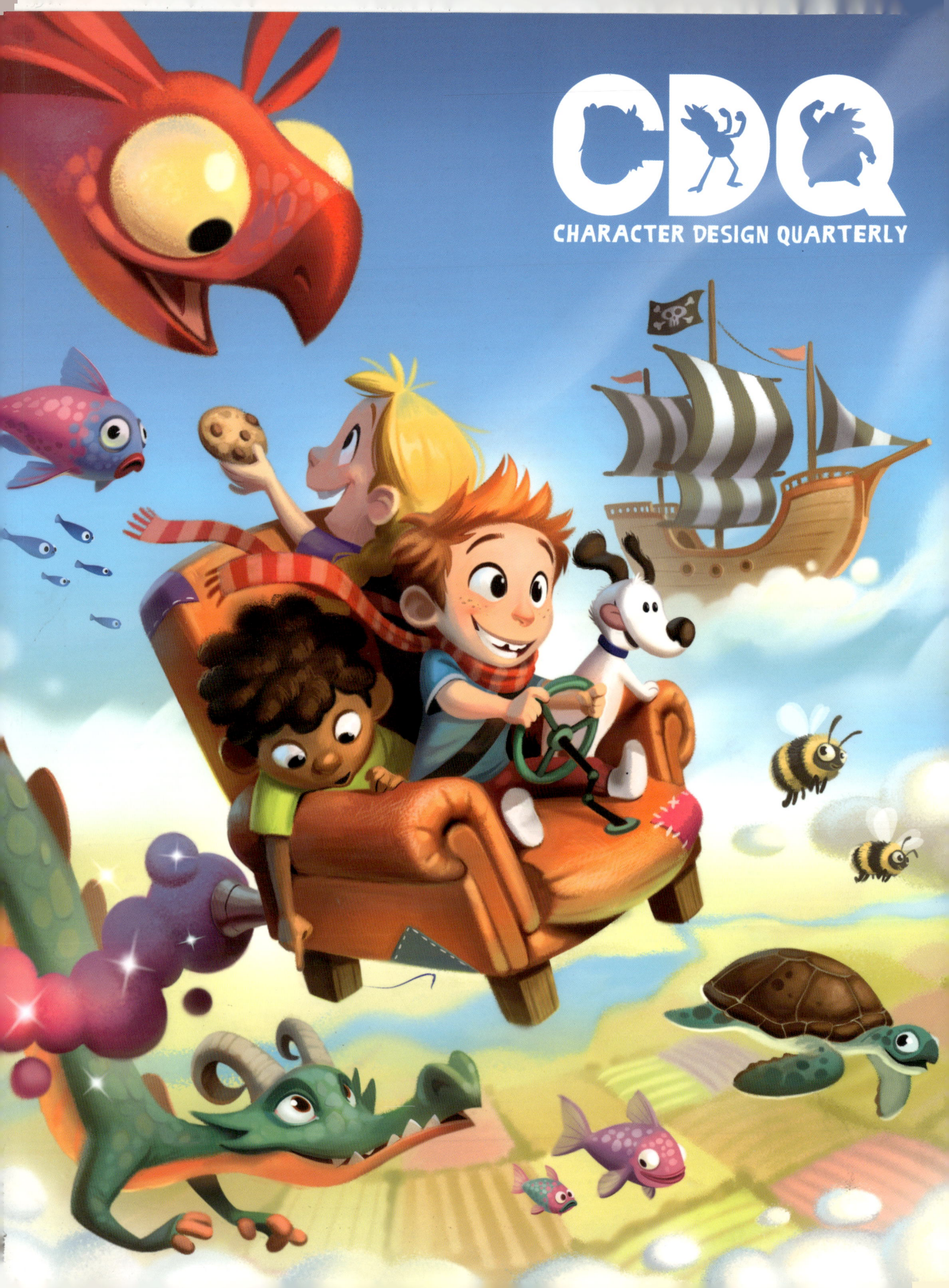

CDQ

CHARACTER DESIGN QUARTERLY

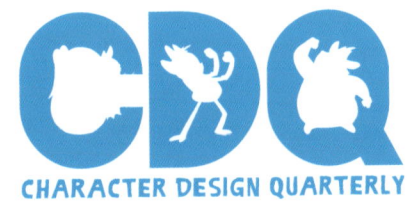
© Lo

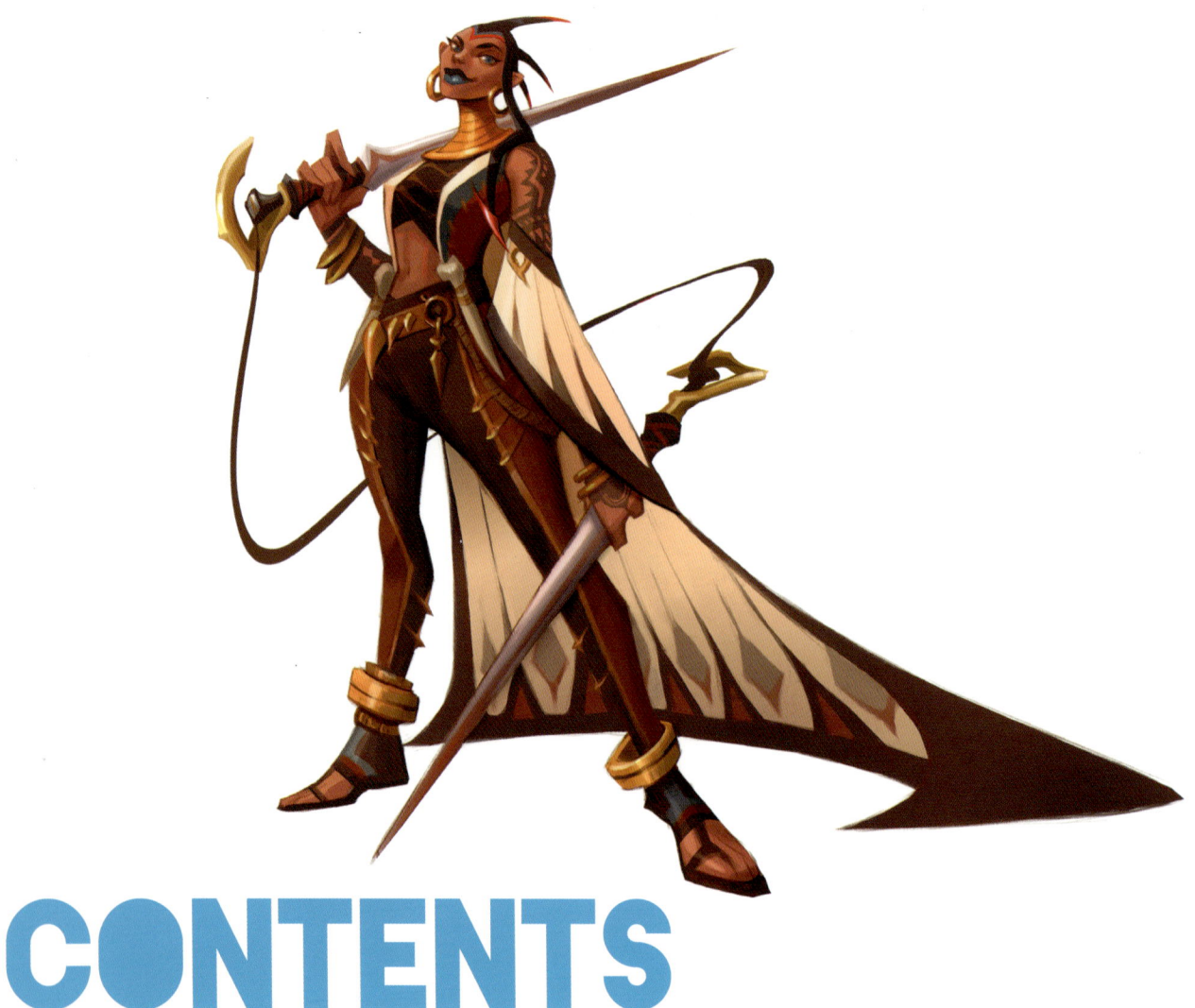

Image © Kaining Wang

CONTENTS

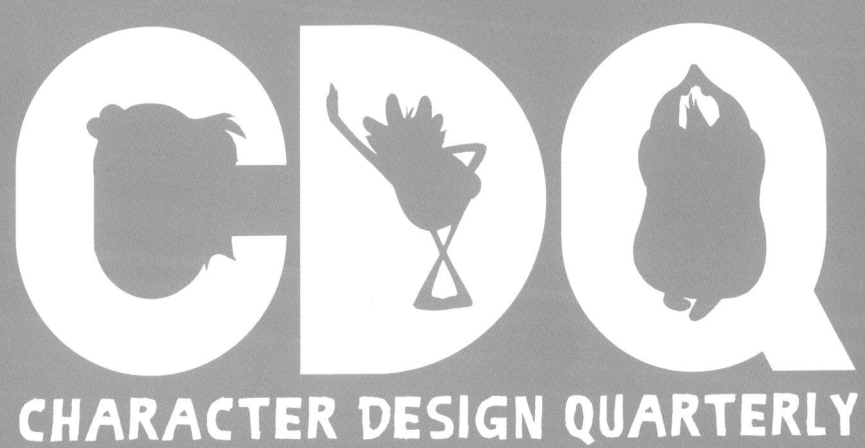

CHARACTER DESIGN QUARTERLY